GET OVER

(maybe not all of

Get Over It

(maybe not all of it)

Brenda Johnson

LUMINARE PRESS

WWW.LUMINAREPRESS.COM

Get Over It (maybe not all of it)
Copyright © 2022 by Brenda Johnson

Cover Design: Kristen Brack
Cover Photo: Big Sky over Mt. Sentinel, Missoula, Montana
by the author. Bicycle added!
Author Photo: Brooke Johnson Nelson

This book is memoir. It reflects the author's present recollections of experiences over time. Some names and characteristics have been changed, some events have been compressed, and some dialogue has been recreated.

Printed in the United States of America

Luminare Press
442 Charnelton St.
Eugene, OR 97401
www.luminarepress.com

LCCN: 2022901956
ISBN: 978-1-64388-885-9

For Bree, Ani, and Brooke
I couldn't do it without you.

Contents

Prologue

2020

My husband of thirty-three years left me in a surprise—not overnight and not a simple disappearance. Disappearing might have been simpler, though no less painful. He hung around another five months, sullen and solitary, after he told me he wasn't happy and before he disengaged from home and me.

I wrote Ed long missives about love and loss and what he had pledged and promised. I didn't deliver most of the self-indulgent letters because no words would have budged the issue off the page. I later shredded the typewritten letters. I didn't want anyone to find them while cleaning up after me, whether I was dead or alive.

Maybe it helped to write down my feelings, maybe not. I played "what if?" on rewind and wondered if I could've or should've done something different. I hoped my husband would return home, and when it was clear he wouldn't, I felt sad for a very long time.

I didn't tell anyone, friends or family, about those weeks when we were miserable and silent in our house. Could the counselors we limped to after Ed's painful proclamation make home, if not me, irresistible and inspire him to rebound? I dreamed of a change of heart and the day he would say, "I'm here. Let's go climb a mountain!"

I cried every morning those first months as I left our sorry house, where the only communication was a dark cloud, and no one hollered "Love you" on my way out the door. It was winter, and I set out for school on my bicycle in the dark. Tears spilled, rain hit the sidewalk, and my bike tires spun through puddles. I arrived at school with tears plastered to my cheeks. I put on a good face and bustled around the classroom to get ready for the cute kids who would soon race each other to be first to class. I taught them to read or to read better. I was good at that.

Hardship is no stranger to my students. Nor is sadness. Many know loss, but they never knew mine. I hid it well until morning recess, when I cried in the staff lavatory. My reflection in the mirror was awful. I washed my face, turned around, and returned to class to welcome my breathless students from the playground.

I cried the minute I closed my classroom each late afternoon and climbed on my bike for the ride home. I cried three miles out of nine on the route through the wetlands. I couldn't tell my own tears from the rain on my cheeks, nor snowy egrets from showy gulls.

Once home, the house was darker inside than out, with no expectation that the man I loved would soon sit down for dinner with me. I liked being in a partnership. I liked belonging. We were in it together, until we weren't.

Carl Jung writes of belonging in his description of a dream after his wife's death.

> Her expression was neither joyful nor sad, but,
> rather, objectively wise and understanding....
> [This portrait of her] contained the beginning
> of our relationship, the events of fifty-three

years of marriage, and the end of her life also. Face to face with such wholeness one remains speechless, for it can scarcely be comprehended.

—Carl Jung, *Memories, Dreams, Reflections*

I wanted to be just that to my husband—so precious that the total vision of me, before or after death, would render him speechless. It's a lot to ask.

The object of my intentions, the one who heard about a student's success, a colleague's baby, or a turtle walking on tiptoes across the bike path, was gone. The sensation of wanting to tell my husband something continued for years, with a sorrow separate from the one death visits upon the soul. The truth is, I had the same sensation before he left, when there were no children at home to anchor us, and Ed didn't have time for the tale I wanted to tell.

In *The Year of Magical Thinking*, author Joan Didion describes the moments before her husband's massive heart attack as so ordinary she couldn't believe his death really happened. Didion recalls the awful days and months after his death, when she repeatedly found herself wanting to tell her husband something. Like Didion, my urge to speak to my husband lasted long after he left.

Alone at home, I didn't busy myself. I *was* busy and did normal things a woman does in an empty nest. I went to work. I baked cookies for neighbors and boxed up more for my distant daughters. I taught Sunday school to middle schoolers, rowdy until the day it dawned on me, they could act out the Bible stories. Always eager to be physical, the boys played with gusto the shunned-but-good Samaritan or the weary traveler, beaten and left for dead on the side of the road to Jericho.

I went to lectures and movies. I hiked and played tennis. I got a new dog and helped my daughter with a new baby. I loved it all. But still I cried my way in and out of every day. No one knew. "Your friends probably think you're better off now," Ed said. Friends didn't consider me the winner. They liked my husband and were surprised at his split. I had imagined I would continue to live every ordinary moment with the man I grew up with before my children grew up with him.

I knew better than to try to stop love or seek closure, that elusive relief that's impossible in most of life's losses. But intellectualizing from dawn to dusk didn't make me less sad. The Rilke quotes I penned in my college calligraphy class and posted on corkboard in my dorm room didn't help. The Rilke quotes are now on tattered pieces of paper in a small binder, along with those from Martin Buber or Dag Hammarskjold, all advising to be patient with what's unresolved, allow loneliness to spur you on, and be ready for the journey inwards.

I continued to grieve the loss of the future I dreamed for my marriage: time, travel, grandchildren, evening walks. Poet Stephen Levine suggests we open ourselves to what's not comfortable. I was wide open, but I failed to do what Levine recommends next, which is to receive the discomfort with acceptance. I was tired of the journey inwards.

I cried and cried some more. Five years, then going on ten, I cried. Now I know the perfect term for what I lived, but I didn't know it then: *Hiraeth, a Welsh word for homesickness and nostalgia, an earnest longing or desire, or a sense of regret. The feeling of longing for a place you cannot return to or a home that never was.* Sometimes hiraeth is irrational; sometimes it's nostalgic. My hiraeth was somewhere in between.

For months, only my pastor knew about my loss. Every prayer, every sermon and hymn, seemed to be directed at me, and I cried. One Sunday, as I left the sanctuary after successfully hiding tears and drying my eyes, I saw my friend Kay, who was undergoing treatment for breast cancer at the time. She had to be worried, for her mother had died of cancer at about her age, but I didn't know Kay well enough to ask. Instead, she asked me a question.

"Oh, Brenda. Are you sick?"

My face must have shown the passion spent and the pounds lost over recent months. A gabardine skirt hung off my hips.

"No. My husband left home, and I'm heading for a divorce," I admitted.

"Oh, honey. You're grieving. I am so sorry," Kay said.

Hiraeth: grief for a place you cannot return to. Kay was right.

Within a few years, I could visit easily with Ed—over coffee or dinner or when our daughters came to town. But watching him leave brought quiet tears for nearly a decade.

What didn't make me cry was writing occasional reports to my grown daughters about what I was doing (climbing to the Tiger's Nest in the Buddhist kingdom of Bhutan), the funny things my students said ("Why do you have a hole in your neck?" in reference to the healthy jugular notch in my throat), or what just happened (a dramatic train ride home from Seattle). I didn't gnash my teeth with Bree and Ani about how their father "done me wrong," but I explored life by writing about a spectacular hike, the pit bulls I met while canvassing door-to-door for the school bond, or how one granddaughter made me laugh and the other made me cry. I wrote about a movie so sad or a concert so beautiful I couldn't get over it. Magnificent events and people I would never want to forget were on my mind, but they didn't drive away the salty sadness, which I was dying to shed. I wrote my girls detailed activity accounts, not to assuage my pain, but for fun, and I had plenty of fun to write about. Many of those accounts grew into chapters in this memoir.

People endure awful, long-suffering divorces that steal souls and drain bank accounts. My divorce had none of that. People lose the barn in a tornado, their home in a hurricane, or their life in a fire. I hadn't even been through a hailstorm. My former husband didn't cast aspersions on me or take anything that wasn't his. I rather enjoyed the cleared bookshelves and empty closet, until I arrived home the next evening. Then I cried.

With so much going for me, what was the problem? *Get over it*, I told myself. *Shit happens.*

Long into my mission to get over grief that lingered longer than I thought was logical for a rather ordinary human loss, it occurred to me that possibly it wasn't right to reprimand myself with "Get over it." If grief was in my bones, yet I functioned normally, even with sadness clinging like a cloud, why was I scolding myself?

My days weren't "bad." My days, always, were generally good, with kids and friends, the garden, a bike ride, and all the things I loved but the husband. I cried because I held onto a sadness. Perhaps tears on the bike path were a simple sigh. *Let it out, whatever it is.*

After my father's premature death, and my brother's many years later, immediate sorrow clutched at my heart, the grieving muscle that continues a steady pace, every pump and pulse a reminder that you are alive. The aching heart remembers that you loved. Long after the grip had loosed on my chest in the months after the deaths of my father and brother, I held a backpack of sadness just over my shoulder. I welcomed the weight of raw pain, for as long as it was there, I couldn't forget the countenance of these people I loved. With each of them, I carried the load for months, until one day the weight simply seemed to lift, and I felt relief.

Was the pain over losing my marriage the "it" I was trying to get over, but not really, to keep the face of it close? Pain held for me that which I loved and lost, but I knew it hadn't kept love alive to mend and maintain a marriage. I lost that option. Could I relax into what was an option—friendship and family, and call it good? The family alliance, rich with daughters and history, wasn't without substance. Could I believe Buber, that the journey might have an unexpected destination?

Hiraeth: grief for a place you cannot return to. The place, heart, home, being someone's someone special, was still taking up space. In time, I would ask grief to take up less space. It took time, lots of it.

The stories in this memoir about my early marriage, my young family, and the days before my husband left are told in past tense. These stories from the past are interspersed early in the memoir with stories after my husband left. The after-departure chapters are told in present tense, as I lived them.

CHAPTER 1

No Wind in My Sails

2003

The October Saturday was brilliant in color. A light wind tossed leaves on the street, on the lawn, on my shoulders. I breezed into the house after raking leaves and said to my husband of thirty-three years, "Want to do something fun today? We could bike to the farmers market for coffee."

Ed looked serious. He positioned himself on the window seat and gave me a pleading, sorry look.

"I'm not happy," he said. "I'm just not happy. I don't know what that means, but I'm not happy." He had been practicing this while I was outside swinging a leaf rake.

What was there to be "not happy" about? It was October in Oregon. One daughter called an hour ago to say she passed the bar exam, the other was two months shy of a master's degree, and the dog had some good years left.

I shouldn't have been surprised. The same person who thought he was dumb as a teenaged kid and never dreamed of going to college was now engaged in nothing but work at the university—grants, research, teaching, more grants. He had been glumly tucked in his office for weeks. With our daughters grown and gone, their father had no soccer games, choral concerts, or graduation ceremonies on his calendar. He had always attended these events with the joy of a dad, but often with an eye on the clock to get back to work when the event was over.

"You know, on your death bed, no one will ask how many hours you put in at the office," I said to Ed one Sunday, mimicking words I'd just heard in a sermon. He didn't respond.

Many times he said, "This is what the job requires." The concession was that he worked evenings and Saturdays in his office at home.

Standing in the dining room that sunny, autumn-streaked afternoon, listening to my husband's words that seemed to come out of the blue—but really came out of a cloud I knew too well, my heart sank. I felt it drop. I knew I couldn't make him happy that moment, and I feared never. There was no comfort to be found in the dining room or outside in a sunny pile of maple leaves.

"Are you going to leave me?" I asked, still standing.

"No!" he answered.

He moved out five months later.

I left the house after Ed's Saturday surprise and biked to the farmers market for a glimmer of the autumn day I wanted to share with him. The day remained glorious, but my heart raced after the dining room exchange that had no end and no glory.

———————

A MONTH AFTER MY HUSBAND TOLD ME HE WASN'T HAPPY, Bree and Ani came home for Thanksgiving. The next morning at the breakfast table, our yellow lab Fenn at our feet, Ani talked with her dad about navigating a difficult professor during the final months of her graduate program. Her father was good at strategy.

Then, after moments of awkward silence, Ed said, "I'm not happy."

Ani looked at me and back at her father. "What does that mean?" she asked.

"I don't know," Ed said.

I was quiet. Bree, soon off to a clerkship with the Supreme Court of Hawaii, and Ani, soon finished with a master's degree and off to somewhere, asked a few troubled questions of their father.

"Are you moving out?"

"I don't know," he said.

Ani wailed and ran upstairs and wailed some more. It was agonizing. Fenn also left the table.

I didn't want my girls to feel the anguish I felt. I was as sorry for them as I was for me. What would become of these breakfasts we loved?

Bree and Ani and I left the house for a long walk through the cemetery. "I guess that takes care of the Blackberry I was going to give Dad for Christmas," Bree said.

We welcomed levity as we wound our way around the good souls at rest.

WHEN ED FINALLY LEFT HOME FIVE TORTUROUS MONTHS after the October Saturday, Bree, an ocean and a few time zones away, called often. Late one night, she asked, "Do you want to be lonely with him or lonely without him?"

"I guess you're right," I said. At the time, it made sense to be lonely without him. With no children at home as welcome distractions, he spent his time immersed in work, with nothing left for singing, talking, or weeping with me.

Years later, I wasn't sure about the lonely without him. I recognized advantages to living alone, but I couldn't say I loved it.

CHAPTER 2

Wetlands

2005

I close my classroom door and climb on my bicycle for the nine-mile ride home. October days are growing shorter, a contradiction in terms. I'll be home well before dark, a gentle wind at my back. Another sunset will be spectacular in a few minutes. I pick up speed on the ride before I stop to turn and look behind me. Orange and purple ribbons of sky drift and dance in ripples just before the sun drops into the ocean. Today, the panorama over the Coast Range is dazzling.

Some days, the sunsets make me weep. Most days in recent years, a hole in my heart makes me weep the minute my bike wheels start rolling. It occurs to me I didn't cry when I hopped on my bike this afternoon or in the last couple miles. Is it the weather, the autumn wonder, the color of the season that gives me a break from heartache? Thomas Merton writes of the crimson and gold of October, a perfect time to mount ambition and begin something new.

I didn't want a divorce. I resisted, tried to plead without begging, asked my husband to go to counseling with me, and hoped he would come out the other side and choose to come home. In the end, I could no more stop this midlife moment than a train wreck.

Divorce is a club I never thought I would be in. Many people are in clubs they didn't choose, and this is not the worst. What makes me cry at the end of the day? Is it going home to an empty house or losing what I thought I had, a marriage that would last into old age? Or what I hoped I would have one day soon, a husband who would take time to talk past dinner, to walk in the neighborhood cemetery of giant sequoias and sprawling oaks, with a view of distant mountains?

Red garden pruners poke out of my bike basket, a reminder to stop in the wetlands I pass every day. Today I'll gather a bouquet of reeds and grasses for church on Sunday. Every fall, I offer a weedy altar arrangement as an alternative to a spray of flowers from a floral shop. I already submitted my blurb for the Sunday bulletin.

> Today's altar is an offering of reeds and greens,
> tufts and tassels from the West Eugene Wetlands,
> in gratitude for open and protected space for all
> to enjoy.

I admire a blue heron standing on one leg in the canal. Herons always do that, and it always amuses me. Seagulls hunt for grubs in the spongy center of the wetland. Even these scavengers, coming and going from the Pacific coast, look elegant against the sky.

MY DAUGHTERS ARE GROWN AND GONE, STRONG AND reasonable. When their father first left home, they couldn't speak to him, they were so angry. Ani finished graduate school the same month and refused her father's help to move her out of her apartment. She asked him to come to the house one late afternoon.

"Dad, I don't want your help this weekend. I've already rented a truck in Seattle, and I have friends coming to the apartment to help me load furniture. Mom and I can pack the rest and clean the condo."

Ani's father sat on the window seat in the dining room, one hand planted on each side of him, ready to push off to leave again. His face moved from confident to crushed as he heard Ani's announcement. Packing and moving was his thing. He worked with big brawny guys at Bekins Moving and Storage every summer of college. He packed and moved our family across the country three times. He was really good at fitting the right things in tight spaces, and he was looking forward to spending time with his daughter.

Ed didn't try to talk Ani out of her decision. He got up to leave, barely holding back tears. "Okay," he said. "Call if you need me." He looked at me with sorrow stinging his face. "Goodbye, Brenda." It was agony for all of us, but mostly for him.

That weekend, Ani and I drove to Seattle and packed the apartment in cardboard U-Haul boxes. Three strong young men came to lift a few pieces of furniture, and we fit all the bags and boxes in small spaces. It wasn't as tidy as her father's packing, but Ani was proud of her accomplishment—a master's degree and a tight move.

In time, my daughters' anger gave way to real life. They conceded their father was dear to them and was not a devil. They don't have much experience, but they were certain death would be easier for me than divorce. It might have been easier on my soul for a moment, only because I might not suffer blame. Whatever it would be, I'd be sorry to lose the friend I care for, and it would be a sorrier loss for our daughters, who have a lot of life left to live. They need their father, and he needs them.

I don't use my daughters as counselors, and after a few years, I stopped going to a real counselor. My counselor was good, but how many tears can I shed on a cushy couch in an office that quivers with decades of anger and sorrow, and how many years can I say the same thing? *I miss my husband, and I would love to just get over it.*

"Join a book group," the counselor suggested. I started one.

"Join a hiking group." I'm in one.

"Join a study group." I'm in two.

The counselor told me I was *guileless*, which I had to look up, and that I loved hard, which I didn't have to look up. What I know is that I don't want to cry for the rest of my life over missing a husband. I would like to get over myself. *Get a grip.*

I have a pretty good grip. I haven't missed a day of work at school in the years since Ed left home. I actually haven't missed a day of school in fifteen years. But I've cried every day since the October Saturday two years ago, when my heart told me my husband was preparing to leave, and on my bike ride home, in a movie, on the phone, or in the kitchen.

For the first months after Ed left, I rarely went to the store, any store. I didn't want to see people I knew. I didn't want them to feel sorry for me, either for what they had heard or what they saw on my face. Left behind by a good guy everyone liked, I felt like less. I didn't want to cry, especially in the grocery store in front of someone I hardly knew.

———

TODAY, I DON'T FEEL LIKE LESS, AND THE MORE I TAKE IN this autumn afternoon, the better. After the sun's dramatic exit on the screen to the west, I set out in search of the perfect bunch of dry, thick-stemmed grasses that will look starkly beautiful on the church altar.

Mine is a good mission this afternoon, to choose weedy, reedy bounty for the altar, in thanks for public space and in honor of God who loves us, no matter our defects or blemishes or slow-to-get-it nature. As my pastor friend Melanie says, we go with God companioned.

Rather than breeze past the wetlands as usual on my bike, I find the right place to stop and put down the kickstand. I might be here awhile. Down the bank is a mound of grasses, crunchy after a long summer and dry fall. Lupine and camas are spent and finished, but the cow parsnip are showy white, perfect in a bouquet of cattails and spiny teasel. I cut a handful and gather enough of everything to fill three altars. Collecting is fun, and it's hard to stop. The next bunch over is more appealing than the last. I wedge a wide load of wild beauty into my bike basket. Grasses stick out every which way, and I pull stragglers out of tire spokes. I'm a picture on this bike. My mother would say, "You look like something sent for that couldn't come."

I savor this crimson and gold October day, short on tears and long on sunset. I draw a big breath before I leave the levee. The day may not patch the hole in my heart, but I will get over what's missing. I'll draw more breath—from memories and kids and connections that weave my life strong as sedges. I'll say, "I can't get over how great this is!" I'll remember I'm companioned.

I set my wheels in motion. Above the bog now, I pass rushes and withered blackberries, riding east toward home and tomorrow's sunrise. I would like to not spend another bend in the bike path feeling sorry about what I've missed.

At home, I unload my basket of the wetlands bundle. The sunset of colored layers that come and go is still with me. Today, I didn't miss a thing.

CHAPTER 3

How Did I Get Here?

1967 and 2005

Ed and I met on my eighteenth birthday in the college commons. He introduced himself by bumping into me in the lunch line, and that night, he stood outside the girls' dormitory and hollered up at my friend Peggy's second-story window.

"What's the name of the cute one with short hair?" he yelled, as Peggy raised her window into the misty night.

I haven't been called the "cute one" since. My friend's nine-year-old grandson recently referred to me as "that girl" who taught him how to cross-country ski, but he didn't say anything about me being cute.

I had a few dates in college with guys who were a shake beyond boys, but they weren't boyfriends. My first date in high school was with Buzz to *Lawrence of Arabia*, four hours of blowing sand and a camel ride.

The boy who called up to Peggy's window was soon asking me to movies at the only theater in town. I didn't know an independent film from a blockbuster, but I liked the small films in a small theater just six blocks from campus, and I liked the boy who invited me.

We saw *To Sir, with Love* and *Guess Who's Coming to Dinner* with dreamy Sidney Poitier and Katharine Hepburn. Both films brought race and class to the screen, not entirely new topics to me, though I grew up in a mostly white town. My parents expressed sympathetic sensibilities about civil rights after morning radio news broadcasts between Maxwell House ads that percolated in the kitchen.

After the film *The Umbrellas of Cherbourg*, a love story told in lilting song, I sang my way back to the dorm and entertained my roommate, Lauri, for the next twenty-four hours by singing my side of our conversations.

Doctor Zhivago, played by impossibly handsome Omar Sharif, entangled in a love triangle with the two loves of his life—his self-sacrificing wife, Tonya, and stunningly beautiful Lara—was the headliner in a sensational film of the same name. I ran out of adjectives to describe the music, love, and landscape to Lauri.

I loved college. I loved everything about it, from roommates to classes to the old growth grove on campus and the library. I loved the academic challenge and professors. I even liked my job in the dining commons, except on Wednesdays, when we served corned beef and cabbage from steaming stainless steel tubs. It smelled terrible, like damp gym socks.

Civil rights shaped me, and college shaped Ed and me together. I began to care about this shy and admiring guy who took me to movies. Our years at college, among the most tumultuous in American history, set the stage for us. The movies and protests, assassinations and elections—the beauties and sorrows of life, would always be with me. I imagined the young man who later was dying to marry me would always be with me.

My movie mate became my boyfriend a year before the 1968 assassination of Martin Luther King, Jr. on a motel balcony in Memphis. When we heard news of the tragedy, we understood the loss and wondered if we would ever be happy again. We walked and talked for hours, weaving in and out of ancient Douglas fir shadows on campus.

In the politically charged spring of Dr. King's death, we drove thirty miles from campus to downtown Portland to see Robert Kennedy pass through town as a candidate for the Democratic nomination for president.

Senator Kennedy's motorcade inched slowly through the crowd, and RFK stood bold as life in the back of a convertible. I worried to see him in such a car, wide open to the crowd like his brother Jack on the terrible day in Dallas less than five years before, the day my parents were so broken with grief that I felt lost. I had no way of knowing the same grief would revisit us many times in the next few years.

Robert Kennedy was handsome, his sandy hair tousled in the breeze. He looked every bit a robust Kennedy. As the car slowed, RFK reached out to shake Ed's hand. Paralyzed by Kennedy's charisma, the youthful sophomore didn't reach back and never got over wishing he had returned the magnetic and vigorous gesture. He speaks of it still.

When Robert Kennedy died three months later in June of 1968 by an assassin's bullet in a hotel kitchen, I felt as sad as my parents did over JFK. My father was broken again. Ed and I were working that summer in separate parts of the country. We were flattened by the second assassination in as many months and exchanged tender letters twice a week, sharing the nation's grief.

"Our biggest and sincerest hope has been assassinated," Ed wrote to me in Wyoming. "My God, I am sick. What… is happening to the home of the brave, America the beautiful? I want to do something to help this country. What can I do, what should I do?"

I penned impassioned letters in return. The letters shrank the distance between us and brought us closer. I was in the Grand Tetons of Wyoming for the summer, slinging hash at a dude ranch, where I began a long shift at 6 a.m., mixing up mayonnaise chocolate cake and spreading chicken salad on a dozen sandwiches for guests on a float trip down the Snake River.

I was not in sympathetic company at Heart Six Ranch, where young wranglers made sport of driving into tiny Jackson Hole in the evening to harass hippies. One morning at breakfast, two wranglers boasted about corralling young men the night before.

"Oh, yeah, we sheared off those pretty golden locks, all right."

I'm embarrassed I don't remember if I said anything.

Still in Wyoming, I listened alone to the 1968 Democratic National Convention in Chicago on a tiny transistor radio I earned selling Christmas cards in fifth grade. Counterculture and Vietnam War protesters met a bank of Chicago police in riot gear. Mayor Daley was fuzzy on the radio but not so fuzzy in his commands to his police force.

Back at college in the fall of 1968, Ed and I went to Portland's Memorial Coliseum to hear Simon and Garfunkel. We saved money from our jobs in the dining commons and library. Students rarely went to the city, and no one splurged on restaurants or concerts or shopping. The concert at the coliseum was brilliant. After springtime assassinations of two heroes who spurred hope in the face of racial inequity and the horror of the Vietnam War, and after riots and the Democratic Convention disaster in the cauldron of Chicago in August, we were ready to be charged with hope.

In Portland's darkened coliseum, we sang from *Bookends*, Simon and Garfunkel's newest album. First "Old

Friends" and then "America." After a season of loss, we felt like lovers who would blend our fortunes together and maybe even take off to look for America. We saw ourselves in every song and verse and for just a moment, we didn't feel weary or small.

VICE PRESIDENT HUBERT HUMPHREY, LARGELY RESPON-sible for civil rights legislation and for vain efforts to convince President Johnson to pull troops out of Vietnam, lost the 1968 election to Republican Richard Nixon. Humphrey stood for much that Ed and I cared about.

My father died six weeks later at age fifty-three of a heart attack. I always wondered if the 1968 election shut down Dad's heart. I was nineteen and adored my sensitive, socially conscious father. He was too young to die, and I was too young to have him die.

Ed came to Montana during those dark winter days after Dad died, and he formed a bond with my mother that was never broken by distance or divorce.

At school, we protested the war, and Ed organized the first Vietnam Moratorium in 1969, with speakers, a march, and handmade signs of antiwar messages scribbled in script or drawn in ten-inch block letters. I admired the commitment from the person who only two years before didn't have an interest that committed him to anything. Our campus joined moratoriums across the country that stopped classes at colleges from Berea to Berkeley and Oberlin to Occidental. Throngs of student activists hoped to put a stop to that awful war. The war didn't end for another six awful years.

In the fall of 1969, Ed and I were college seniors, reading Keats and Kierkegaard, Kafka and Camus, engaged in heady discussions with professors and classmates about Sisyphus pushing that rock up the hill or about how mourning becomes Electra. Between study dates at the library and cheap independent films, we planned to get married in June.

We were engaged in the same studies, working for the same causes, and we wanted to be together our last semester. We moved the wedding up to Christmas break. A seamstress made my wedding dress in a soft, white wool with a nice drape and the same dress for my little sister in a heathery blue, a good winter color. Ed bought his first suit. Women in the church made pumpkin bread.

On a November Saturday before the wedding, I spotted my wedding ring in a window display at Goldworks in Portland. I chose the handcrafted design by Art, the gentle man who owned Goldworks. It reminded me of a cross section of a Montana ponderosa pinecone. I love it still, on my right hand. It doesn't make me sad—it represents a time, a time Simon and Garfunkel sang of, a time of innocence and confidence.

I hadn't set out to buy a wedding ring in Portland. I certainly didn't plan to buy my husband's wedding band with my friend Sue, rather than the groom himself. But there it was in the window, next to mine, simple and beautiful but more substantial. I hoped Ed would like the motif I was drawn to. I paid seventy dollars out of my campus paycheck for the two gold bands. I smiled at Art as I pushed through the shop's glass door into a winter night on Broadway.

"DO YOU LIKE THEM? THEY'RE ONE OF A KIND," I SAID, when I showed Ed my ring and the matching one I bought for him. "You would have loved Art, the artist."

"I do like the rings," he said.

Decades later, I think I should have asked Art at Gold-works to hold the larger band until Ed could look at it and choose it himself. I did what made sense to me. The ring was there, it was a beautiful match we could afford, getting to the city wasn't easy, and time was running out. During the three decades we lived together, Ed might have said I was too practical on several occasions. This was one.

We slipped on the handcrafted bands on a snowy, star-studded January night in Montana. Our wedding was simple, as planned, and candlelit and quiet.

———————————

THE FOLLOWING SPRING, ANTIWAR PROTESTS HEATED UP across the country. A demonstration at Kent State University in Ohio ended in National Guard troops gunning down four students. This tragedy, six days before our college graduation in May 1970, brought the Vietnam War painfully close to home. It was a somber week on campus.

The keynote commencement speaker was president of nearby Lewis and Clark College. He didn't acknowledge the grave tenor of the time or the heavy hearts in his audience but offered an uplifting message: "You can be anything you want to be in this great country." I wanted to be out of there.

As much as I wanted to walk out, I didn't. My husband, president of the senior class, was the next speaker. He came a long way to that podium, and I wouldn't have missed it.

The grief for lives and innocence lost at Kent State was palpable on the May afternoon that should have been jubilant. Ed connected with the communal sentiment. He named the victims, who were all of us.

"We can either fight the plague—the plague of militarism, the plague that suppresses dissent, and the plague that inhibits expression…or we can silently accept our death," he told graduates, many in tears and others eager to toss their mortar boards. I was so proud of him—the courage, the allusions, naming the four slain students. I'll never get over the tears and the sun that warmed the day, and I won't forget the students' names.

The young man who responded to a sorry time in American history with an inspiration from Camus had been, only four years before, a skinny teen from Hawaii who didn't know college was an option, didn't know fir trees came any bigger than Christmas trees, and didn't know what he didn't know.

"I skipped class one afternoon and bumped into Coach Bafaro, who invited me to come to the mainland and play college football," Ed told me. "It was about that simple."

Ed had no idea what college meant, but he knew football. A few classes in, he learned he was smart. He learned to care about thinking and learned life was bigger than an island. Despite the series of national tragedies we will never get over, we were young and resilient. We were just getting started. We spent more than thirty years growing up together.

"If it weren't for you, I would have gone back home after graduation and certainly wouldn't have gone to graduate school," Ed told me. I wasn't sure I wanted the responsibility. Was showing him new possibilities what caused me to lose my marriage? Occasionally I was on a pedestal, and from there, I could always fall. "I think of you as perfect," he said, which could only end in disappointment when I wasn't.

We made big decisions together, yielding to Ed's work. Where we would live, when we would vacation, if we could put demands on his time. I bought and sold houses before the moves, and we bought cars together. Ed always wanted a second car, but I didn't see a need for a second and held out for only one. I think it was a wedge. It was practical, like my purchase of both his wedding ring and mine.

Our alliance was agreeable because Ed made all our living when the girls were young and most of our living later, when I worked part time. We were good parents together. I managed most of the household and the yard, which seemed right, considering Ed's workload. He cleaned the kitchen after dinner. "Pass me the broom," he'd say. "Hawaiians don't sweep after dark. It's bad luck." Hammering after dark is also bad luck, but we had less occasion to hammer.

———

It will soon be forty years since that day in the lunch line at college, the day I turned eighteen. Most days, when I bike home from school, my wheels turn on what I could've or should've done to save my marriage or what my husband could've or should've done. I don't spin answers on the ride, but I can think of a few.

CHAPTER 4

What's Google?

2005

I've come to Montana alone, to visit my mother and step-father. This summer, I feel the changes. My daughters are grown and gone, out of graduate school, and on to real jobs. My husband is gone. He loved it here—the pot roast and huckleberry pie my mother made to welcome him the first evening of every visit. He loved Mom's humor and looked up from his computer or yellow legal pad to josh with her in the kitchen. He worked at the dining table every day of vacation, but he was here.

I've always wanted a house you can see all the way through, from front to back, where the garden in the back-yard comes right inside. My mom and Dick's house in Montana is like that—from the street, the view goes straight through the picture window into the living room and out the kitchen into the raspberries. Sunshine floods the kitchen. It looks like the petunias spilling over a window box outside are growing out of the Wheaties box on the table inside.

The house is a relaxing space. Scandinavian furniture reminds me of a dentist's office but better. The comfort-able couch on slim hardwood legs with tight-weave wool upholstery has a couple pillows that don't match. The big sky outside sends light inside. There's no clutter, one of many reasons I love to come home.

The coffeepot is always on. Friends and relatives stop to see Mom and Dick and come away saying, "I have to get rid of some of my stuff!" I share the sentiment. Something about Barbara and Dick in that simple little ranch house on the farming edge of Missoula, with a view of Lolo Peak that gets better in winter, makes people downright envy their life. It looks like the two of them never really wanted to be anywhere else.

For more than a dozen summers, cousins have grown up here. My sister Brooke's kids and my kids lined up sleeping bags in the backyard and counted stars six layers deep. They rose early to drag flannel-lined sleeping bags out of the path of the sprinkler that Gramps set to go "ch ch ch" in an arc over the garden early in the morning, before the sun came up. We played rousing games of croquet, my mother the most enthusiastic contestant of all, and sprayed each other with a garden hose once the sun heated the day.

This has been our favorite vacation spot for years. We've eaten out of the garden, fed carrots to the horses next door, tried to beat Grams at rummy, and slept with the windows open.

Not long ago, I sat on the edge of my mother's bed as young Ani wiggled on the other side of her grandmother in the early morning. We talked and giggled while Mom had her first cup of coffee.

"Coffee, coffee," Mom yelled in sing-song from her bed, the minute she woke up. Dick served Mom's first cup the minute he heard her holler, before he went to the garden to move sprinklers or pick raspberries.

I knew the time would come when these summer days, with kids in this comfortable house with a window on the garden, would end. I'm afraid my time as a daughter is slowing down.

I didn't think my marriage would end, in any season. My time as a wife slowed to a stop over a year ago. I don't feel like a failure because I'm alone, but I miss Ed here this summer. When I see old friends in town, they ask about him.

"How's Ed?"

"He's fine. He doesn't live with me anymore." Friends hear resignation in my voice. They know I didn't have a choice.

"I'm sorry," one friend says, outside Butterfly Herbs downtown or at the Wednesday night band concert in Bonner Park.

"Me too," I say. "I'm just getting used to it."

Brooke is here with me this week. It's hard to reckon with our families no longer enjoying this sun-and-garden-infused vacation into the next decade. My mother is finally showing her age. It took a long time for her to get really gray. It took a long time for arthritis to really slow her down. Now she's talking about giving things away. She tells Brooke and me to go to the little red barn on the other side of the garden and find things to take home with us.

"Which one of you wants that walnut bedroom set?" she asks. "It was my mother's, you know." I do know.

"Do you want the picture in the guest room? Take it with you. And what about that Arizona poster?"

"Mom, if you die, Dick just might want a picture on the wall," Brooke says.

"Oh, he doesn't care," she answers.

Our stepfather, Dick, is fit as a fiddle and probably doesn't care. He's a quiet Hoosier, born and raised on an Indiana farm. He likes a new truck and travel trailer but doesn't care much about decor.

On a recent visit, I helped Mom sort through her closet, spare compared to my own, with hangers sliding easily across the rod. We sorted out a few thrift store items that "didn't do a thing" for her.

"No, Mom," I said about the gray polyester blazer she modeled for me. "It's saggy, and the color makes you look like a sidewalk." We howled at the bargain that looked great hanging in the thrift store but looked like a paper bag hanging on my mother. She was shrinking and didn't know it.

IT'S SUNDAY, THE LAST DAY OF MY SOLO TRIP TO SEE MOM and Dick. I love Montana. It's home. Sometimes I wish I lived here. I don't look forward to walking in my own back door to an empty house, but it's time to go. I return to school next week, and I'm ready for that. By the end of summer, I'm tired of myself and eager to see kids, lots of them.

As we pull into the driveway after church, Mom breezes through the screen door and heads for the bedroom down the hall to change her clothes. Her speed in peeling off her church clothes reminds me of Sundays when I was a child, when Mom swept in through the back door after church, threw on her outdoor clothes, and tossed together a picnic, whatever the season. Then she hollered, "Let's go!" and we headed for Lolo Creek or Pattee Canyon or Blue Mountain. It was good living.

This Sunday, Dick comes in the back door with green beans in one hand and a few ripe tomatoes in the other. "We'll have more tomatoes later today. If somebody wants to pick 'em, we'll have more green beans too."

Never bothered by distractions, Dick picks up the fat copy of a Teddy Roosevelt biography he's half finished, takes a seat in the glider, and pulls out the bookmark.

Mom returns to the kitchen in a plaid blouse and shorts and pours her third cup of coffee before settling at the table with the Sunday paper. She reads bits of local and national news to anyone in earshot.

A month ago, Brooke called to tell me about a weekend visit, when Mom was reading the Sunday paper like she is today. Mom hollered to Dick, who had just started Edmund Morris's nine-hundred-page Roosevelt biography.

"Have you had your ducts cleaned lately?" Mom said.

"What?"

"Have you had your *ducts* cleaned?"

"What are you talking about?" Dick asked.

"Your furnace ducts—have you had 'em cleaned?"

"No, we don't need our ducts cleaned. We hardly have any."

Mom took a drink of coffee and flipped the newspaper to a new section. She read silently for awhile and then called to Brooke this time, down the hall. "I bet you wish you had some of that Google stock."

Brooke answered, "Uh huh." She grinned to herself and counted to five, knowing what was coming next.

"What is Google, anyway?" Mom asked, from her place at the kitchen table.

I WILL MISS THE CHARACTER THAT IS MY MOM WHEN SHE'S gone. I tear up, my face pressed to the window, as the plane lifts off and heads west, Lolo Peak and Grant Creek behind me. I wonder when I'll see my mom next.

Only a few minutes after I arrive home, Ed calls. "How was Montana, and how is Barb?"

"She's okay—great natured. But she's failing a little," I say into the phone, confirming his absence in Montana and here.

I don't tell him I know Mom missed him this week. It's a nice thought to convey, but I don't want to make him feel guilty about not being there. Ed will also miss the character that is my mom. He will never get over her. Neither will I.

CHAPTER 5

Mom

2006

I was walking with my visiting cousin on the same wetlands path I bicycle every school day, counting crows and exclaiming over winter cloud formations that drift in from the Pacific, when Brooke called. I fumbled through my backpack for the flip phone I brought for this very reason.

"Mom died a few minutes ago," Brooke said.

"Oh, gosh," I said. I knew it was coming. I cried.

I pictured Mom, tiny in a hospice bed in the living room of the sweet little house she shared with Dick on the edge of town.

"I think she was ready," Brooke said. "Just before she took her last breath, she said she was ready 'to go out the back door.'"

At the same time my mother was going out the back door, my stepfather was dialing the hospice nurse to ask if he could add morphine to Mom's drip. Brooke called him to the bedside. "Dick, I think she's going. We don't need the nurse or morphine."

Mom died several months after my summer visit of chattering and church and tomatoes and green beans from Dick's big garden under the big sky. All that garden bounty kept Mom perking along quite well, considering her diet for decades of aspirin and prednisone to treat rheumatoid arthritis, before modern biologics for the disease.

TODAY I'M BACK IN MONTANA TO REMEMBER MOM IN the church that was mine when I was growing up. I'm sad and I miss her, but I'm more full hearted than broken hearted. My adult daughters sit on either side of me on a wooden pew, their father next to one. Brooke and her family are nearby. We will commend my mother in this warm, familiar sanctuary.

The minister welcomes guests. "Barbara and Dick attended more memorial services than anyone in this congregation, out of respect for this community of believers and friends." My stepfather offers a gentle smile. This serious Hoosier is warm and grateful.

The church is full of memories. Late winter light finds its way through yellow, blue, and ruby glass bricks and glances off the back of oak pews polished by decades of squirmy little girls in satin dresses and women in wool coats. The natural wood interior, with a courtyard view on the world, was the right place to remember my forester father a Christmas season decades ago. At nineteen, I appreciated the treasure that he was.

On the day of my father's memorial service, the chancel was flanked by two ten-foot alpine fir trees that Dad had chopped down in the woods, to decorate the church for Advent and prepare hearts for the birth of the Christ child. At the memorial, two University of Montana campus ministers spoke of Dad's steady sense of justice during the civil rights era and the Vietnam War. Friends shared my heartache in this green, beautiful, and somber space.

A few years before that December afternoon, a childhood friend fainted on Christmas Eve, very near where I sit today. Brad and I were thirteen-year-old rumpled shepherds. Brad, mesmerized by the flickering flame of the candle he was holding, buckled at the knees and crumpled to the floor. Nervous parents blew out candles throughout the sanctuary.

A springtime before that, my shy little sister sang "I'm Called Little Buttercup" in a musical upstairs. "You have such a nice voice," I said in preteen surprise.

I was married here on a snowy January evening thirty-six years ago, our humble wedding scheduled between college semesters. No one we knew held a three-day wedding event like couples have today—volleyball and raft trip on Friday, ceremony and farm-to-table dinner on Saturday, and breakfast buffet and Frisbee on Sunday. A destination wedding was unheard of among our young friends. Today, the man who wrote and recited vows with me in this space on a winter night, traveled to Montana for the service to honor his mother-in-law.

The adult daughters next to us were baptized in this church as little girls, touched with a drop of water and reminded they are beloved children of God. Bree sang in her first children's choir on the steps before us. Ani went to preschool downstairs, where she colored her pictures solid black, each one looking like night. I wasn't worried, but her artist auntie was.

The last memorial service I attended here was for my brother Bruce, remembered with exclamation points as a character. He also died too young, and I felt part of me was gone.

Today, another part of me is gone, though he's here. With me but not really with me. I'm glad my girls have their father with them. And I'm glad for him. Ed telephoned this week in support and tears, missing Mom. It would have been nice to have him at my side, like he was when Bruce died.

Ani begins the afternoon memorializing and looks beautiful, strikingly like her grandmother, as she stands to address the congregation.

"My grandmother called me Puppy Toes," she says. "I never knew why. Grams was different from other grandmothers, and I loved that. There was no mystery, no hidden agenda, no dramatic emotion with Grams. Instead, what we experienced as grandchildren was a woman of good humor and terrific faith. The simplest explanation is she truly let life happen."

My daughters remember their grandmother—her quirkiness and keen card games—with affection.

When it's my turn, I say, "Thank you for coming today to honor my mother, Barbara. Our family moved to Montana from the wild and scenic Selway River in Idaho when I was nine years old."

My mother missed the Selway rolling past her kitchen window when we first arrived in Missoula, where she looked out her kitchen window at the big "M" on Mount Sentinel. It was good, but it wasn't the river.

"I'm grateful my mother and father brought our family to this church," I say, "for that move in 1958 had everything to do with how I would shape my life and how my daughters would shape theirs."

As I speak, I tug at the back of my blouse, my customary way to maintain composure. My voice cracks, but I keep the tears at bay. I want to talk about Mom. Ed is tearful, but even watching him, I don't cry. I imagine he feels a little lost here today, a place where he once belonged, but now not so much. I'll cry later.

"Thank you for holding my mother in the warm embrace of this community of lifelong friends," I say to the congregation. The truth is, Barbara sometimes embarrassed us with stern silence, even here, in the most forgiving of places. Her secret insecurities were few, but they ran deep. She brushed off compliments and thanks. Only one time did she share with me her insecurity about living in a college town with many intellectual women friends. She never got over missing out on college. When Mom finished high school, she went straight to business school.

"The War was on, and after business school, I went to work at the Pentagon," Mom said. I was always sorry that my wonderful, solid mother felt like less.

"Mine was the mother my friends wished was theirs," I tell the friends gathered at church. "We ate oatmeal cookies two at a time out of a ceramic pig cookie jar. My friends still talk about the cookies and Mom's clinking silver Navajo bracelets stacked on her wrist. And her humor. They all loved her humor."

Everyone did. When I look up, friends, cousins, and acquaintances nod in recognition of Barbara's funny side. Everyone here has a story. Eyes all around me are smiling and brimming with tears at the same time, but only Ed, sitting between Bree and Ani now, is crying. Full-on weeping. He loved my mother, and she was crazy about him. He was the only person in her circle who could call her "Barb." Together, the two laughed and forgot their insecurities.

"You might know that our family hustled home from church every Sunday to head out of town for a picnic," I continue. "Every Sunday in every season, Mom packed the wicker picnic basket she purchased with green stamps and told us to get in the car. She couldn't wait to get outside. In winter, my father built a fire in a tree stump, set a can of B&M Baked Beans in the coals, and settled a heavy grate on the fire to grill hamburgers. Mom pulled a runner sled up the hill with the kids." I tell about the Army-Navy surplus snow pants my mother wore on those outings, wool thick enough to ward off weather in the Aleutian Islands. On top, she wore a wool sweater with holes at the elbows.

"We often stopped at Barrett's Grocery for a can of baked beans on the way out of town. I stayed in the car," I confess, "to avoid seeing anyone I knew. Forty years later, I dressed the same way."

"My mom took us camping without a tent, danced to the Beatles in front of the picture window on North Avenue, and took my friends on family vacations," I say. "Mom also welcomed my best friend Ginny to live with us during her last year of high school, when her family moved away. I wasn't sure I wanted to give up my hard-earned single bedroom, but Mom said, 'Do you want more space or more happiness in this house?'"

Not much riled my mother. She often said, "It'll be okay," and it almost always was. When my husband left, she didn't say it would be okay. She may have been as sorry for herself as she was for me. She was fond of Ed and knew he was fond of her. I dreamed of sons-in-law one day who would care as much for me.

Near the end of her life, I sat on the edge of Mom's bed and talked with her, as I did on every visit. "Maybe he'll be back," she said about this son-in-law she loved.

"He's not coming back, Mom." I didn't tell her I still hoped he would, one year out. Instead, I said, "It'll be okay." Mom gave me a faint smile and turned away on the pillow. When she turned back to me, she told me for the third time, "Ed gave us that plant on the patio, you know. It's still blooming three months later."

I WISH I WAS BLOOMING IN THIS MOMENT. I'M GLAD TO be here with all these people who loved Mom, doing what I'm doing, but what I'm missing is clear. At the end of my message to the good souls in church, I say, "From my mother, I learned values of simplicity and friendship, loyalty and generosity, faith and justice."

From the unfairness of teenage slights to the beauty of loyal friends, I have remembered her message, "It'll be okay." This dimension of my mother is no secret to anyone here today.

Ed sits before me, a red bandana folded over his tears. He catches my eye, and I see his sadness. We share so many intimacies about my mother that it feels odd to be this distant. With his loss in layers, Ed may wonder if it will be okay. I do.

Many people in these pews remember at least one of Barbara's pithy expressions: "It'll never show on a galloping horse." "Six of one, half-dozen of another." "Keep the faith." "Don't wish your life away."

Indeed, don't wish your life away.

CHAPTER 6

Lakoloa Place

1971

"We hated my mom, growing up, and she hated us," Ed told me, when we were in college. "She was pretty mean. She called us the 'dirty Russians' and said, 'You lucky you get adopt.'"

Ed and his twin brother were *hanai* kids, an ancient Hawaiian tradition of giving away the firstborn child, the greatest of all gifts. Even after World War II, families gave children to family members. Ed and John's birth mother gave the twins to her uncle and his wife, who had no children. Jeannette had suffered two miscarriages, and I always wondered if she had no choice in taking the boys as her own.

"My mom had a stroke when we were in third grade. It left her deaf and with a weak leg. She was an easy target for my dad, who flipped over his dinner on the TV tray if something wasn't right. Or he knocked my mom to the floor. Then he'd say, 'Pick up your mudda.'"

The twins lived the sorrow and shame of their mother crumpled on the floor and the blows their father dealt each of them. I had no experience with rage or such a shadow on a child's psyche. I thought experience and a strong will could soften the harsh effects of childhood.

Ed called mine the Ozzie and Harriet family, not because my mother wore a housedress like Harriet on television, or spoke adoringly to her husband and children, but because we had fun and talked to each other and ate dinner together, where we talked more, often about social issues and politics. I never doubted my parents loved me. I could count on them.

I was grateful Jeannette got a second chance to love her son—and show it. She was proud of Ed and kind to me, and later, she was a loving grandmother.

Proud as she was, Jeannette didn't want her son to get married his senior year of college, certain his grades would fail, and least of all to a *haole*. She didn't want him to think so much of himself that he wouldn't return to Hawaii to work for the fire or police department.

I introduced myself to my future mother-in-law by mail, hoping a nice hand on delicate stationery would make me more than a haole who thought too much of herself. From my first letter, Jeannette addressed thin blue airletters to her son and me.

———

WHEN ED TOOK ME HOME TO HAWAII IN 1971, I DIDN'T know what to expect, beyond paradise. The flight into Honolulu was beautiful—Pearl Harbor gleaming on one side and Waikiki touching the sky on the other. Giant coconut palm fronds clacked in the breeze outside the airport.

As we drove into Lakoloa Place, Ed said, "You'll see more of the neighborhood tomorrow. Kalihi has a rough reputation." What I did see was a street lined in flowering everything, avocado trees drooping with heavy emerald fruits. I had never seen anything like it.

I slipped off my sandals on the back porch and lined them up with rubber flip flops and bamboo slippers in order.

I didn't know this would endear me to my new mother-in-law. I only knew it looked like the right thing to do.

Jeannette hadn't heard us arrive and sat in the living room with her hands in the dip of her cotton sundress. As we walked through the kitchen, she shifted her weight to rise off the chair on her right arm and reached for my face, kissed me on each cheek, and then pulled her son's face toward hers. "Ahh, Noa," she crooned. She had signed her letters "Mom Jeannette" since we married eighteen months ago. I felt it.

Afternoon breeze cooled the living room through wide plantation shutters. Ed slipped an album of old Hawaiian music out of its cover, onto the turntable. The music was foreign to my ear, a combination of high notes and agreeable warbling, but I liked Genoa Keawe's falsetto the moment I heard it. In the coming days, Jeannette shared more old albums with me. She couldn't hear the music but remembered the Hawaiian masters from years past. "I feel vibration," she said.

A large pot of fish head stew simmered on the kitchen stove our first evening at Lakoloa Place. I smelled it before I lifted the lid to see if anything else brewed in the bubbling pot. All fish heads. I looked at my husband and winced.

"You'll love it," he teased. "Eyeballs are the favorite."

Jeannette filled a bowl to the brim with shimmering broth and opalescent heads and moved to the carport to eat the soup with rice. I pretended to ladle a bowl for myself, passed it to Ed, and scooped a bowl of rice for me. Ed used chopsticks to dip rice in mocha-colored poi, the soupy paste pounded from taro root that sits on the table for every meal. "Want some?" he asked. I sampled a bit. It's an acquired taste. I ate fresh pineapple so sweet I speared more—and more. I peeled a mango and sliced it into thick, fleshy chunks before I washed the dishes and went outside to say good night to Jeannette.

Ours was the back bedroom, painted in flat, institutional green that camouflaged geckos crawling near the ceiling. I shooed away three silver-dollar-sized cockroaches skittering in the bathroom sink before I climbed into bed.

Roosters crowed at the break of dawn. I opened my eyes wide and looked straight into Ed's. "Oh, yeah. Forgot to tell you about the roosters," he said. "Lots of people in this neighborhood keep roosters for cock fights."

"What are cock fights?" I asked and wished I hadn't.

We found guava juice, more pineapple, and rice for breakfast and packed a lunch of the same to take to the beach.

At the beach at Ala Moana, I swam into the waves and felt like a child, buoyant on my first dip in the Pacific. Ed moved farther out to catch big waves and body surf, while I laid out the towel with orange stripes parallel to the ocean and slathered my pale legs in baby oil. I fell asleep in the noontime sun and woke an hour later. I knew the moment I looked at my shining shins that I would pay for the first day at the beach.

By evening, the flaming sunburn was radiating heat, and a giant canker appeared on my bottom lip. My husband was sympathetic. "Can I do anything?"

"Find some vinegar," I said.

"I should have warned you. People all over Waikiki look like tomatoes. Bright red bellies and bald heads."

"At least I don't have either of those," I said. "But I look like the tourist I am."

THE NEXT DAY, ED AND I WENT TO KAMEHAMEHA Schools, a diamond on the hillside above the city, Honolulu Harbor and Diamond Head in the distance.

"When I was a kid, it wasn't cool to be Hawaiian," Ed said. "We couldn't speak Hawaiian in school." A curious edict at a school for children of Hawaiian ancestry.

"But we could sing Hawaiian songs."

Sing they did—in classrooms and contests, kindergarten through high school, and in late-night gatherings with friends, where they "talked story" and poked fun at each other, parents, and teachers.

Near the bus transfer station, Ed said, "Dad's 1954 Chevy embarrassed us when we got to high school, the passenger door tied shut with a piece of rope. We didn't want anybody to see us, so we asked Dad to drop us off a block from the bus stop. 'Thanks, Dad. We'll walk from here.'"

Ed recalled an experience that haunts him still. "The building up there is where I told my guidance counselor I wanted to take Japanese. She said, 'You can't, Ed, you're too stupid.' The worst is not that she said it, but that I believed it."

He recalled more high school days as a gangly teenager. "I was six feet tall and 130 pounds in the ninth grade. My dad called me Big Head. Sometimes he called me Neck."

When I think of my parents' pet names for me—Gwendolyn or Honey—there was never a reference to my gawky teen features.

When we passed the gym, Ed described a day that branded him. "I got kicked off the basketball team for drinking." I had already heard this story. "I was the only one the coach nailed. My dad didn't come to games, so he didn't have to know." Basketball was the one place this lanky teen could match his classmates, point for point.

Hope was dashed in a flash. "I was embarrassed the rest of my senior year," he said.

"My dad had one hope for me—to graduate from Kam Schools and walk out the front door. I did. John got kicked out, but I finished. At graduation, many classmates wore a stack of a dozen leis, but I was proud with three leis from my aunties—orchid, pikake, and ginger. After the graduation ceremony, I walked up to my dad, thinking he might congratulate me."

"He said, 'Neck, go find yo' mudda. Let's go home.'" The graduate left the celebration stoop shouldered, to find Jeannette and the Chevy.

Ed suffered a punishing portion of shame by the time he was eighteen. No reading Kafka or comparing Shakespeare's tragic characters could fix that. The world of literature would only illuminate the wounds.

"I was so insecure," he said to me, about many things, including growing up with his twin brother. "John was the life of every party, everybody's friend."

———————

JEANNETTE AND I COMMUNICATED WELL JUST A FEW DAYS into our visit. I understood her pidgin, and she read my lips. I liked my new mother-in-law, who filled in more of Ed's story, that he was slow to read. "We thought he mental retard," she told me.

Jeannette gave me an eight-by-ten-inch black-and-white photograph of this little boy with a gentle smile, sitting with other sweet-faced, barefooted five-year-olds at a low table in a Kamehameha Schools classroom, high on the hilltop. The children looked bright and secure and darling, in a classroom bathed in sunlight, noisy birds in swaying palms outside the open door.

"My husband, Bill, pure Hawaiian," Jeannette said of the man who came after work and left after dinner every day for the last ten years. "We still married," she said. "I never give up my husband." I sensed her hurt. Now I know a wife's hurt when a husband decides he's not hers.

When Bill came home to Lakoloa Place at the end of a workday during our visit, he was serious and quiet. He served himself dinner from the stovetop and ate alone at a TV tray before he left for Dottie's house. There was no threat of him upending his dinner tray. One evening, Ed came into the kitchen after sitting with his father in the carport.

"That ten-minute conversation with my dad is the most I've ever talked to him," he said.

I was starting to get it during the week in Hawaii, why Ed called mine the Ozzie and Harriet family. At his house, I felt the gifts of a culture and losses of a family not lost on him. I had a peek into paradise, a culture rich in story and song, and a childhood Ed might never get over.

CHAPTER 7

Selway River Memorial

2006

i miss her much more than i expected
i mowed the lawn all afternoon
baked in the sun
thought about how i'd fill the new void
in my montana soul
i won't
i won't fill the void
i won't try
the emptiness is meant to stay
to give shape to the
landscape
family
my heart and
remind us why we love
the big
big
montana sky

—ANI

Yesterday, Ani and I drove over the mountains from Mom and Dick's Missoula house, where Ani mowed the lawn and remembered why she loves the big sky. This morning, I rise early and climb out of my tent on the bank of the Selway River. My family, in various stages of waking up this morning, is here in the perfect place to remember my mother. We will soon spread her ashes.

The sun glimmers on the river as it rolls past O'Hara Campground. It's August, and the water is low and slow. The cascades of Selway Falls are upstream. Maybe we'll drive twelve miles up the dirt road this afternoon to walk on the massive boulders below the falls and wonder at the power of the river. There is no place I would rather be right now.

The Selway, named a wild and scenic river in 1968, was among the first to receive this divine designation, a memorial to Idaho's extraordinary gentleman senator, Frank Church. In forty years since protection, the Selway looks the same. No hotels or hydroelectric dams will ever crowd the banks or stem the flow of the river.

———

I LOVE IT HERE. WHEN I WAS A LITTLE GIRL, WE LIVED two miles down the road. My father was ranger at Fenn Ranger Station, on the Nez Perce National Forest, built by the Civilian Conservation Corps in lasting wood and river rock. Dad's office, filled with oak armchairs and file cabinets, smelled of linoleum. The amber fir-paneled walls were covered with maps and black-and-white photographs of young men on fire crews, standing next to pack mules bearing heavy burdens.

From the ranger's house, a small wood-framed bungalow heated by a wood-stoked furnace, we watched deer cross the road to drink from the river and stood wide-eyed on the porch as a massive moose lumbered through the yard.

On summer mornings, especially when our cousins came to visit, we walked up the path to the cookhouse, where cheerful Ruth Bullock cooked for a crew of firefighters and summer workers. We pulled out a wide drawer lined in wax paper and helped ourselves to a warm maple bar.

For nine years, my brother and sister and I, with the same visiting cousins who have come today to remember their Aunt Barbara, spent hot summer days at the river. We learned to swim, played in fine white sand, and built elaborate houses of river rock until we were brown as berries and had to go home for naps or dinner or both.

Today, I stand on the riverbank to watch the Selway move downstream. In a few miles, it will merge with the Lochsa to form the Clearwater, which will enter the Snake at Idaho's border and roll on from there to the mighty Columbia. The water is so clear, I can see the river bottom, layered in green and tawny and black-speckled rocks where fish of the same colors hide. I wonder how many salmon from the quiet eddy below me will travel six hundred miles to the Pacific Ocean. How many will finish the arduous journey back to spawning grounds?

My mother loved it here and returned every summer since 1958, the year our family moved to Montana. I miss Mom at this place she loved, and I miss Ed, whose first experience in the echo of a wild and scenic river was right here. We camped as newlyweds across the river and upstream a bumpy mile or two. It was hot and dusty on the road, but Rackliff Campground was an oasis in the shade of towering Douglas fir and cedar. Camping was uncomplicated fun. When we started to sweat in the heat of the day, we plunged in the river.

Ed would like to be here, as much as he enjoyed my mother and all my family. He's been gone only two years, and I couldn't pretend, in the intimacy of a family campout, that it was easy to have him here. Tears flow in time with the river. I miss Ed and Mom both.

―――――――――

My stepfather Dick arrived at O'Hara Campground late last evening, after dinner and before dark. I walked over to see Dick and Bea, his lady friend, after he backed his shiny new trailer into a site with hookups. He seemed anxious, revved up, and gave perfunctory responses to my lightweight inquiries. "How was driving over Lolo Pass with your new rig?" I asked.

"Fine," Dick answered. I couldn't tell if he was happy to see me or not.

―――――――――

This morning, I unfold myself from the bench on the sturdy picnic table and ask the kids, Brooke's two and my two, all young adults and hardly kids, if they're finished with the Corn Chex. My nephew Micah pours another bowl. I fold the wax paper liner and put the milk carton in the cooler. If Mom were here, Dick would be stirring up huckleberry pancakes. He would feed the campfire that's taking the chill off the morning and griddle the cakes next to the bacon he just fried to a ripply crisp. Two of the kids would ask for hotcakes, as Dick calls them, without bacon grease.

"Oh, a little bacon grease won't hurt you," Dick would say.

"That's right. Can we use a different skillet, Gramps?"

Dick is the only grandfather my girls and their cousins have ever known. He's afforded them dozens of summers of garden bounty and campfires. They're fond of him and managed in their early years to josh this Hoosier out of his taciturn ways around the fire or at a game of hearts after dinner. He refers to them as his grandchildren—not Barbara's and not step-grandchildren, but his. Dick even calls me his daughter. We've been sharing Barbara a long time.

This morning, Dick emerges from the screen of choke-cherries bordering his campsite and walks up with a hitch in his get-along. Bea is by his side. In unison, the kids say, "Hi, Gramps" and walk around the firepit to give him a hug. Dick's hug is as stiff as always, but no stiffer. I'm proud of the four as they follow their greeting to Gramps with, "Hello, Bea." I wish she hadn't come on this day set aside for my mother, but I'll be a good sport.

"Good morning, Oompah," I say. "Hello, Bea."

"He'llo," Dick says, his voice high and quick, hiding any sentiments he might have about this moment and why we're here. This Indiana-bred forester is so good at hiding sentiments that sometimes I wonder if he has them to hide.

My cousin Susan throws back the flap of a small tent and climbs out. She is long and lean in stripes and shorts to her knees. Susan wears thin, strappy sandals and looks as put together this morning as when she enters the kitchen of her own house on a sunny morning wearing a print poplin duster with a wide ribbon tied in front.

Aunt Bette, my mother's only sister, moves slowly down the aluminum steps of a travel trailer and walks over to our picnic table in a white cardigan, canvas Keds, and short pants that she and Barbara called pedal pushers five decades ago. Susan and I called our mothers the Queen Bs when we were girls and laughed at their pedal pushers. Now we call them capris and wear them ourselves.

"How is everybody this morning?" Aunt Bette says, with the customary smile in her voice. She radiates at all times what the rest of us would like to radiate sometimes. Like

Susan, Bette looks put together, from earrings to painted nails.

When we were kids, the highlight of the year was when Aunt Bette arrived with Susan and her brother GB for two sweet summer weeks. Gleeful cousins slept under wool army blankets on cots in a canvas wall tent. Moonlight spilled in through the tent flaps, and we listened as crickets chirped all the way to the river. At lights out, the boys used government-issue flashlights with a powerful beam to cast spooky shadows across the canvas ceiling and terrorize their little sisters.

THIS MORNING, AFTER BREAKFAST, I GO BACK TO MY TENT and riffle through a bag to find the manila folder containing copies of an old hymn. I feel a catch in my throat. I don't want to cry when I speak about Mom at the riverbank in a few minutes. Other than missing Ed as I do, this is about as good as it gets. Mom is here.

I wave to everyone to come down to the shore. The river glints in the morning sun. Smooth moss-covered rocks stack their way up the bank. I move down to the river's edge, and others follow. The sough of wind in the trees upstream makes this spot an apt choice for our memorial.

Brooke picks up the red and black urn she shaped from clay and fired at home last week. The urn is both comical and beautiful, with a fat belly, a lid with a peak, and little feet to stand on. Young cousins scramble down the riverbank carved by high water, and Aunt Bette's grandson takes her arm as she picks her way along river rocks. Dick and Bea follow and stand just behind the circle of family.

Brooke walks into the river in flip flops, holding the pottery urn with both hands. She steps gingerly over slippery rocks that shimmer green and gold in the ripples. Her daughter, Zoe, follows in a tank top and shorts, looking as young as she is at nineteen. She stares at the river bottom and blinks away tears. The river swirls around her muscular legs.

Brooke opens the moment. "We've gathered here because this was Barbara's favorite place. She lived down the road at Fenn Ranger Station for eleven years. When our family moved away, she missed the Selway and brought us here to camp every summer."

Brooke releases the twine that holds the lid in place and tips the urn toward the river. Pale gray ashes spill into the water in heavy plops. Some float downstream. More sink and settle on the river bottom to form a large imprint that doesn't move.

"That's Mom sticking around to watch what's going on," Brooke laughs. We all laugh. Dick says, "Have a good swim, Barbara." Perfect. My mother never saw a body of water she didn't want to swim in, but her favorite was this one.

Everyone in the circle, shading themselves from sun or tears, has a moment to offer up a memory. Ani, her cap with a Frisbee team logo protecting her eyes from the river's glare, speaks with affection for Grams, the one different from all other grandmothers. Micah cries, his heart swelling with memories of this character grandmother.

Dick says, "Barbara loved the Selway, and we camped here together for thirty-five years."

My Aunt Bette cries and says, in the way that is hers, speaking every syllable of a name, "Bar-bar-a loved it here, and we loved it with her so many times. She'll be happy in this river."

I pass around copies of "Shall We Gather at the River," and we sing the shaky and beautiful hymn. GB and his wife have music in their bones, and they carry the tune for us. Dick doesn't sing. He doesn't ever sing.

We close our circle and move up the bank to plan a triathlon. Mom loved this summer tradition and served as timekeeper. Each team had a champion in one event: Zoe a runner, GB a biker, Ani a paddler in a fat inner tube. This morning we form teams. Dick is timekeeper.

After lunch, we drive downriver to our favorite swimming hole at Johnson Bar, named after no one in our family, but we claim it as our own. This could be the last time some of us walk the path to the beach, lined on both sides with chokecherry bushes, heavy with berries in dusty ruby clusters in dry August. We swim and float on tubes and talk about Mom and her zany expressions, like "You'd be taller if you didn't have so much turned under at the ankle." The family favorite was Barbara's exclamation when telemarketers called at dinnertime. After a cursory conversation, she would set the receiver in its cradle, return to the dinner table, and say, "Who gives a rat's ass how I am tonight?"

Brooke and Susan and I sit at the river's edge. The water laps at our ankles and washes away caked sand. It was here that Susan and I spent hours as girls, washing the beach with buckets of river water, searching for the dime-store rings with sparkling stones that we lost while building sand castles.

We talk about Dick, who grieved ten short days before he took up with Bea. When Dick told Brooke about his new lady friend, whose three husbands over many years had each died, Brooke said, "Grampa, are you sure this is a good idea?" A refrigerator magnet in Bea's kitchen reads, "Eat, drink, and remarry." A yellowed cartoon taped to a cupboard door says, "Women grieve and men remarry."

For the empty weeks after Mom died, Dick was on a tear. He couldn't clear out closets fast enough. He sold his house in a fire sale to a friendly neighbor. He called Brooke and insisted she rush to town to pick up a bedroom set. He partnered with Bea, and they went everywhere together. Brooke and I thought Lucille, who walked across the road with a chicken-and-green bean casserole that sad night after Mom died, might strike Dick's fancy.

Weeks later, Dick told Brooke how he felt those first empty days. "I took care of your mother 24/7 for so long, I just couldn't bear being alone without her. I'm the one who knocked on Bea's door—she didn't come to me."

I had to get over my judgment of Dick for squirreling from here to there and my assumption that Bea was the one in a hurry. I admired Dick's devotion to my mother. It was enviable. He didn't forget Barbara. He was grieving and needed to keep going.

I know a little about how to keep going. I have practice at being alone, and I'm pretty good at it.

When work kept Ed from coming to a family campout on the Selway River years ago, he enjoyed the report of Barbara cheering triathlon teams of bikers and runners as they crossed the O'Hara bridge and the finish line. When I return home in a few days, he'll call to ask about Mom's memorial.

"Did you spread Barb's ashes?"

I'll tell him Mom hung around to be remembered in the best way. He knows a little about hanging around.

"I'll never get over the shape of Mom's ashes on the river bottom," I'll say. I won't tell him how much I missed him on the banks of the wild and scenic river.

CHAPTER 8

Possum—or Was It Opossum?

2009

A summer evening in Oregon is almost always heavenly, perfect for a bike ride home. Tonight, I enjoyed a potluck of salmon quiche and blackberry cobbler with friends. The dog greets me from the yard as I cruise down my street and up the driveway.

In the kitchen, I soak the baking pan and go outside to the glider in the backyard. I love the way the cool air rises from the grass. With today's newspaper under my arm, I switch on my headlamp and push the screen door open.

Tinder, named long before the fiery dating site of the same name, is in the middle of the yard. "Hello, Buddy," I say and expect him to follow. Next to him on the grass is a small mass of something I can't make out. I lean closer to pick it up, thinking it's a limb off the fir tree. My headlamp catches enough of the something to illuminate a stray possum, not a stray limb. I see blood.

It's late. I can't rush to my neighbors for help. Furthermore, I don't want to be that woman, the one the tall, strong men and boys in the neighborhood shrink from when they see me coming. I can manage this.

In the five years I've lived alone in this house, I've asked for help only half a dozen times for the pesky jobs that require a tall reach, a strong arm, or a stomach of steel. My young neighbor Tim dug out a huge fern and root ball one Sunday. Jack used a power screwdriver to reinforce hinges. Zach pounded two nails to hang the Yankee Clipper sled Santa brought when I was six years old. Jeff buried the rat my hunter dog shook back and forth after he caught it. I can still hear the flapping.

I turn on my heels and call the dog to come in the house. I'm not particularly squeamish, but I don't like possums or rats, dead or alive. Or raccoons. Sometimes I hate nature. My friend Jacque has trapped a dozen rats. "They're just creatures," she says. "They don't know they're creepy." Jacque is generous.

Possums don't mean to be icky, but they are. However, this sharp-toothed, naked-tailed creature keeps rats and mice in check. I must keep the dog at bay on summer nights.

The slow, pale member of the animal kingdom we spot as roadkill on the roadside, or worse, in the middle of the road, is actually an opossum, cousin to the possum, an Australian marsupial. Marsupial is a more attractive label than rodent. With friendly familiarity, we call our own North American marsupial "possum," leaving off the proper "o." We feel like we know him, or her, the one carrying the babies.

The correct name for this sleek animal is a little like the correct name for the wedge-shaped wheat-and-oatmeal biscuit enjoyed every day in marsupial-rich Australia. The Brits and Aussies call the biscuit "scon," but we call it "scone."

I feel pretentious ordering a scon or telling a story about an opossum.

The name doesn't matter tonight. I have to do something with the lump on the lawn.

My dog sits next to the carnage like a big brother, as if to say, "I maybe hurt this furry being, but it's mine." The dog is serious, no racing around to get me to chase him in the dark. He comes a few steps my way and returns for a nervous spin around the possum. I call him again. He hesitates but finally leaves the lump in the yard and follows me through the screen door.

I holler and moan and wonder what to do. I assume the animal is dead, but even if it is, I don't think I can bury it. I walk out into my quiet, moonlit street to see if either of the two men I might ask to bury a possum is awake at this hour. No and no. Why am I looking for a man to move this carcass? It's not beyond my reach or too big. I've lived alone long enough to know how to do some heavy lifting, and this is not my heaviest.

Jeff did say, "Anytime" when I thanked him for burying the rat. He is always up late, his computer screen glowing in a front window, but he's been down with a summer cold. From the looks of him this afternoon, he probably went to bed early. It would be a lot to ask him to help me tonight, even if that computer screen was lit.

Twenty minutes pass. I tiptoe onto the patio to see if the bloody possum was playing possum. In the dark, I see a white head move. Maybe he and I will both be lucky, and he'll be gone in the morning.

It's hot tonight, but I am not sleeping on the screened porch, for fear of opening my eyes to catch the wounded nocturnal mammal slinking along the fence. What if I hear him struggle in the shrubs? I go to my bedroom upstairs and open the window wide.

I sleep fine and wake early. I've forgotten about the possum until I come downstairs. There he is, in the middle of the yard, evidently quite dead, not playing possum at all. He's just a few inches off last night's position.

Can I catch Jeff walking his Bernese mountain dog? He will still have a cold this morning. He's probably sleeping late. I can do this. I have to do this. I cannot leave the possum in the hot sun for the day. I find a shovel in the garage and go to an out-of-the-way spot to dig the deepest hole I can dig in the sunbaked earth. I hope this is the hardest part.

In the yard, I aim the shovel at the silvery body. I try not to look. It won't scoop. It won't load. I push the rigid lump around the yard with the tip of the shovel. I can't get it to slide onto the concave steel blade. I holler and gag. I use the Lord's name in vain and appeal to a higher power. My impulse is to push the carcass onto the shovel with my free hand, but I don't.

Finally, I get half the bloody body onto the shovel. I tip the blade and slide it under the possum's other half. He's much heavier than I expected. I gag again and walk through the gate, my arm and shovel extended in front of me. I look away and maintain my footing. At last, I drop the possum in the deep hole. It lands with a thud, naked tail pointing straight up.

I'm dizzy but satisfied. I wish my children could see me now. I wish Ed could see me dig, load, and bury a possum. I can get over living alone as well as I can get over burying this critter. When Ed lived here, he would have dug the hole and easily scooped the possum to fill it, but in the last years of his residency, he left yard work to me and smiled at me from his office. I pruned and planted, trimmed and tamed but never made as close contact with wildlife as today. I can do this. I did do this. I can do more, not just managing, but being here in this house alone, making it work.

By all appearances, I have finished dealing with the heavy mammal, though I half expect him to rise up out of the soft dirt I piled over him. I watch the mound on the other side of the fence for days, to make sure the opossum wasn't playing possum.

I have a quick talk with Tinder about preserving possums that eat ticks and mice and other pesky critters. I hop on my bike and head for the YMCA to Cardio and Strength class.

If one of my fitness friends says, "How's your morning?" I'll tell her.

CHAPTER 9

Contacts

1971 and 2008

Biking home from school in the afternoon, my glasses fog up, not from crying, but from the misty cloud I'm in. I seldom see clearly, for my glasses are either dirty or fogged over. Some of my students are grimy, but they don't grab at my lenses like a baby sitting on your hip. I slip the glasses into the pocket of my raincoat. Maybe I should look into contact lenses.

I've never worn contacts, but I used to have a frequent dream about them. In the middle of a vivid one, I stumbled into Ani's bathroom a few minutes before midnight, wobbly after only an hour of sleep. Ani was home from college with a friend, and the two stood at the sink, each with toothbrush in hand. They stepped aside to make way for me to open a cupboard door and reach inside.

"Mom, are you looking for your contacts?" Ani asked.

Suddenly awake, I was embarrassed and returned to bed.

Ani had witnessed this odd nighttime behavior enough to know what I was up to—or why I was up. I awakened in the night to hunt for something I didn't have.

I've worn glasses since college. I've never had contacts to lose. That night in my daughter's bathroom, searching under the sink for the contacts I didn't have, was one of many like it.

Each time I climbed out of bed in a dreamy state and began to root around in a search, I realized my folly within seconds and went back to bed. Sometimes, instead of looking for contacts, I looked for a ring with a precious stone. I didn't own a ring with a precious stone either. The odd dreams persisted.

***

WHEN I STARTED HIGH SCHOOL AS A THIRTEEN-YEAR-old in wool skirts and sweaters and a corduroy jumper I sewed myself, my mother gave me a ruby ring that her mother had given her when she started high school. I was proud to wear something so delicate and beautiful that had passed down mother-to-daughter and again. I wore the ring every day until a gold prong in the setting pried loose, and the ruby fell out.

I searched for the stone in every shirt and shoe I'd worn in recent days. I scoured every fold and pocket and pulled out drawers and pulled them out again. I never found the small ruby, red as a cardinal's throat.

When I went away to college, my mother gave me another ring, her aquamarine birthstone in a rosette setting. The faceted stone was the color of water. I held it up to look at the sunlight through the watery gem. I admired it on my hand and wore it often. I don't know why I didn't wear it when Ed and I left our little wood frame Wisconsin house to spend the summer in Montana.

We had been married over a year, college graduates a year, and Wisconsin residents almost a year, since the day we moved across the country from Montana with everything we owned in a yellow Opel station wagon. We camped our way, making a stop in the towering Grand Tetons and then a straight shot through Nebraska and Iowa cornfields, to arrive in a sleepy, tree-lined town in the center of Wisconsin for our first real job. We served as house parents to eight teenaged boys at a residential treatment center, and yes, we were in a house with boys, but "parents" was hardly an accurate moniker. We were twenty-one and twenty-two years old and as naïve as ten-year-olds in the art of parenting, especially troubled teen boys.

We didn't know anything about behavior, bad behavior, or managing behavior. We were better at managing the house. Several days a week, I wrestled five pounds of ground beef out of white butcher wrap and deliberated what to do with the greasy mound this time. Meatloaf. I would add shredded carrots.

Ed did laundry for eight boys every day of the week and sorted black and brown socks until he was dizzy. He also supervised showers. If no one checked on Ron Moon, fourteen, he would turn on the shower and flatten himself against the metal stall, fully clothed.

At the end of our first year at Sunburst Youth Homes, we weren't stellar house parents, but we were better. We learned to set boundaries for the boys, went ice-skating in winter, and tossed a football every summer evening. But we didn't love the role and were relieved to be hired as teachers in the campus school for the following year. We liked Wisconsin, we liked Sunburst and kids, and we were immersed in a circle of idealistic young friends and coworkers. We campaigned door-to-door for George McGovern in the 1972 presidential race. He won the District of Columbia and one state. It wasn't Wisconsin.

In June, I made my last meatloaf in the boys' cottage, and Ed folded the last pair of brown socks. We set pedal to the metal in little Opel and drove 1,300 miles back to Montana for the summer, to finish graduate work.

Before we left town, we sublet our house to perfect strangers. No deposit, no worries. The ring with my mother's aquamarine birthstone, set in gold wire shaped like a flower, was in a faux leather jewelry box upstairs.

We returned to Oak Street in August and found a few things missing—a curious expression, for we didn't find them at all. Among the missing items was the aquamarine ring. I telephoned the not-so-perfect strangers to ask questions. Tami said she hadn't seen a ring with an aquamarine stone.

It was a full thirty years beyond the good years in Wisconsin until I dreamed about losing a ring with a precious stone or losing contact lenses. When the peculiar dream entered my sleep, I didn't explore its meaning or why I leapt out of bed in the middle of the night to scramble in cupboards and drawers, even a jewelry box. The dream just came back.

Five years after the curious night-time interruption began, my husband moved out. From the day he left, the dream didn't return. Not once. I was seeing an adept counselor at the time, who made literary allusions and pulled the perfect poem off his bookshelf to accent our conversations. I told him of my recurring dream about something I didn't own. I added that since my husband left, I no longer jumped out of bed in the middle of the night to search for a lost something.

John didn't skip a beat. "You finally lost that something you didn't have enough of and feared losing."

I had longed to be more valuable to my husband, more precious. I didn't know I was afraid of losing our alliance altogether. I knew Ed harbored his own longing, perhaps missing as much in his middle-aged soul as we were missing as immature house parents. He worked and worked some more, and when that didn't fill the hole in his soul, he looked for more and left.

A few years after we divorced, when the exchanges were less raw, Ed shared time with me as friend and father to our girls, our family in his fiber and mine. He too had a good psychologist who opened his eyes to the half-dozen adverse childhood effects he endured as a child. He confessed to me how insecure he was all those years—teen, young adult, middle adult—all of them.

Ed became the person I had hoped would emerge as my husband, offering attention I had missed on my side of the office door. Now we could talk over the table about books and music and kids. This wasn't how I planned it would unfold, and I cried when he drove away, but it was better than missing a piece in the family.

I left my counselor after three years and a lot of tears in his office, before he left town in retirement. During our final session, John read another poem that exposed my own longing and that of many women. In "The Unsaid," Stephen Dunn writes about searching for solace by being understood without having to ask.

I hopped on my bike and pedaled to the bookstore to buy Garrison Keillor's *Good Poems for Hard Times*. Poets master an economy of words to explore a wealth of human hardship and heartache. I can pull out my own Robert Morgan or Mary Oliver poem to define a moment. I'm done dreaming. This is good work, finding words to describe the human condition.

I left the bookstore and biked home to dog-ear a few choice poems for choice moments.

CHAPTER 10

Phone Calls

2010

E d always calls about 9:40 p.m. He doesn't call to chat. He knows I don't like to chat on the phone. He calls to ask if I have time for coffee or dinner this week, if I survived the ice storm, or if I've heard from Bree or Ani. I appreciate our connection over our daughters, though I'd prefer the whole connection to half.

Early in my independent tenure five years ago, I looked at the clock when the phone rang late in the evening, to confirm it was 9:40. Sometimes I didn't answer. *I have nothing new to say.*

Always when I do answer, even now, Ed greets me with a surprised, "Oh, hi, Brenda. You're home. How are you?" He tried earlier when I wasn't home.

"Okay," I say. I haven't answered, "Great" to anyone's query about how I am for years. I don't cry or stammer at my end of the line.

I cry later, after I hang up. I used to hang up first. *I'll be the one to say goodbye.* In our early years apart, Ed cried when he saw me, emotional over a reunion or love or loss— I'm not sure what. There's been a lot of crying.

Ed doesn't know that for months after he left, I cried at school, between classes of squirrely first and second graders who pumped life into me. I didn't tell him, on the phone or in person, that for a very long time, I thought my heart would shatter.

Nor do I tell him how long I hoped he would come home, really come home, as in be devoted. I cried in the kitchen, in the garden, always on the ride home from school, and I still do. But no one ever sees me cry.

Why do the tears flow the moment my tires hit the bike path at the end of the school day, heading home through wetlands, past the blue herons and blackbirds? It's a lovely way to end the day. Why cry? I don't tell Ed that I miss him still, especially now that he's generous with time.

Ed worked more than eighty hours a week in the years before our marriage ended, and I couldn't admit he had a problem. I couldn't admit I had a problem. I didn't want to watch his back at his desk for hours on end, but I didn't add up the hours until he was gone.

Today we can visit long over coffee or dinner. I don't do lunch. I'm not sure why. Maybe it smacks of privilege to me. I avoid fundraising luncheons and send a check. However, I don't have a problem with the privilege of going out to dinner. I love dinner out. Ed and I talk easily about old friends and new books, about our thoughtful daughters and time-out for a two-year-old. "Parents have to be really consistent," Ed says. I agree.

Nice as it is, this alliance is transient, and I don't always welcome it.

It doesn't seem right, the tears, the stuck gear. It has taken years to let go of the hope for a relaxed future with my husband. I liked our family together. Do I miss the image? We're doing okay, spread out as we are, and my mind no longer runs the reel of what I might have done differently.

In the same years since Ed left, figuratively or "for real," as kids say, I've danced at two weddings and adored new grandchildren. I've watched brilliant, sympathetic Barack Obama share his good humor, get elected president, and appoint two women Justices to the Supreme Court.

My husband didn't try to cheat me out of anything but himself. He made certain I was provided for when he left, partly out of guilt and, once he got out of a tailspin, out of genuine regard for my welfare.

"This doesn't change retirement or anything," he said, on his way out the door. He simply, or not so simply, found another person at the depth of longing for a meaningful life. He is the first to say the hole in his heart had nothing to do with me, which is hard to believe when you're left with the house, the dog, and the empty place at the table.

I have friends, a job, and purpose. While I tell myself to get over it, I remain uncertain what "it" is, with its claim on my head and heart. It's getting in the way.

Bree often calls after she puts her girls to bed.

"How are you?" she asked on a recent night.

"I'm okay."

"No, what's wrong?"

"I'm tired of being sad," I said. "Really, just get over yourself."

"You'll get over it when you do," Bree said. "Don't punish yourself." She might be right.

"Should you see someone for help?" she asked.

"I've gotten lots of help. I went to counseling for three years. I finally stopped because I did what John said, followed his advice, practiced what he told me to practice. He said, 'You love hard.' No one knows but you and Brooke—and the counselor, that I can't shake this," I said.

"Do you think you're depressed?" Bree asked.

"No. I function well all around. I'm pretty well-glued.

Every mindfulness guru has a version of 'Wherever you are, be there.' I'm there, all right," I said.

WHEN BROOKE CAME TO VISIT IN THE SPRING, SHE wrote a poem.

My Sister

My sister couldn't fall apart at the seams,
So she unraveled like a thread on a sweater.
After so many years, the sleeve is gone.
She feels like she lost an arm.
She misses the him he is now.
Not the him she had before,
But the new him the new she has now.
Lighter, attentive, a grandpa.
She thinks she'll have to sew up the
seam where the sleeve was,
But I tell her no, get a new piece of yarn
And start knitting like mad.
　　　　　　—BROOKE JOHNSON NELSON

CHAPTER 11

In-flight Music

2010

On a cross-country flight to visit Ani in Washington, D.C., I sat next to the most interesting in-flight conversation I've had the privilege, not punishment, of overhearing. I was in the window seat, and the two gentlemen to my right began to talk politics, then climate and philosophy. They looked my way, to include me. I did want to be part of this, to listen, if nothing else, for the two were illuminating topics I've thought about. I wanted to know more. I liked the pensive gentlemen, ruminating about things that matter. They weren't pontificating or trying to outdo one another.

In my sixth year of living alone, I missed conversation with a companion in my house, though conversation was harder to come by as Ed logged more hours at his desk.

The man in the middle seat was Ted. After the satisfying communication between three strangers, we parted ways in the Denver airport, but not before I registered the street address on Ted's briefcase. I couldn't make myself ask him outright if he would like to continue the conversation. What if he were married? Or committed? It would be embarrassing.

I wrote Ted in Portland. "I was your seatmate on the flight to Denver. I enjoyed the conversation. If you're not attached, I would be pleased to continue the conversation." Or something like that.

Ted responded immediately. We met in Portland for dinner on a few occasions and continued lively discussions about race, urban life, progressive churches. We heard Sister Helen Prejean, of *Dead Man Walking*, speak to my congregation about the death penalty and caring for the convicted's family with the same mercy we offer the victim's family.

"Timothy McVeigh's father doesn't have a proud photo of his son on the mantel to prompt conversation about his boy," Sr. Helen said.

———

TED AND I SPEAK THE SAME LANGUAGE—POLITICS, RELIgion, kids. I tell him little about my loss but learn about his. He suffered an unspeakable one. I don't know it's unspeakable when I ask, carefully, "How did your son die?"

"He took his life," Ted says, not easily, but it's a well-practiced response. "He was a junior in high school." Ted has regained his moorings, and he doesn't dodge or obfuscate, but death has visited a shadow upon his soul.

My eyes brimming in tears and wishing not to sound insincere or shallow, I say, "I don't know anything worse." Ted has doubtless heard every standard sympathetic expression, from "God wanted him" to "At least he's out of pain."

"How did you get through it—I mean, at the time?" I ask. "I can't imagine getting through it, not to mention over it." Later I ask Ted about his younger son.

I know about the toll losing a child takes on a marriage, but I don't ask that question. I don't know Ted well enough yet. I know the toll real life takes on a marriage. I know grief and loss, but not like this.

———

TED'S IN TOWN FOR MY FAVORITE CONCERT OF THE YEAR, the Mozart Candlelight, a glowing performance of chamber music in the radiance of flickering candlelight at a church in the round. I want the warm relationship to glow in every way, but it doesn't. I haven't told my daughters about the good man with good conversation. I think I'm embarrassed.

I like Ted and the way he considers and expresses the details of life, from the gravest of griefs to choir practice. In addition to erudite conversation, Ted is quick and funny. I need that, but I don't feel the spark I want to feel. On a long hike in the park, I know I should tell him, for this might be our last rendezvous.

"I am sorry," I say. "I enjoy your company—a lot. Could we continue the good visits about religion and politics and go to a concert now and then?" Ted is a great singer. He'll always be up for a concert.

"Sure, but I was hoping to travel and more," he says.

"Maybe we could travel together and just stay in separate rooms."

He chuckles. "Well, that wouldn't be any fun."

Ted and I don't go to another concert. If there was more, more of everything, I would invite him to the Mozart Candlelight again next year. He calls to ask how I'm doing. We talk briefly about a new Australian minister at his church and President Obama.

Maybe we'll take in another concert some day. We do speak the same universal language, music.

CHAPTER 12

Wednesday With the Spielmanns

1975

I n 1975, Ed and I moved across the country from our first home in Wisconsin, driving a blue Dodge sedan and towing a tiny U-Haul trailer filled with everything we cared to keep. Ed was expert at packing, stacking, and stuffing after working several summers with Samoan movers who carried refrigerators on their backs. We landed in Oregon, where Ed aimed to be expert at graduate school.

We were house sitters our first months in the new state, in a rambling old house several miles from the University of Oregon campus. Photographs of the elegant home in the shade of giant oak trees looked charming. House sitting would save us money, but money saved, the house was dark and dank, Sparkles was a yappy, unpleasant dog, and I was lonely out on the edge of the college town where all the hum was at the center.

As luck would have it, the homeowners returned two months early, and we moved to Amazon Student Housing, the U of O complex of a peculiar name and ramshackle strip houses behind buckled fences. I wiped mold off the baseboards and threw open the windows. I loved it there.

Amazon, a quick, temporary response to a housing shortage after World War II, sat next to the Amazon Canal.

It was not home to exotic hardwoods, monkeys, or large snakes, and the area regularly flooded, until the Army Corps of Engineers diverted a narrow creek into a wide channel. The temporary housing on the Amazon Canal was in its fourth decade when we moved in.

Doug and Sue moved into the apartment above us and cranked up the Pousette-Dart Band with lots of bass. We tapped our toes and tapped the ceiling with a broom handle on Saturday mornings, to let Sue, an accomplished baker, know we were ready for breakfast. We liked the arrangement.

Later we moved to a less moldy single-story Amazon apartment, with a view of a running track. In Track Town USA, runners of every shape and stride circle the track in every stripe of weather. I liked living with nearby neighbors in much the same boat—pregnant wives, a host of small children, smart men and women chasing advanced degrees, most of us poor. I liked Amazon because everyone else seemed to like it too. We shared everything from casseroles to childcare.

Ed started graduate school, and I signed up to substitute teach in local high schools. Still months from delivering our first child, I decided to boost my income with something I was even better at than substituting. I put an ad in the local paper: "Fast and thorough housekeeper." Two people called immediately, one of them Mrs. Spielmann. I hadn't cleaned house for pay since I was twelve, when I shined my neighbor Mildred's house for a dime. That was ten cents for however long it took me, not per hour. I learned to be fast and thorough.

ON THE LONG COUNTRY DRIVE TO THE SPIELMANN house, I looked like a storybook character peering over the steering wheel of our Dodge Dart with a Slant Six engine.

I didn't know then and don't know now what a Slant Six engine is, but I knew it was desirable.

I arrived with apron in hand and rang the bell and waited. Mr. Spielmann had to know I was there, just like the last six Wednesdays at 9 a.m. He surely heard the baby blue Dart spit gravel as I drove up. At last, he opened the front door.

"Good morning. How are you today?" I said.

"I've been better. I don't like this weather."

Why did I ask the same question every week? I knew Mr. Spielmann would never greet me with anything but grousing. He would never say, "I'm fine," and he certainly wouldn't say, "And how are you?"

Next Wednesday, I'll surprise him. "Mr. Spielmann, what a handsome sweater you're wearing."

My first day at the house, Mrs. Spielmann told me about her husband's career and why they moved to a stone house in the country in a new state.

"My husband was an aerospace engineer for Lockheed," she said. "When he had a heart attack at forty-six, his doctors said he should retire that job, it was too stressful. They told him to move out of California."

Mrs. Spielmann, nine years younger than her husband, was a sweet, round woman who spent most of her waking hours sitting on a Vellux blanket on her king-sized bed, watching soap operas on television and embroidering pictures with thick, woolen thread.

The second week, she told me about her wedding. "We were married at the Beverly Hills Hilton, because that's where my mother-in-law wanted the wedding." This couple didn't fit my image of a wedding in the gold-gilded and crystal glitter of the Beverly Hills Hilton, but I didn't doubt her. It was clear her mother-in-law was in charge.

Each Wednesday, Mr. Spielmann closed the front door behind me and faded into his office, while his wife came to say hello in the hallway. I liked her, and I was glad to see her.

"How have you been this week?" I asked.

"Oh, I'm okay." She sounded wistful and asked about me. She knew I was a few months pregnant. "How are you feeling?"

"I'm fine," I assured her. "I feel good, actually."

Mrs. Spielmann told me to help myself to anything in the refrigerator if I got hungry. Did she know there was nothing to eat in that refrigerator? The gleaming white interior was filled with bare chrome shelves. Each week, I found nothing but supermarket yogurt with artificial fruit flavors and individually wrapped cheddar cheese kisses. I tried each once.

Opposite the barren refrigerator was a solid wall of cookbooks, floor to ceiling. Julia Child's *Mastering the Art of French Cooking*, Betty Crocker, Crock-Pot cooking, books on bacon, books on pies. Hundreds of cookbooks of every size and ethnic influence and dietary persuasion. Twenty-minute meals, the best of Greece, all-chocolate desserts, more Julia Child. There was no evidence that anyone had ever used a cookbook. It didn't look as if the glossy dessert book, a slice of crimson cherry pie on the cover, had ever been opened. The slick, white pages were clean and tight. Not a single casserole cookbook was greasy with finger-prints. Books of casseroles in thirty minutes, casseroles in forty-five minutes, casseroles for a busy household, and a Sunset volume of casseroles for entertaining stood in tight vertical stacks. I can't imagine the Spielmanns ever ate a casserole, and I was certain they never entertained. It was a book club subscription gone berserk.

Time was ticking, and I wanted to get started. David and his father were in the middle of the entry.

"Hello, David," I said as I walked around father and son.

David, sixteen, didn't answer but said in a loud staccato, "Father, what's for lunch today?"

"The usual," his father answered, which meant two Herfy's burgers and fries. So usual they had the same lunch every day.

I pulled a broom and dust cloth out of a closet and moved toward the basement. David and his mother were now in the hall.

"Mother, tell the maid not to touch my TV. Tell the maid not to touch my typewriter." Each word offered a punch, wrapped in singsong.

David's awkward manner was not so different from students I knew at Sunburst Youth Homes, the treatment center for children with emotional troubles or learning disabilities where Ed and I worked the five years before moving to Oregon. I remember twelve-year-old Randy, who called me a bologna sandwich when he got angry and raised the middle finger on each hand to illustrate just what a rotten bologna sandwich I was. I thought of Raymond, who answered my request to get back on-task with, "Might as well. My day's pretty well shot anyway."

Mrs. Spielmann told me earlier that David didn't attend school because his father didn't think the schools in town were good enough. Neither were the doctors or shopping. And the weather—the weather was never good enough. Leaving sunny California might have been a mistake.

Each morning after greeting me, Mrs. Spielmann retreated to her room and picked up her latest embroidery project. I counted thirty-seven stitcheries on the walls of the cavernous house my first day there. Most pictures were flowers, with a rooster and a fruit bunch here and there. I recognized crewel, the stitchery my grandmother did when she sat silently at the end of the couch in our living room and pulled wool yarn through linen.

Always eager to get it out of the way, I started cleaning my least favorite room of the sprawling house, the little bedroom dedicated to the family cats. I didn't get close enough to count the cats, but I think there were nine. The room was filled wall-to-wall with three mattresses, three litter boxes, and many cat dishes. Grateful to be without a sense of smell because of a head injury a few years before, I vacuumed the mattresses and carpet with breakneck speed and didn't touch the litter boxes, a hazard to pregnant women. The cats were elusive, a good thing. I didn't like cats, and I sure didn't like them in great numbers commanding their own bedroom.

Another set of cookbooks, packed solid as matchbooks, covered a wall in the basement family room. I didn't dust the cookbooks or pull one out to flip through pages. A steel sculpture of a dozen birds in flight, which I did dust, was mounted over the fireplace in the same room. One Wednesday, Mrs. Spielmann told me about the time her husband ran hell-bent into a bird's sharp wing tip.

"The tip punctured his forehead, and he ran across the hall to lock himself in the bathroom," she said. "There was a trail of blood from here to the bathroom door, but he refused to let me in to see how serious it was."

I shudder. "How did it end?" I asked.

"He doesn't like local doctors, and he wouldn't drive into town to have the gash stitched. He should have. He used three Band-Aids at once and replaced each as it filled with blood. The scar on his forehead isn't bad, considering."

I hadn't noticed a scar on Mr. Spielmann's forehead, for I always scurried around him to escape his sullen silence. I told Ed the story about the wing tip. He knew something about stern and sullen fathers in a rage.

WHEN DAVID AND HIS FATHER LEFT THE HOUSE ON THIS Wednesday for Herfy's Burgers, I bustled into David's room to clean. It was a teenager's room, full of stuff.

David's grandmother made known her disdain for her daughter-in-law by demanding her son or grandson when she telephoned. The grandmother sent gifts to David on any and all occasions, always practical and always by the dozen. One dozen pairs of athletic socks. One dozen pairs of pajamas. I worked around the bedroom closet over-flowing with these and dozens of other pieces of clothing. I pitched dirty laundry into the hallway and straightened the desk only slightly.

I had never touched David's television or Royal type-writer, and I didn't plan to touch them today. I glanced at a page rolled in the typewriter and moved on. I turned back. I read the first line and the next. I couldn't stop. Was I violating David's warning? He had written a full page in the voice of Lynette "Squeaky" Fromme, sentenced just two months before to life in prison for an attempt on President Ford's life. I read as far as I could read without rolling the paper in the Royal.

The onion-skin page read, "No, I'm not sorry about what I did."

At first, I thought this was a parody, but there was noth-ing exaggerated or funny about it. The strange imitation was filled with frightful attention to detail. News reports highlighted Fromme's difficult relationship with her "tyran-nical" father. Lynette Fromme's father was an aeronautical engineer. This was creepy. Squeaky Fromme was a devoted member of the Manson family. That was creepy.

I had more to tell my husband. He knew about special kids. At Sunburst, he taught teen boys who ranged from distant or dyslexic to disturbed or delinquent. He brought predictability to their lives, and they liked him.

I finished vacuuming David's room and stacked a dozen new dress socks in the closet. I didn't open drawers.

Back upstairs, I swept around Mr. Spielmann's island of African violets in the dining room. Two hundred and fifty of these strange grandma flowers filled wire shelves on a tall rack on wheels. My job didn't include watering the violets or dusting their fuzzy leaves. As far as I knew, Mr. Spielmann was not a would-be botanist, but he must have liked African violets. I should have asked him why, but I didn't.

The Spielmanns' high-end house next to the woods was 3,500 square feet of stone and tile and glass. It might have been beautiful, but it wasn't. It was cold and lifeless. I doubted this was the reason Mr. Spielmann was planning a new house in a high-end Portland suburb. He suggested life would be better there. I didn't tell him the weather would be the same. Maybe the doctors would satisfy him. Maybe he would find a satisfactory school for David. Maybe someone in the house would open a cookbook and make dinner.

Father and son returned to the house with Herfy's burg-ers. The two passed the kitchen, each with a white paper bag in hand, and trailed off to eat lunch in separate bedrooms.

Soon Mr. Spielmann was on the telephone, talking construction materials and deadlines. I heard him mention the washbasin in a packing box that I stepped around in the basement. The ruby red sink was beautiful, ready to drop in place in the new house. Would the new bathroom be different from bathrooms in this house, with fiberglass shower stalls and harsh lighting over the mirrors? Mr. Spielmann was sure to move the African violets north to Portland. The indoor climate would be the same.

Back in the basement, I started the laundry. I heard Mr. Spielmann close a bedroom door upstairs and speak to his wife, his words barely audible. It sounded like they were talking about the new house, until the exchange took on a serious tone. Mr. Spielmann was louder, as if to assure his wife or avoid something he sensed was coming. I sensed urgency and pleading in Mrs. Spielmann's voice.

"I can't do this anymore. There must be something else. I can't live this way."

I knew Mrs. Spielmann was lonely, and I sympathized. I had been lonely in a big house across town just a couple months ago, but my husband moved with me to a rundown multiplex near the university.

Mrs. Spielmann talked to me every Wednesday. She didn't have a friend in the county or state but me. Maybe she knew it wouldn't be better 100 miles north. She knew she didn't belong in this cold stone house—or anywhere to anybody. Mr. Spielmann, scarcely middle-aged, would still wander the house and complain. David wouldn't go to school. He would bang on his typewriter and occasionally answer a phone call from the Los Angeles grandmother. Mrs. Spielmann would be at home, sitting on the same bed in a different bedroom, finishing another crewel embroidery for another wall. The TV soap operas would be in the next chapter.

I ached for this woman. Only ten years older than I was, her life was already old.

The conversation upstairs grew loud, then muffled, then loud again. Mrs. Spielmann was crying and crying out. When I left her, she was on the spongy blanket on top of the big bed I had just made. I imagined her still in the black jersey bathrobe, her soft little body quaking in spasms.

"It will be okay," Mr. Spielmann said. "I can…"

How did this man keep 250 African violets alive while his wife was wilting?

I didn't know what he should do for her. I doubt he knew, but I thought of twenty things that might make her smile. Go to a movie. Walk on the beautiful property. Find the synagogue. Bring her flowers. Let her drive to town. Touch her on the shoulder.

The words upstairs continued in waves of tears and silence. The agitator of the washing machine blocked the back-and-forth conversation. I knew if I left, I wouldn't get the laundry in the dryer, but it didn't feel right to stay in that basement. I wanted to say, "It will be better tomorrow," but it wouldn't. I wanted to be gone.

I climbed the stairs, where Mr. Spielmann met me in the hall. I caught a glimpse past him of the rumpled figure of sorrow on the bed. He asked, "Could we pay you next week?"

"Of course."

Leaving the front porch, I felt grateful not to live in a big, empty house with so much money that no one had to work. Maybe the money came from the Los Angeles grandmother, which made it all the grimmer. Large bills by the dozens.

ED AND I AGREED THAT THE SUMMER DAY WE LEARNED I was pregnant was the happiest day of our lives, to be eclipsed by the day our daughter was born. I knew I could look forward to more happy days. On the drive down the hill into town, my own shoulders slumped as I thought of Mrs. Spielmann, folded in half on her bed, looking forward to nothing, here or north of here.

That night at home, I told Ed of the mounting misery and emptiness in the stone house in the country, and how powerless I felt to fill it. He knew down to his bones about a house that's not a home, and while he might never get over what happened or didn't happen in the house on Lakoloa Place, he was determined.

"It sounds familiar. Our house will be different," Ed said, as he emptied his briefcase on the small table in the tiny kitchen of our little student apartment in rundown student housing. "Even here. Just wait 'til that baby arrives. I dreamed a couple nights ago that we had a little girl. She had dark hair—it was so clear."

I would return the following Wednesday to the house at the end of the winding drive. Maybe the weather would be better, and Mr. Spielmann would wear a handsome sweater.

CHAPTER 13

Gabby

2012

Bree and Azra join me in Seattle's King Street Station while I wait in line for a seat assignment on Amtrak.

The woman in front of me speaks to my four-year-old granddaughter. "I like your sparkly shoes."

"Thank you," Azra says to the friendly stranger and fades into her mother's hip.

The woman shifts a large cloth bag covered in grommets and jewels to the other shoulder.

"Where did you get those nice shoes?" she asks.

"They're TOMS," my daughter answers for her own daughter.

"Oh, good. Nordstrom's sells TOMS. I could pick those up at Nordie's for Maddie. That's my granddaughter's name. Her name is actually Madelyn. I'm going to Portland to get Maddie and bring her back to Seattle. She's about your age," the woman tells Azra with a broad smile. Maddie's grandmother wants to chat.

I want to hold Azra's hand and talk quietly with my daughter. I gently turn a shoulder and speak to Bree about the spectacular King Street Station lobby, under renovation and a mess of construction for years, now nearly finished. The dropped ceiling and clumsy acoustic panels are gone, and this expansive space will soon be restored to 1906 glory.

Most of the ornamental relief on the forty-five-foot ceiling is now gleaming white.

"Aren't the tiles gorgeous?" I say. "I wonder if they're original." Tiles in tiny squares of green and gold make a shimmering ribbon around the lobby walls. Some walls remain behind scaffolding, but I can see the tiles glimmer.

This massive waiting room has seen the quick steps of business travelers, dragging steps of weeping lovers, and racing steps of children, leaping into grandparents' arms. Wealthy lumber barons first walked through here with East Coast investors. Railroads were the ticket to moving Easterners out West.

When we reach the train platform, I hang back a couple passengers. I don't want to be paired in a double seat for four hours with the bejeweled woman now talking to several people in line. When I reach the conductor with a clipboard, I ask for a window seat.

I pick up Azra and hold her for a moment. "Goodbye, darling." I kiss Bree on the cheek. "Goodbye, honey. Thanks for everything. I love you."

"Love you too. Thanks for all your help, Mom."

I climb the iron steps, turn into car 7, and find my seat by the window. My seat partner appears to be a quiet young woman, already reading her hardback, *A Thousand Splendid Suns*. I leave her to reading and don't tell her I loved the book.

Hand-in-hand, Bree and Azra turn to leave the platform and look back at my window, spattered in rain. I wave a last time and wish we lived in the same town, but I don't want to move to Seattle. The traffic would kill me, one frazzled nerve at a time, and I'd never feel safe enough to commute by bicycle.

It's beautiful along Puget Sound, morning light reflecting sun on the water. Runners and walkers and bicycle riders weave in and out on a path that stretches for miles between railroad tracks and the Sound. The Amtrak historian-geographer, a volunteer with a sense of humor, comes on the loudspeaker.

"The white stone complex on the bluff across the water is not a place you would want to spend time for the last 136 years, even though the view is mighty nice," he says. "That's the McNeil Island federal penitentiary. It closed a short time ago, but closed doesn't mean quick release. If you were locked up at McNeil, you were probably moved to Airway Heights or Clallam Bay or Coyote Ridge."

I didn't know I was looking at the penitentiary every time my Amtrak coach breezed north or south.

As the Coast Starlight lurches southward, I walk to the observation car, checking my balance on a seatback. I settle into a seat with my book and a view to the east, hoping for a glimpse of Mt. Rainier.

The woman who was chatting liberally at King Street Station climbs the narrow stairway from the club car into the observation car. She announces two cranberry vodkas, her French nails, painted in blue tips, firmly gripping a plastic cup in each hand. She has a lot to say, and I think of her as Gabby.

"Now that you know all about me, tell me about yourself," Gabby says to a slight woman about twenty years her senior, who follows up the steps from the club car.

"I was just visiting my granddaughter in Seattle. Karla is eleven years old. I'm Grannie to her. That's what she calls me. G-r-a-n-n-i-e."

Grannie continues. "Karla is my daughter's daughter, but my daughter is not capable of being a mother. She's on

SSI with mental issues. She can never get her own little girl back, so they placed Karla in an adoptive home."

Gabby says, "I know it's important for children to have continuity in their lives, but what if your daughter wants to get her girl back one day?"

"She will never get her back," Grannie says. "They put Karla in a family with eight children. Why would they do that? Why would they put her in a family with so many children? Luckily, I'm allowed to visit her. Karla says to me, 'I want to come see you this summer, Grannie.' I don't know if she knows summer is a long way off."

"My daughter is also on SSI with mental health problems," Gabby tells Grannie. "Maddie is my daughter's daughter. She's five, and she's my pride and joy."

The historian on loudspeaker announces the Mount St. Helens volcanic eruption of 1980. "The explosion sent one side of the mountain sliding into the Toutle River. The landslide washed an entire campground into a river of mud and ash that flowed toward the sea." I like this. I haven't been on the train with a volunteer guide before. He points out the ash still visible near the tracks thirty-three years after the eruption that filled the river and delta.

Gabby finishes one cranberry vodka and begins the other. She tells Grannie that she chose to separate from her husband of thirteen years just this week. "He's fifty-four and has a good job. He's been away on vacation for a week, so we haven't really played out the separation yet."

Gabby continues, "We own two vehicles and a fifth-wheel travel trailer. I'll get one or two of the vehicles in a divorce."

I shift in the vinyl seat, my feet propped on the window ledge as I watch the view to the east. I'm reading a good book—or trying. I'm eavesdropping, and I'd rather not hear every word of the two women sitting at the windows facing west, but I can't help it. Their echoing conversation can be heard from any seat in this car. I could return to my seat in coach, next to the quiet reader, but this is interesting.

"The house my husband and I share in Portland is really my house," Gabby tells Grannie. "It's in my father's trust. My daughter lives next-door, and Maddie comes and goes through a gate in the fence. It's very convenient. When my husband left earlier this week, he said, 'Please don't bring Maddie over anymore when I'm here, before I move out.'"

"It would just crush him," Gabby continues. She becomes weepy as she talks about how much her soon-separated husband loves Maddie. "Maddie is his pride and joy too."

I was fifty-four when my husband left me. I hope Gabby's husband's heart doesn't take the hit mine did. Our granddaughters are equal pride and joy to their grandfather and me. That's a good thing.

Gabby takes another sip of the cranberry drink. She remembers the volcanic explosion. "Have you ever been to Mount St. Helens? I've been up there to Windy Ridge. Trees blown down everywhere, but a lot has grown back in thirty years."

Gabby turns to Grannie and changes the subject. She reveals that she has cancer. "It's stage 1 breast cancer, the hardest kind to treat. What's it called? I can't remember."

"Is it in your family?" Grannie asks.

"I'm adopted," Gabby tells her. "Get this. All three of us were adopted. One brother died of breast cancer at forty. Yes, a man with breast cancer. The other brother died of lung cancer. He smoked. And we're all adopted from different mothers—what are the chances?"

Gabby changes the subject back to Maddie. "I'm picking up Maddie at the house in Portland and taking her back to Seattle. I have an apartment there. I don't have a car in Seattle because everyplace is a six-dollar cab ride. I used to drive, but I don't anymore. Then I have to get Maddie back to Portland on Monday for Head Start."

The Seattle-to-Portland Amtrak run is nearly over. "Where are we?" Gabby asks. "I'm picking up Maddie at 2 o'clock and getting back on the train at 2:45. Where am I? I forget which place I'm in, Portland or Seattle."

"You're almost to Portland," Grannie says. "If you get back on the train to return to Seattle, you'll be riding all day."

The steam engine pulls the Coast Starlight across the Columbia River into Oregon. The wheels screech against steel rails as the train slows into Union Station. Gabby stands and falls back into her seat. She stands again and moves toward the door that opens with a touch of her empty hand.

It's 2 p.m. as we arrive for a brief stop in Portland, where the conductor warns everyone to be back onboard at 2:20 p.m. or be left behind. I walk a few lengths of the platform, but I don't go inside the station. I don't know if someone met Gabby at Union Station with little Maddie in tow, or if Gabby has to make her way across town to pick up her granddaughter. If by a stroke of luck the two meet up in time, they'll board the train and ride Amtrak back north, arriving in Seattle near dark. Gabby will hail a cab, because she doesn't drive, and take Maddie home to her apartment. The two will be in Seattle less than twenty-four hours before Gabby rides Amtrak back to Portland to get Maddie to Head Start Monday morning.

It sounds like Gabby will get over her divorce. It's her idea. She has two homes, maybe two vehicles, and one granddaughter who brings her joy. She seems to be less confident that her husband will adjust to the divorce, at least to losing Maddie in his life. The more I listen, the more I know everybody has a challenge to face or manage. Today's exchange makes my loss of seven years look simple. My daughters are healthy, I have one house, and I didn't have to learn to drive or park a fifth-wheel.

I hope Karla feels loved in a big adoptive family with lots of children. Even if she does, she may never get over missing her mother. I hope Maddie grows strong. She may miss her mother now, even though she lives with her. She may never get over missing the grandfather who soon, by report, won't live on the other side of the gate.

The grandfather of my grandchildren calls when I arrive home to ask about the cute things Azra is saying and her baby sister is doing.

"How's Bree?" Ed asks. He's in touch with his girls, but he likes to see them through my eyes as well. We can never get too much of them.

When I hang up the phone, I cry. I miss the little girls, I miss my big girls, I wish Ed were here to talk about them. I would tell him about Gabby, whose daughter is suffering, whose granddaughter may be suffering, and whose husband will be lonesome.

I would tell him about Grannie and Karla, who may have more to get over than Gabby.

The grammar isn't right, but everybody's got something.

CHAPTER 14

One -ana to Another

1983

I loved living in Montana for three years after Ed got his degree. Our house was a few miles from picnics in Pattee Canyon, a few blocks from my parents, not far from my sister, close to my old grade school and Bonner Park, within reach of my best childhood friend, and between neighbors who loved our children and made every day a good day. I belonged there.

We decided to move from Montana to Indiana, home of Purdue University, in 1983. Ed stayed home in Montana with the girls when I flew to Indiana to buy a house early that summer. I was good at selling houses—I had already sold two, and I aimed to be good at buying one on my own.

For three long days of house hunting in West Lafayette, I felt out of place. The sky was low and gray. Oppressive heat and humidity pressed from every direction. My host, the wife of one of Ed's new colleagues, closed every drape inside her air-conditioned home as stifling heat outside squeezed the breath out of the house. I knew I had a few things to get used to. Even the water in north central Indiana tasted bad, like the steel pipes were in need of a Brillo scour.

Ed and I talked about houses on the phone. "Trust your gut," he said. My gut said we didn't want an old house that required undoing tacky updates. I saw a lot of dropped ceilings and Z-Brick on my home tours.

LATE IN THE SUMMER, WE DROVE EAST FROM MONTANA toward the plains and cornfields of the Midwest. In the center of Montana, still a solid three hundred miles from the North Dakota border, four-year-old Ani said, "There are no mountains here." Wait 'til you get to Indiana. No mountains. No bluffs. Scarcely a knoll. Indiana has soybeans as far as the eye can see. My gut said I needed to open my mind to new landscape.

Once in Indiana, Ed said, "Lots of smokin' and not much jokin.'" He was right. People were serious and didn't appear friendly, but soon, friendly folks turned up everywhere. Hoosiers aren't chummy and don't hug much, but that's not the whole story.

The new house I chose was an old bungalow, Mrs. Knauer's home since the 1940s. She left prayers taped inside the kitchen cabinet doors, the cellophane tape yellowed by years. I liked her for this comforting habit and for not ruining the beauty of the bungalow with bungled remodels. The house had great bones, as my artistic friend Pat would say, and of all our houses across the country, this small Craftsman was the architectural winner. I spent our first days stripping and refinishing oak woodwork, and at the end of each afternoon, hot and grubby from grimy work, I took the girls to the city pool.

Late one night, as I perched precariously on the sill of an open window, scraping forty years of cracked lacquer off the woodwork, I saw my first possum, or opossum, in the light that spilled from the dining room onto the lawn below.

I watched the silken marsupial slink in the grass. She may have had six or eight honeybee-sized babies riding along, for she turned her beautifully ugly head back my way, as if to scold me for the bright light disrupting her night.

We lived a dozen blocks off the Wabash River. Before we moved to Indiana, I thought the Wabash was a cannonball train in a Johnny Cash song. The river was wide and slow and murky, and there lived, on that river, a dozen bats with thousands more, until that dozen made a home in our chimney.

During our first weeks in the house, bats flew into the living room one at a time, as soon as dark set in. When summer nights turned cooler, the bats arrived with more frequency. One evening, when I was humming away on the sewing machine in an upstairs bedroom, I heard "ththth." I turned to watch not one, but two bats crawl out of a heating vent just three feet from my feet and take flight in the tiny sewing room.

This was the closest I had come to the nocturnal intruders, and I let out a bloodcurdling scream. I leapt from my sewing machine, bolted out the door, and slammed it behind me.

"Ed," I hollered down the stairs, "there are two bats in the sewing room. Grab the tennis racket—it's in the breezeway."

We couldn't kill the endangered bats, nor did we want to, so we caught each mammal with delicate see-through membranes between a towel and tennis racket. As Ed inched his way in the sewing room with both implements, one bat escaped to the stairwell.

"It's over here…" I said. "Wait a second. Hold still."

While Ed waited, the bat swooped toward us and headed for another corner, out of reach.

Every chase brought out something primal in us, and we flailed about while the girls slept in the next room. Once we captured the soft velvet creatures on wings, we released them to the dark of night and back to the Wabash River, where they ate their fill of mosquitoes, which was good for everyone. Only after we had danced circles around a dozen bats did we locate the crack in the chimney where they found their way into the living room.

A few months after that hot summer, Indiana suffered the coldest Christmas in decades. On Christmas Eve, radio DJs alerted listeners, "Local churches have closed their doors tonight. Do not venture out in the minus 30-degree wind chill." The DJs warned that car engines would freeze and batteries would die in the silent night.

We knew winter in Montana, but it was mild by comparison. In Indiana, icy wind funneled east from the prairies and south from Lake Michigan to rattle the wavy, single-pane windows. Occasionally, the west wind was so fierce, it blew the fabric-covered Styrofoam insert I fashioned for the drafty window right out of its squeeze.

Our neighbor, Mrs. Beck, turned seventy-five our first season in Indiana, about the time Ani turned four. When Ani rose from a nap each afternoon, she hurried next door for *Sesame Street* in Mrs. Beck's carpeted living room. This was a happy partnership. We had no cable TV nor *Sesame Street* at our house.

One day, Ani bounded in the front door the minute *Sesame Street* went off the air. "Can I eat dinner with Mrs. Beck and Woody?"

I agreed, and Ani sprang back to Mrs. Beck, waiting on her front porch. The Becks still ate dinner at 5 p.m., on farm schedule, though they had sold the farm and moved to town long before.

Ani had her first hotdog that night and returned home exhilarated by the new experience. The next day, she launched out of bed after her nap and dashed next door. Before Bert and Ernie wrapped up for the afternoon and Oscar the Grouch pulled the lid over his trash can, Ani tugged at Mrs. Beck's apron.

"Can I eat dinner with you again tonight? My mom's a slow cooker."

Ani belonged on the block.

I belonged on the block. I liked our family life next door to Mrs. Beck, with friends up the street and a progressive church with a good choir and good minds nearby. Bree and Ani were happy at their international elementary school, and Ed was happy at Purdue. I directed the Tippecanoe Arts Federation and created *Over in the Meadow*, a children's radio program, for Purdue Public Radio. With content children, great neighbors, and a husband who liked his work, what was not to like?

I came to appreciate the landscape, but I didn't belong to it. I missed the West, a feeling in my bones I couldn't get over. I gave my all to Indiana for three years. In the fourth year, I knew I didn't want to give the middle of my life to the middle of the country.

As a gesture and concession to me, Ed applied for a job at the University of Oregon that would begin after he worked on a one-year project in Washington, D.C. We loaded another U-Haul with essentials and moved to D.C. for a year, where we lived in the home of Americana, our third -ana, and the home of inspiring luminaries over the course of our nation's young history. We never tired of reading inscriptions of wise words that line walls and monuments up and down the National Mall, from the U.S. Capitol at one end to the Lincoln Memorial at the other, where Abraham Lincoln, wisdom warming his face, sits vigil in a wide marble chair. In 1987, women's inscriptions were sparse, certainly not because their wise words were rare.

"Who wants to go to the Kennedy Center with me this afternoon?" I asked on our first Sunday afternoon in the nation's capital.

"Can we go on the Metro?" eight-year-old Ani asked. "What's playing?"

"Yo-Yo Ma, Yehudi Menuhin, and Emanuel Ax."

Ani at least knew Yehudi Menuhin, and she would go anywhere with me if we rode the Metro train. At the Kennedy Center, I bought the first of many standing-room-only (SRO) tickets I would buy that year, at $7.50. Ani stood on a wooden box behind the back row of the theater, where we swayed to the pure joy of our first Yo-Yo Ma experience.

Our final theater event in Washington was *Cats the Musical*, at Ford's Theater. Ani stood tall on a box next to the aisle, and as the lights dimmed, Mr. Mistoffelees appeared and stood next to her, waiting for his stage entrance. He swiveled his shimmering golden head, wide as a house, to raise an eyebrow and grin at her.

It was a great year in Washington. At the end of it, we picked up everything stored in Indiana that we hadn't needed for a year and drove west across the wide country to Montana for a visit and on to Oregon for our longest residence.

CHAPTER 15

Kindergarten

2013

Walking my five-year-old granddaughter to school, I delight in the gentle touch of the small hand she happily slips into mine. Today Azra wears school uniform leggings in navy and a white turtleneck that's almost gray. She's darling, all the same. We gather in a sea of children of every color and size on the playground, each in a variation of navy or white tops and bottoms. The morning buzzer blares and bounces off the brick building. Students leap off monkey bars and ladders and enter lively lines for class.

When we arrive in the kindergarten classroom, the teacher is on the telephone, trying to reach Mahir's parents about a permission slip. She tells Mahir three times how important the paper is.

Mrs. Wilson's first words to the group are, "It's the usual kids who are the loudest," followed by, "Who came late?" She knew I was coming to visit today, but she's not trying to impress me.

The teacher tells the children they will go to the carpet to study the baby pictures on posters they brought to class. They will write down the classmate they think is photographed on each poster.

"The red table is excused to the carpet except for Antonne, the blue table except for Valentina, and the green table except for Tyrone. Tyrone, you're out of control. Time out." Tyrone puts his head down on his desk.

Mrs. Wilson speaks to me for the first time, across the room. "Help Tyrone with his numbers and letters. He can't be in the circle."

I'm delighted to have a job. *Which numbers, which letters?* I find a piece of paper and a page of the alphabet and begin where it seems reasonable. Tyrone is eager for the attention and wants to please. He gets right down to business.

The students in the circle spend fifty minutes on the carpet, guessing who is pictured in a variety of baby photos. They look at the poster board, write their guess on paper, return to their place on the carpet, and wait in silence for all classmates to do the same. "It's not your turn—sit down," Mrs. Wilson says to Bella.

What is the objective here? What are students learning in this big block of time?

Tyrone has been working with me on "stop" sounds: *b, p, t.* I whisper to him, "Raise your hand to see if you can join the group." His hand goes up.

"No," Mrs. Wilson says to Tyrone, allowing him no time for a question. "I need to see you controlling yourself, not throwing your arms." Tyrone puts his hand down, looks back at me, and we take up stop sounds again.

With no transition, Mrs. Wilson passes out geoboards to the students, still seated on the carpet. They each hold a square grid of thirty-six nails bound by a few rubber bands. Tyrone raises his hand again, but the teacher ignores him. She tells the sitting students to use rubber bands to make a "rectangle or other four-sided figure on the board." Soon the teacher holds up a geoboard and asks, "Did he do it right? No. What did he do wrong? Everybody's hand should be up. Mateo, you're not listening."

I want to scream. *Do you want any four-sided figure, or do you want a rectangle? Model it.* Show them a rectangle. I'm distressed by what I see and hear. It's obvious today is not an anomaly.

As students in the front row hold up their boards, Mrs. Wilson points to several and says, "It's not a corner. It's not a corner. It's not a corner." She says it twelve times. Twelve students don't have it right. Most of them have made a corner, but it's not a right angle. They haven't been taught rectangles or right angles. Mrs. Wilson doesn't model the angle or shape she wants. She continues to tell the students they're wrong.

Azra's grandfather would be horrified. He knows instruction, and this isn't it.

While one group demonstrates geoboards, the back row of students must sit perfectly still. No shifting on their haunches, no plucking those tempting rubber bands.

"Give your board to me, Nat. You weren't supposed to do it yet. I said just the first row," the teacher scolds. The kids each have a board covered with nails and a dozen rubber bands in hand, and they're expected to sit stone still. No exploring shapes, no talking, no fun.

Tyrone leans on his elbows on the desktop to see what this nail and rubber band business is about. "Sit down, Tyrone," Mrs. Wilson insists. "Valentina, what are you doing?"

After ten excruciating minutes on the carpet with geoboards, students move back to their desks. "The humming and talking has to stop," the teacher says. I didn't hear any humming and scarcely any talking.

Mrs. Wilson passes out a narrow sheet of paper to each child for a spelling test of five "short-o" words. She warns against cheating. She doesn't review the "short-o" sound or provide examples of words with a short o.

"Cover your answers, Carl," the teacher says as she nods toward Valentina. "She's looking." After providing the first short-o word, Mrs. Wilson says, "David, I can take your test to the garbage if you're looking at your neighbor's paper." She tells Bella, "Do not get an eraser out of your desk. We say it every week. Just cross it out."

After dictating five words, Mrs. Wilson has five students come to the chalkboard to each write a word. Four students spell their word wrong. The teacher tells the class that "mop" is not spelled *m-a-p*, but she doesn't show them the correct spelling. So much for short o's. Even my granddaughter, a strong reader, misses three of the five short-o words. She hasn't been taught.

Ed would have choked by now. I wish I could teach the kids short o this very minute. It would be fun, and they would get it.

The remaining eagerness in these twenty-four students astounds me. It's January—what keeps them going? Five-year-olds are dying to please. Mrs. Wilson could have these wiggly enthusiasts eating out of her hand if she praised anyone for doing anything right. "Thank you for sitting quietly, ready to read." "You spelled 'mop' correctly, m-o-p." I can't bear it. Mrs. Wilson finishes the spelling lesson by telling students to throw their spelling papers in the trash. Nothing gained, nothing learned, nothing to take home.

"Mahir, you need to move to another seat. You have been wiggling around since you came in. You haven't done anything you're supposed to do. We're still waiting for your father to bring in that form. If I were you, I'd be worried," the teacher warns.

From short o and Mahir doing nothing right, the teacher moves to the walrus. I don't see any context as Mrs. Wilson passes out twenty-four simple line drawings of a walrus and tells the children to color it reddish brown. As they begin to color, she looks at their papers and tells one student after another, "That's not reddish brown, that's just brown. A walrus is not brown."

As students color and cut, Mrs. Wilson calls three children to her desk to read. She says "good" to each reader one time, the first positive word I've heard in three hours.

The teacher dismisses the class for lunch and tells six children to stay in the classroom. I stay back with them.

"Why are you still here?" I ask the six kindergartners, all black, brown, and Asian.

"We didn't finish our work." They hadn't finished coloring and gluing the reddish-brown walrus. The same students the teacher assigned one infraction or another this morning, from flailing arms to cheating, are now looking at a rumpled walrus on the desktop. I help them finish and wait in the classroom eight minutes before an education assistant returns to lead them to the lunchroom. I wonder if they often spend time alone here. It's probably illegal. It's at least very bad practice.

After lunch, Devin is sitting in the hall. He must have committed a violation I didn't see. I ask at the office if I can meet with the school principal. Mrs. Tannen receives me directly. I share notes from a November visit to the kindergarten classroom and notes from this January day.

"This is not acceptable," the principal says. "I'm surprised."

Really? You've been here the same fifteen years Mrs. Wilson has, and you're surprised? Do you ever walk by Room 10? Did Allie's mother tell you she withdrew her five-year-old to home-school her, that Allie was losing weight from stress?

I say only part of what I'm thinking. "I believe this class-room is a serious problem. How many of these kids, especially students of color, the ones who haven't been 'listening' all day, will decide by age six or seven that school isn't for them?" I continue, "The students are pegged. A couple weeks ago, my granddaughter told her parents that she walked Mateo to the office because Mrs. Wilson said he was a liar when something was missing from the classroom. My daughter worries Azra isn't learning compassion or empathy."

I tell Mrs. Tannen the teacher doesn't teach the students what she expects or wants, yet students are punished for what she doesn't want. "Five- and six-year-olds are eager to please. She doesn't show them a model of a rectangle or a spelling word but punishes them for not listening. What does 'listen' mean? She and her students could easily model the behavior she wants. That's what makes kindergarten work."

The principal continues to agree and act surprised. She assures me she'll address the issue, but as I leave her office, she says, "It would be more meaningful if you talked to Mrs. Wilson than if I do." I can't believe this. Now I see the problem.

I return to Room 10 and find Devin in the same place in the hall, next to the classroom door. He's no doubt been here the entire hour I was away. I pull up a chair at a back table and whisper to Azra, "Do you do artwork back here?"

"No," she says. "I never come back to this table. It's just for the kids who don't listen." Azra knows who those kids are.

I haven't heard Mrs. Wilson use a single kindergarten jingle to help shape cooperative behavior. Not "One, two, three, eyes on me," nor "Sit criss-cross, applesauce," nor "Clean up, clean up, everybody clean up." Children spend most of their time waiting quietly and doing nothing.

Ed will call when I arrive home to learn about my visit. He'll ask about Azra's kindergarten class. We've been looking forward to this experience for her. I wish it were better, and we were facing it together.

Ed will be as troubled about this classroom as I am, not just for his granddaughter, but for all the students. When our kids were young and we moved to a new town and new school, we didn't request the reportedly "best" teacher. We figured we could handle new or challenging situations as well as anyone, and our daughters could too. We were better at talking about our daughters and what they needed than we were talking about ourselves and what we needed.

Bree told me, before enrolling Azra in kindergarten, that she had heard bad things about Mrs. Wilson from another parent. "Should I request another teacher?" she asked.

"I don't think you can make a judgment on a sample of one," I said. "You don't want to be that parent who makes a demand before you even know."

Back in the kindergarten classroom at the end of the school day, Angel's mother serves a Filipino chicken-and-rice-noodle dish to the class. Every student gets a VIP week, celebrating their family or culture. Today is the last day of Angel's VIP week.

"Angel, tell us about your snack," the teacher instructs.

"This is Filipino pasta," says shy Angel in a soft voice.

"No, rice noodles are not pasta. Don't call it pasta," Mrs. Wilson insists.

Angel's mother offers me a paper plate of chicken and rice noodles.

"Thank you," I say. "Do you know why these kids don't have a plate?" I ask, gesturing toward the six students with a blank desktop in front of them. The usual suspects are Tyrone, Ali, Mahir, Antonne, Valentina, and Devin. Devin is still in the hall.

Angel's mother shrugs and says, "I guess they didn't listen."

Before dismissal for the weekend, Mrs. Wilson allows two of the six outliers a plate of the Filipino chicken. Ali doesn't eat his.

Children dismiss for the Martin Luther King, Jr. weekend. It occurs to me the teacher didn't mention Dr. King today, or peace or love or cooperation.

Mahir's father at last appears with the proper form, and Mrs. Wilson provides a scorching report of his son's day. Eager children run to parents' arms and bump up against siblings. A few cast a "goodbye" back toward Mrs. Wilson, and the room is soon clear.

I ask the teacher if we could visit for a few minutes and give her time after the flurry of dismissal. We sit down in tiny chairs at a low table and exchange pleasantries. I tell Mrs. Wilson I saw things today that trouble me.

"I know. I'm troubled by this behavior myself. Somali parents can't control their children at home, and they count on me to teach them how to behave."

She sees herself as the behavior manager between home and school and thinks the students' behavior is bothering me. I try to clarify that I haven't seen severe behavior today or any that couldn't be redirected.

I tell Mrs. Wilson I'm a teacher too. "A child like Tyrone needs seven positive comments to every negative one. You could point out what kids are doing right rather than wrong, to get everyone onboard. Kids this age want to please you."

"I don't have time to say something positive to him seven times. I have twenty-four students to take care of," she insists. "These children can't learn until they learn to listen."

I listen for the next forty-five minutes. I don't tell Mrs. Wilson that kindergarten classrooms at my school have thirty-one students, managed and taught by adept teachers with a pocketful of positive reinforcements. I don't tell her their classroom population is twice as challenging and unprepared as hers.

"I'm frustrated, and I worry about some students every night," she tells me.

Mrs. Wilson may have empathy I didn't give her credit for.

I say, "We use a program at my school called Second Step, developed here in Seattle. It teaches classroom expectations and reduces our behavior issues to only a few." The staff in my school is extraordinary, and I would eagerly enroll my grandchild in any teacher's classroom.

When there is nothing more to say, Mrs. Wilson concedes, "You've given me something to think about over the long weekend. Maybe I'll have some new ideas on Tuesday."

When I arrive home on the Martin Luther King, Jr. holiday on Monday, Ed will call to ask about my weekend with the kids or invite me to coffee.

I'll write the principal and ask Ed to help me shape a direct, yet diplomatic, letter. The two of us were good support for our girls in school and advocates for children who didn't have an advocate. We made more than one visit to the principal's office, not regarding our own children, but about a classmate's struggles that troubled our own. Bree's first grade teacher sent six-year-old Ben to the hallway every day. It's hard to learn anything in the hall. Ani had a teacher who sometimes twisted another Ben's arm behind his back in math class. It took a long time to determine why Ani didn't want to return to school after lunch at home. Her next class was math.

I can't get over Tyrone sitting on the sidelines today, eager to join in. I can't get over Devin in the hall for seventy-five minutes, Mahir threatened about the important form, or Ali and Valentina watching as classmates ate the not-pasta snack.

I'll never get over Mrs. Wilson's kindergarten. I'll lose sleep over what I saw until I do something.

Today begins a commemorative holiday weekend. Cooperation, love, tolerance, resistance.

CHAPTER 16

Do Fence Me In

1983 and 2013

The house tucked at the end of Crum Court, near the Purdue University campus, was a welcoming place. Music spilled out the screen door onto a front porch wide enough for Saturday breakfast. Neighborhood kids rode bikes and played ball in the street. They climbed on the tire swing and ate lunch on the porch swing.

An Army surplus canvas hammock swayed in the breeze in the backyard. Kids piled in, erupted in spasms of laughter, and tumbled out. On the autumn morning Bree and Ani opened the white canvas to find a dead rabbit in its fold, they erupted in shrieks of horror.

That day, we bought lumber to build a fence between the Sigma Alpha Epsilon (SAE) fraternity foot traffic and our back-yard. The fence would serve a second purpose. I didn't like the traffic on the thoroughfare just beyond our yard, where cars and trucks streamed across the bridge over the Wabash River.

"Think of it, Babe," Ed said. "The traffic won't bother you if you can't see it. It's like the cicadas. You tolerate their racket if you don't have to look at their bug eyes." The fence would block auto traffic from view and keep fraternity foot traffic from drifting into our yard.

On Saturday afternoon, legions of football fans streamed up the busy street behind our house to the stadium, where they joined fifty thousand other Purdue Boilermaker fans, dressed in black and gold from wigs to socks. Ed and his friend Pat dug eight post holes to the backdrop of stadium roar on an autumn Saturday. They poured concrete and set six-foot fence posts as big and square as life into the holes.

The next morning, I woke at dawn and went out the back door to see if the posts were straight as rods, anchored in concrete.

They weren't. They were gone. I followed the trail of posts littered along the sidewalk, into the SAE front yard, where the last three were jumbled on the porch steps. The brothers who heaved the heavy posts out of the concrete stopped short of dragging them in the front door of their fraternity house.

It was too early Sunday morning to knock on the door to chat with the young men, though I should have banged on it. Ed dragged all eight posts back to our yard, broke off the hardened concrete with a hammer and screwdriver and said, "At least they didn't take the holes."

The next Saturday, Ed and Pat started over, early in the day, and clawed concrete chunks out of last week's holes to make room for a new pour of concrete. When the new, improved fence was firmly in place, we could hear the brothers, late into Saturday night, hollering back and forth, their conversation punctuated by "f_ _ _" this and "f_ _ _" that. The young men were out of view on the other side of the fence, and the fraternal order never again left its signature in our backyard.

――――――――――――

WHEN ED WALKED HOME FROM WORK AND UP THE FRONT steps of the Wedgewood blue bungalow late on a Friday afternoon, it meant one thing to Bree and Ani. They ran to the door.

"Can we start the story now?" Bree asked.

"We were just at the scariest part," Ani said. "Tell us about that bad guy again."

"You could say, 'Hello, Dad. Sure nice to see you,'" Ed said, pretending to feel slighted.

"Hi, Dad," Ani obliged. "Now can we start the story?"

For weeks, Ed had been telling the girls tales on Friday afternoons that he made up in the telling. Ani and Bree, six and nine years old, waited seven full days for the next installment, and by Friday, they were ready for the story-teller to scare them out of their skin again.

Ed opened his office door and tossed in his briefcase of bumpy fake alligator skin, scales worn to nubbins. He sat down in a wide chair, where the little girls joined him—sitting on the chair arms, in his arms, on his lap. It was a mess of little arms and legs quivering with anticipation.

"Okay, Dad. Go." Ani was ready.

In twenty minutes, Ed wrapped up the chapter for the week at the peak of suspense.

"Please, Dad, just the next part."

"No, we'll pick it up next Friday," he said.

"Okay. Please, will you play Lion with me?" Ani asked.

"Let's play in the morning," Ed answered. "It's almost time for dinner."

The last time the two played Lion, their game of hide-and-seek on all fours, Ani scrambled up the oak stairway and around the corner at the first landing. The lion had stopped roaring, and she was sure she had lost him. Then, just a few stairs behind her, the lion let out a ROAR-R-R that rattled the windows in the 1920s house. Ani, levitating on the top stair, let out a scream that might have cracked the glass. The lion opened his arms for the lamb quaking in gleeful terror. When she recovered, she said, "Can we do it again?"

Saturday morning was special in the house on Crum Court, or any house we lived in. While I put Danish Puff, strips of eggs and butter that puffed in the baking, into the oven, Ed played guitar or put a Windham Hill album on the turntable. We never got tired of George Winston's *Autumn* or *December* or *Plains*. "Cloudburst" filled the house with sounds we knew in the Midwest. We listened to strong women and cranked up Holly Near and Judy Collins, and later, Tracy Chapman and the Dixie Chicks. Bree and Ani spun Michael Jackson's *Thriller* over and over and sang and moonwalked with abandon, thrilled with themselves.

I loved our family time in our Hoosier state house. We were good in that house with original windows framed in oak woodwork. I liked being married, Ed and I were crazy about our kids, and I liked coming home, where we belonged.

CHILDREN REVEL IN SIMPLE DELIGHTS OR FRIGHTS AND beg to repeat them, over and again. Adults in marriages are something like children—ordinary delights or rituals are grounding reminders that we belong. When it was obvious Ed was leaving our marriage seventeen years after the lion chase and after Michael Jackson rocked the living room, I wanted to say, "Can we do it again?" I wanted to get it right.

I miss my kids and their father, the only person who loves them the way I do. I miss the significant other who called to say he was leaving his office and would be home soon.

For much of our marriage, Ed said, "Bring me a treat" on my way out the door to do errands. It seemed a sweet way to secure my return, always with a token of whatever I was about when I was out. I gave it some thought. I stopped at Euphoria Chocolates and considered the popular new sea salt caramel chocolate but settled on the standard dark-chocolate cashew cluster I knew he liked.

I went to most events alone after our children were grown and gone. I took in book talks, concerts, and even birthday parties on my own. From those ordinary events, I brought something home, usually more than an edible morsel. I shared with Ed an evening lecture at the university.

"The guy was unbelievable. He did a gorgeous slide talk on the ethnobotany of seven continents without a single note in front of him. You would have loved it," I said.

I should have known. In our final months together, Ed turned toward me when I stood next to his desk to tell him something exciting or not, but the tension in his face and body made it clear I should wrap it up and leave. I loved him but was losing my belonging. The guy called "Big Head" who never heard any praise at home or school, was now a wildly successful professional, immersing himself in work and more work.

When Ed said, "I'm not happy" from the window seat in our dining room, when he was working close to ninety hours a week, there was no space or place for me. By the time those words came out of his mouth, he had one foot out the door.

A few months later, when my husband told me he was moving out, I mourned losing him and the creative imagination that marriage demands. He was gone, and nothing I said, no minister or counselor, could turn him back. While I wore sadness on every sleeve but still wanted to be fenced in by the security of marriage, I think Ed bore the dreaded sentiment, especially for men, of shame. How could he forget that his father humiliated him or that two mothers gave up on him, if only for a while? Nor could his proud profession erase the sense of never being enough.

The same person who was a gangly college senior three-and-a-half decades earlier, who spoke about *The Plague* to an audience of graduates expectant about the future and heavy hearted about the present, was now a middle-aged man who wanted a new life and a jumpstart to the heart.

I hoped a new romance would be transient and my husband would return when it dawned on him what he gave up, before the sorry finality of divorce details on legal documents.

It wasn't and he didn't. A new relationship became a partnership, and our alliance became history. My former husband's new partner was an infant when police dogs lunged at Black civil rights demonstrators for eight days in Birmingham. She was a baby when Ed Sullivan welcomed the Beatles to the American stage and the United States sent troops to Vietnam. She was too young to watch and too young to absorb television news that Martin Luther King, Jr. was assassinated on a Memphis balcony or that Robert Kennedy was gunned down in a hotel kitchen. While Ed maintained our history together shaped him, the history felt erased. I felt erased.

TODAY, NINE YEARS AFTER A CLIMACTIC DEPARTURE, ED would give me all the time I ask for, but I don't ask. I join him for coffee or dinner, and we talk about kids or current events, informed by forty, even fifty, years of history. He would probably say I'm precious to him, but I don't ask.

My divorced friends have no illusions of what might have been. They don't miss their husbands. My married friends are happy in unions, not out. They talk with their husbands about family, politics, religion, the dog. They jostle and disagree. They make fun of each other's frailties and themselves. They take on each other's family, referring to their husband's father or brother as their own. They climb into the front seat of the car together because they belong. I miss belonging to someone and his broader life. I liked saying "We…"

I had been missing that kind of belonging for awhile when Ed stood up, his shoulders caving in on his heart, and repeated, "I'm just not happy."

I don't suffer low self-esteem, but the niggling feeling that I'm less because I was left isn't easy to shake. Is that why I cry in and out of the day?

Ed tells me his exit was less about me and more about his searching. He is the first to say I wasn't too anything—too smart, too dumb, too silly, too serious, too pretty, too ugly.

I miss the friendship and familiarity of a primary relationship. I spent much of my adult life looking forward to the day my husband would take time for walks and vacations, to laugh and play his guitar, to drop everything and run to hear a quartet in a church or tavern. I thought the day would come to reward me for devotion and time invested in a long academic career, to reignite or reinvent our love for each other. We would walk the beach on the nearby Pacific Ocean, waves lapping at our heels. I would remember "A Dog by the Sea," a David Salner poem of a couple revisiting old affections, walking the dog by the sea, holding hands and feeling the other's heartbeat.

I'll walk by the sea myself and hold the leash of my silly little dog.

CHAPTER 17

Granny Camp Is Over

2013

Granny Camp is over today. The last six days went too fast. My three- and six-year-old granddaughters are almost all fun. Their grandfather will be here any minute to pick them up. I've dreaded this moment all morning, but I don't let the girls know.

When her father first left, my wise young adult daughter, the mother of these two children, said, "At least Ani and I aren't six and nine, and you don't have to pass us off once a week with a bag of our stuff." At least. It must be excruciating for parents—tear this beautiful part of me, of the trusted us, away and leave me standing here. I am grateful my own kids were in graduate school when their father left. But here today, I'm parting with little girls, and I wish I weren't.

The week with Azra and Kiele began with "No-Tangle Tuesday Trim," a quick haircut to reduce the hairbrush holler every morning. I swept a barber cape, the same slick one my mother used, around their shoulders. I handed the young customer in the chair a mirror and began work as Helen the Hairdresser. This week, I was Belinda, "your server," when I offered the kids tomato with cheese sandwiches for lunch. I called them Melody and Magdalena, and while I suggest a new pair of names every season, Melody and Magdalena continue to be the names of choice. I tried Susie and Snap, but the names didn't take.

On Wednesday morning, we biked to *Jungle Book*, a play in the park. The Mad Duckling Children's Theater is a lively group of creative young, roving thespians. *Jungle Book* was good, with plenty of funny surprises, but it wasn't hilarious like *Cinderella*, last summer's Mad Duckling production. Azra liked *Cinderella* so much that we spread a blanket on a grassy knoll two mornings in a row to watch the light-hearted romp. The fairy godfather, dressed in Sunkist juice bags, told Cinderella to get a backbone.

"Tell your stepsisters to make their own lunch," he instructed Cinderella. Azra asked why the stepsisters weren't nice. I told her they just hadn't been taught. After the play, she watched with adoration and waited to speak to Cinderella herself, adorned in thick messy braids tied in ribbons and a funky pinafore with puffed sleeves and ruffles.

The little girls and I biked to the public swimming pool every day this week and bobbed our way between hundreds of bouncing bodies in the heat of the afternoon. It took steady coaxing to get them to go down the curly slide. We climbed the ladder to a second-story platform, waited shivering in a stiff breeze near the top, and braced ourselves for the race down the slide in tandem. On my first run with Kiele, I shot down so fast that I was flung flat onto my back and couldn't hold her out of the water at splash down. She took in a noseful, and no matter how fun I consider the curly slide, Kiele won't try again. Maybe next summer.

Playing with a bucket of spray bottles, squirt bottles, and medicine droppers in the sprinkler is as much fun to the kids as the city pool. They tinkered with a tiny trickle of water from an old steel sprinkler with three yellow arms and filled and refilled bottles, made suds from a foaming pump, and asked, "Would you like whipped cream with your coffee, Ma'am?"

"Are you kidding?" I said. "I wouldn't think of it. I take my coffee black." The girls have well-developed imaginations. They play restaurant in and out of every open window and always have a fruit smoothie or burger on hand. "Here's your burger/no cheese, Ma'am." My daughter credits Waldorf preschool with teaching them the art of imaginative play. When I first visited the preschool, I couldn't find any books. No books.

"We tell stories and use song," teacher Violetta told me. Indeed they did, with flowing fabrics and fairy dust and big wood blocks to build the castle. Azra and Kiele were all in.

At Granny Camp this week, we tried story time at the public library one morning, but most of the children were toddlers, bouncing from knee to knee. We listened politely to a story, then made knowing glances at each other and slipped out the door. Kiele wanted no help choosing library books. I pulled one picture book after another off the shelf. "This looks good," I said, with cheerful enthusiasm, "about a dancing pig. Or how about this book about a mouse family that lives in a pumpkin?" Kiele chose chapter books, all print, no pictures.

I pulled the girls in a trailer behind my bicycle to the pool and the library. I can still bike them up the hill behind my house. In another year, they may be too heavy. Maybe not. They are slight little things, and the pediatrician wants them to put on pounds. Bree is afraid the doctor thinks she feeds them nothing but bean sprouts and bamboo shoots.

"We feed them everything. They just can't eat enough!" Their parents are in constant search of calories.

"Do we have to have cream in our mashed potatoes again?" they moan.

LAST NIGHT WE GEARED UP TO BIKE DOWNTOWN TO Mezza Luna for pizza. Bike trailer hitched, helmets on, harness buckled. The orange flag waved behind the trailer to alert everyone on the road to precious cargo.

"All set?" I asked.

"Yes, Granny. Let's GO. We're hungry."

I climbed on my bike, pushed the automatic garage door button, and began pedaling down the steep driveway. I set out at a good clip when CLUNK, the hub of a trailer wheel caught on the garage door frame and stopped the whole parade. The door came down and bounced off the bike trailer. I pitched tail-over-tin cup and landed on my hands and knees in the driveway.

With grave expressions, the girls asked, "Are you okay, Granny?" I was not. I said some bad words, hobbled into the kitchen for ice, and returned to nurse my wounds in the driveway. It could have been bad. Kiele examined my palms. No blood, just a wide swath of cement ground into my palms.

The bruise on my knee didn't bloom and shine right away. Azra, still buckled into position, waited patiently, careful not to sound insensitive. At last, she said, "Can we still go for pizza?"

"Yes. I just need a couple minutes for the sting to go away." In five minutes, we rolled out of the garage and down the driveway.

The friendly people at Mezza Luna served "Say Cheese" and "Funny Feta and 'Choke" pizza and made conversation with the girls. We biked home before dark in the cool evening, past a chorus of frogs in the wetlands. I pedaled gingerly, my knee throbbing in rhythm with the frog song and the best of summer.

At home, the kids climbed on the bottom bunk on the screened porch, where we read the last chapter of *Wind in the Willows* to the sound of crickets in the nighttime, chirps filling the dark beyond the screen.

"I'm the best reader in my class," Azra offered, when we finished the story and before I turned off the light.

"I bet you are. Do you know the best way to get smart?" I asked.

"Reading?" Azra wondered.

"Yes, that's true, but it's really learning new words, and the best way to learn new words is to read. It's vocabulary that builds brain power."

"Yeah, like *ass*," Azra said.

I thought she said "aft," as *Wind in the Willows* characters Mole and Rat are in the aft of the boat. No.

"Remember, Granny," Azra reminded me, "Rat calls Mole a silly ass when he tries to row the boat. It's too hard."

She was right. Mole is full of jealousy and pride on his first boat ride with Rat. He jumps up and grabs the oars, ignoring Rat's warning that it's not as easy as it looks. In the whole wonky process, Mole overturns the boat.

Later, after being plucked from the river, cold and wet, Mole regrets being foolish. "I am very sorry indeed....I have been a complete ass, and I know it."

While Kenneth Grahame uses "ass" benignly several times in *Wind in the Willows*, it's a testament to Azra's parents that she hasn't heard the word at home.

I write a daily account of Granny Camp for Bree and Ani every night, but after I tucked Azra and Kiele under quilts on the screened porch and put *Wind in the Willows* back on the shelf, I was tired and bruised. I would send the bicycle and rowboat report tomorrow, after the girls leave with Pop Pop.

———

TODAY IS FRIDAY, DAY OF DEPARTURE. KIELE IS READY with her canvas bag of everything. On top is a big fuzzy blanket she clutches when she sucks two fingers and watches the world go by. I'd like to cut the grimy green blanket into fuzzy little squares, but I don't dare.

Azra is gathering books and shoes and a swimsuit off the line to drop in her bag. She remembers "purple one," one of several soft little cloth squares that babies snuggle up to and children hang onto until kindergarten and beyond. Azra has a purple one, pink one, and new one. She brought the purple one to Granny Camp.

Ed drives up in his girlfriend's shiny black rig before noon. He walks up the driveway and greets me as he always does—a slightly tentative, "Hi, Brenda. How are you?"

"Fine," I say, my chin up. I turn and go to the back of the garage to gather bags. *I'm swell, but you're about to drive away with my granddaughters. Remember the oversized chair we bought ten years ago to read to the grandchildren we hoped we would have one day? Now we have them. The chair is still in your old office.*

Next, this grandfather will ask about my week with the girls. I would rather share them with their grandfather than report on the good time we had.

"Hi, Pop Pop," the girls say in unison. They hug him and pull an art project out of an open bag to show him.

I help Ed move car seats from my car to the new car. It gleams. The girls climb in the back as we anchor their safety seats. They notice the drop-down video screen and ask if they can watch a movie on the way to wherever they're going. They kiss me on the cheek and buckle in.

Ed says, "Goodbye, Brenda. Thanks."

Yeah, thanks. He turns around the new Honda Pilot, shining in the sun, and heads out of town to his cabin. *This is hard.* The girls wave. They're smiling.

This is good. Children can never have too many people who love them. But how do I compete with a drop-down screen and a dock on the lake?

I don't want a Honda Pilot or a cabin in the woods. I just wanted to walk in and out of the office while Pop Pop read to the kids in that big, wide chair. Maybe I'm Mole, jealous of time.

This isn't so different from any other departure of these lively little girls. I cry when their parents turn around in the driveway and head home, because I don't like to see them go. They're fun, and they fill the house. I unhitch the trailer from my Bike Friday, hang it on a hook in the far reaches of the garage, and grab the broom. The dog moves out of the way. I sweep dust balls and chalk dust out of the garage and bawl like a baby. Tinder looks up at me and cocks his head, again.

I'll get over this, and I will power this boat, front and aft.

CHAPTER 18

Joy of Sax

1985

All music is what awakes from you
when you are reminded by the instruments.
—WALT WHITMAN

Our young family found good music wherever we
lived, from Washington, D.C. to Oregon, and two
states in-between. Ed and I took the girls to concerts in
church basements and concert halls, in auditoriums and
the Kennedy Center. Even Broadway. We heard Yehudi
Menuhin at seventy and Midori at thirteen. We heard
Judy Collins with the Eugene Symphony and Taj Mahal in
a tavern. We listened to the unparalleled Sweet Honey in
the Rock indoors and out. Everything about this a cappella
ensemble is heavenly, from gorgeous baritone to costumes.
Everytime I hear Sweet Honey sing "Sometimes I Feel Like
a Motherless Child" or "Let There Be Peace," I come away
saying, "NOW I'll be a better person." I would walk on my
knees to hear them again—the voices, the history of Black
experience, the political discourse.

When Ed worked longer hours, I often took the girls
to concerts alone. On a warm February Sunday in 1985, I
made the familiar drive with Bree and Ani. eight and five,
from West Lafayette, Indiana, across the Wabash River to

Lafayette, to a concert by the Joy of Sax. I didn't know the chamber group, but I liked the creative name, and we all liked saxophones.

The February Sunday of the Joy of Sax concert, near the end of a cold Indiana winter, was sunny and warm. The wind had stopped howling on its way from Nebraska, and most of the ice on sidewalks had melted into a few gritty ridges and a patch of dirty snow.

On our way out the door to cross the Wabash River to the concert, Bree and Ani called back, "Bye, Dad." Ed liked saxophones too, but the quiet afternoon afforded him a few hours to work in his office.

The girls were Suzuki violin students and played classical pieces on their quarter- and half-sized violins, from Bach's "Minuet in G major" to Brahms' "Lullaby," welcome sounds after early training on "Twinkle, Twinkle, Little Star." We played "name that composer" on the radio and took in many concerts. This afternoon, we chose Joy of Sax, a quartet with a sense of humor.

We arrived at a white, clapboard church in downtown Lafayette and took the front steps two at a time, feeling lighter in the late winter sun. We found a seat toward the front of the sanctuary, slipped off winter coats, settled into a polished church pew that gleamed in fading daylight, and waited.

A faint stream of low winter sunlight struck the chancel, and in the moments before the concert began, the sun was gone. Two pillar candles glowed on the altar. The hushed sanctuary was nearly dark.

A gentleman offered friendly words of welcome, and we waited in the cavernous space until a lone saxophonist began to play in the balcony and took measured steps down a stairway to the chancel. Before that player took his place, a second saxophone returned the haunting sounds from the opposite balcony and came down the steps. A few lights lifted in the shadows as two more saxophones entered from the rear and picked up the melody, then the refrain, of a Bach piece we knew. By the time all four shiny brass instruments came together, they had reached an interlude.

From the ensemble of a distinctive name came sounds of joy, the call-and-response and echo of the instruments. Saxophones glimmered in soft light. Near the end of the concert, the musicians began Pachelbel's well-worn "Canon in D." There was nothing tired about the sweet, resonant harmony of this piece under the influence of four brass saxes. The golden sound drifted from rafter to rafter, filling every dark and silent corner of the sanctuary. Ani smiled at me as she recognized Pachelbel from our George Winston record album.

As the Canon continued, Ani leaned into me, face in her hands, and began to cry. At the same moment, her sister slid down the mahogany pew and stared at her shoes. I knew what these girls were thinking. I had seen moments like this since our move, when suddenly, without warning, they pined for Montana.

"I miss Auntie Brooke," Bree would say from the back-seat of the car.

"I miss Zeke," Ani followed, remembering Brooke's bouncy golden retriever pup.

They missed our old neighbors. They missed the foster baby we kept for a week after his birth, until his new family was chosen and made the long drive across the Big Sky State to take the baby home as their own. We called the infant boy Elliott, from the recent movie *E.T. the Extra-Terrestrial*.

Our first month in Indiana, a neighbor girl asked Ani who the baby was in the photo on the fridge. Ani said, "That's my baby brother, but we had to give him away."

AT THE THE END OF THE JOY OF SAX CONCERT, I WAS awash in the tenor of the evening and the tears beside me. I loved every moment, my kids knowing and feeling the music and remembering.

Ed was still at work in his office when we arrived home. He greeted the kids with wide arms before they tossed their coats and ran upstairs.

"How was the concert?" he asked me.

"I can't get over how lovely it was." I told him about the saxophones and the tears. "You would have loved it."

"I bet," he said, in earnest. I wished he had been there with us.

Joy of Sax was a lucky find, the moving music solace for the soul. I missed Montana as much as my daughters, the landscape and more. I knew I would never get over the place, which was how I liked it. I was grateful for the roots that connected Bree and Ani to people and place and would take us back, over and again. There was something sweet about their pining for Montana in tears. I understood it.

CHAPTER 19

Mouse in the House

2013

Ed arrived for dinner at my house last night, moments after I flung a broiler pan and a toasted mouse onto the driveway. I met him on the porch and made my first request for household help in the nine years since he left home.

"Would you pry that mouse and trap off the broiler pan for me?"

He did exactly that—popped the trap and charred mouse off the pan with a stick in a swift motion and dropped the melted mess in the garbage.

This is the seventh mouse I've trapped in five days. As soon as I button up the kitchen for the night and turn out the lights, mice come in from the cold and make themselves at home. I can hear them scurrying in the oven, warming their dainty gray bodies near the pilot light.

One tiny mouse made a whale of a noise flailing around the oven in an exhaustive effort to escape a trap. It was awful. I could hear the wee thing struggle and the wood trap clatter. I biked to the hardware store to buy a better mouse trap and brought home a package of two traps with quick jaws and plastic housing to hide the captured. I positioned the new traps in the cozy oven each night.

The cellophane wrapper on the pair of traps reads "quick-release," both good marketing and an attractive feature. In the morning, I pinch the spring hinge and drop each mouse into a paper bag, fold the top, and walk it outside to the garbage can.

WHEN ED CALLED TO ARRANGE A VISIT OR ASK HOW I was doing, he added, "Do you need help with anything before winter?"

Yes, I'm overrun by mice. Do something!

I invited him to dinner.

As I prepared dinner, I slid lasagna out of the refrigerator, into the oven. Not until the thermostat clicked at 350 degrees did I remember I had placed a new mouse trap on the broiler pan early that morning, certain I would remember it before I turned on the oven.

When I did remember, I pulled out the broiler pan, ran shrieking out the front door, and hurled the pan, mouse and trap stuck in place, onto the driveway. That's when Ed arrived.

After he eliminated the mouse and hosed off the pan, he said, "I don't know if you want to keep this pan."

"I do," I said. "It fits the oven drawer. Look—right there next to 'Flavor Well,' it says 'spatter proof and smokeless.' That mouse didn't spatter or smoke."

I poured boiling water over the broiler pan, scrubbed it with SOS, and poured on more boiling water.

TODAY, I CALL ALL NATURAL PEST ELIMINATION AT 8 a.m. on the dot. I'm sure I'm Kelly's first customer.

"Do you take care of mice?" I ask.

"Oh, yes," she says. "We find where they're getting in. This is the season for that."

The All Natural inspector arrives at 2 p.m. for his 3 p.m. appointment.

"I'm sorry to be so early, but I finished my last appointment not far from here," Jon says. "I hope it's okay."

It's quite okay because I've had nothing but mice on my mind. We talk first in the kitchen, where I describe my problem. Jon tells me I should have been ordering pest and rodent inspections once a year.

I've been in this house twenty-five years—who knew?

"Our products are all natural—no noxious chemicals, no nasty residue," Jon assures me.

Jon is nice and he's funny. I also tell him about my fruit fly infestation. He recommends a trap for fruit flies, or maybe they're drain flies. They're a lot alike, and it's hard to get a good look at the face.

"I'll show you a trick." Jon asks for a bottle and vinegar. He mixes water and vinegar and fashions a tinfoil cover to the bottle, complete with a hole for a straw. "The good thing is, fruit flies can enter but can't get out," he says.

"I found that remedy online," I say, "but it hasn't worked. The bugs just gather on the outside of the bottle and multiply." All Natural's website is nobuggy.com. I need this company.

I've been a madwoman thrashing about my kitchen with a towel for days. I'm swatting at dots on the counter that belong in the counter's pattern. I've had a preview of Hades, which is where I may end up.

Jon tells me he won't have any trouble locating the source of the mouse problem. "Don't worry. I'll suit up and go under the house to find where those mice are getting in, and it won't be all that bad." He'll start in the crawl space under my house.

"How can you stand to go under houses with mice and dead possums and worse?" I ask. "I can only imagine the icky things you run into."

"The truth is, lots of times I would rather go under a house than sit across the kitchen table from people. It can be bad, really bad, in some kitchens. You, on the other hand…" Jon waves toward my dining room table, clear except for a small vase of asters, "have a lovely home."

Jon goes to his truck to put on a hazmat suit and returns looking like a Pillsbury doughboy. He disappears in the shallow space under the front of the house. In a few minutes, he catches my attention at the kitchen window and pulls down his facemask. I crank open the window.

"Do you want to come look at the pond under your house?" he asks.

"No," I answer and go outside to look. It's no pond— it's a lake.

Jon shines a large-beam flashlight another direction. He sees support pillars under water, some of them lined in mold. This is bad, really bad. In the brief time he was under the house, Jon found a three-inch hole. He's certain mice have fashioned a freeway from there to the kitchen. These mice might also be swimmers.

"I can't take care of the hole until the water is gone. It's too deep to go in the crawl space to patch the hole and tack up insulation that's torn away," Jon says. "You'll need a sump pump to get the water out, and you'll have to take care of that mold on the support structure right away."

I don't doubt him. We've had days of torrential rain, and we'll have more. The water is backing up. I live at the bottom of a slope, in the path of an underground spring. Run-off and fresh water stop here. I need the sump pump.

I can thank mice for alerting me to the crawl space and mold. I'm surprised the water hasn't seeped through the kitchen floor. It was close.

"You'll be lucky if you don't have dry rot," Jon says. He's worried. He opens the glossy All Natural Pest Elimination three-ring binder on my clean kitchen counter.

Dry rot would take a $6,000 fix to a $20,000 problem, or more. Jon recommends Plan B from the binder and cranks up his phone to find an installer for the sump pump tomorrow, Saturday.

To sweeten the deal, he offers a bonus roof treatment.

"We can take care of the moss on the north side of your roof. Like everything we use, it's green and won't hurt your plants or anything downstream."

Maybe it was a chunk of moss under the chimney that caused the DRIP DRIP from the ceiling in last night's downpour. That's another story. Early winter is raining a raft of problems on my house. The chimney needs flashing.

I've had leaky skylights replaced one month after the ten-year warranty expired. I've had big trees limbed before the next big storm. I've pruned and pruned some more. I've stored lawn furniture and hauled it out in spring. Last summer, I installed a watering system in my garden with tubes and timers and barbs and bubblers. Sometimes the system sputters. Usually, it sprays a circle or half circle.

Home ownership might be for the birds. This water problem under me is the first big-ticket item I've managed as a single homeowner since I had the house painted. It took me three weeks to choose a color off a paint chip of eight yellows, from Eggnog to Creamy Caramel. Or maybe it was Custom Camel.

Jon is an affable fellow, and we joke about what could go wrong but hasn't yet. He doesn't ask if I need another person's signature on my contract with All Natural, nor does he talk to me like I don't understand mice and mold, sump pump, and sinking pillars. I can do this.

Back in the kitchen, I offer Jon my credit card as he secures all procedures for tomorrow and the coming week. I've checked Better Business Bureau to make sure All Natural is on the up-and-up, but I don't have time to get comparative estimates.

"How do your prices compare to other green companies?" I ask.

"We compare quite favorably," Jon assures me, "and we've been around twenty-five years. You can't beat us for customer service. We'll come back anytime you need us."

I hope I won't.

I thank Jon as he wraps up his business and mine and leaves. It's lucky he was an hour early—flood and mouse and pump arrangements took two solid hours. I gather myself in a hurry for an appointment across town.

I'M SCHEDULED FOR A DEXA SCAN TO IMAGE THE POROUS bones on my small frame. I've been doing more weight-bearing exercise to stave off osteoporosis, for bicycle riding just doesn't do it. I hope today's scan shows improvement.

The drive to the radiology center is dark and foggy. My headlights don't split the cold, dense cloud of fog but disappear into it. My skeleton will soon be under review. I imagine the velvety mouse's fragile skeleton. It's creepy. I'm grateful for the goose-down jacket that's keeping this small frame warm.

After checking in at the radiology desk, I wander the waiting room and admire large Northwest photographs before I'm called to another waiting room. There I hang my purple jacket on a coat hook and sit on a bench to wait. Across from me is a woman even tinier than I am. She's completing a form on a clipboard.

"I won't let them inject any radioactive isotopes into my body," she says. "I know a young woman who did that in 1978. By 1982, she was blind and had no eyelids."

I don't think isotopes will be part of my DEXA scan. The woman plucks her purple puffy coat off a hook and shows it to me.

"I have the same color jacket as you, but without the pink piping." She pulls a necklace from the pocket. "These purple fluorite beads go with your coat too." I hear *fluoride* and can't imagine fluoride comes in stones. I tell her the beads are beautiful, which they are, but I don't ask questions about fluoride or fluorite. I look it up later at home. The word is indeed fluorite, a mineral consisting of calcium fluoride, which usually appears as crystals. It makes the perfect purple bead.

The radiology technician calls me in. April is soft-spoken and nice. "I did your DEXA scan three years ago," she says. "I'm sorry—I have to ask you to take off that cute skirt. The metal buttons will interfere with the scan."

"I don't mind. I'm wearing tights."

"Your tights are cute too," she says.

Before April gets me into position on the table, she asks the standard questions about smoking, drugs, alcohol.

"Would you like a blanket?" she asks.

"Oh, yes."

I'm chilled to the bone from the icy fog outside. The warm blanket just out of a toaster oven is heavenly. I could stay right here under this blanket in this room with harsh lights and forget about mice and dry rot. Or was it wet rot?

April moves my limbs from place to place, and the machine clunks as it takes images from every direction. "We're all done," she says. "Would you like to stay under the blanket a few more minutes?"

"Oh, yes." While I enjoy the warm quiet April offered, she reviews my scan without a word. She can't talk about medication or weightlifting. It's not her job. For a few minutes, I revel in the warmth folded over my body and don't even think about mice seeking a heat source. I swing my legs in thick striped tights off the table, pull on my cute skirt, and drive home through the fog that's thicker and harder to navigate than it was an hour ago.

At home, I push the three-ring no-buggy binder out of the way, pour myself a glass of wine, and pull a bag of salt-and-pepper pistachios out of the cupboard. By the time I twist the bag closed, the fruit flies have lined up on the rim of my wine glass. Three have fallen in. I sacrifice that glass to the bugs, pour another one for me, and toast both fruit flies and mice.

Maybe the sump pump and Plan B from the binder will rid me of mice, even fruit flies. It would be easier to have someone to lean on when the water rises. I had to make decisions in a hurry about mold and dry rot and deep water. I'll make more on how to treat my bones. There's no three-ring binder for that.

WHEN ED AND I SAT DOWN FOR LASAGNA LAST NIGHT, the scoured broiler pan in the drainer, I wasn't thinking about my skeleton and the DEXA scan on the calendar for today, but I was thinking about mouse patrol and living solo. There's certainly no binder for that.

When Ed left after dinner, I thanked him for tackling the mouse mess in the driveway.

"Anytime," he said.

CHAPTER 20

Company

2013

Many years after Ed left my house and had his own pretty house on the river, with partner and pets and resplendent blueberries hanging in heavy clusters in a veritable grove of blueberry bushes, our six-year-old granddaughter asked a question.

"Granny, when we all go out to Pop Pop's house for dinner, why don't you come?"

"Well, usually," I said, taking time to think, "when people get divorced, one partner doesn't want to be divorced. That's how I felt, so it's not fun for me to go see Pop Pop's whole new life."

"Why did he leave to make a new life?" Azra asked.

"Well," I said again, searching for the right words but not too many words, "sometimes people reach middle age, like Pop Pop and I were then, and feel something missing. They want a new and different something, possibly excitement, in their lives. They want to feel good, and maybe they don't want to be fenced in anymore."

"So, after he found something," my granddaughter wondered, "why didn't he come back?"

Good question for a six-year-old. I don't know if I had a good answer. I probably said Pop Pop liked what he found and didn't need to come back. I didn't say, "even though he was torn at first and may have wanted to." That would have been too much information.

I LIKE HOME—GOOD ART, SATURDAY BREAKFAST, A FRONT porch, a perennial garden with scarlet runner green beans to eat off the vine. All our houses have been friendly places. Was my challenge losing the family life I loved as I aimed to "get over it"? Maybe the challenge should be to find someone who needs a home and needs to belong here, rather than me long to belong to the man who is gone. Or any man. What is belonging?

Was I experiencing *hiraeth, in the context of Welsh culture, a deep longing for something, especially one's home; homesickness tinged with grief and sadness over the lost and departed?*

In the early months of being alone, I didn't go to the store with the strain and stain of tears on my face. Later, I had a hard time going home. Hiking California's Trinity Alps or rafting white water or pulling Azra and Kiele on a sled at Holden Village, deep in the North Cascades, were all such good times, that it was hard to come home to an empty house, no one at the table to tell stories about clear streams, wildflowers in bloom, or rafting a blue-green river in Patagonia. It has gotten easier, coming home to the dog, the garden, the neighbors.

OVER OUR YEARS TOGETHER, ED AND I HOSTED MANY dinners with close friends but rarely invited people that we, or I, wanted to know better. Ed was less inclined toward this kind of social engagement, though he was good at it.

Sometime after I began life alone, after the tears dried enough that I didn't look like I just crawled out from under a rock, I invited people to breakfast and dinner again. My cooking or potluck, indoors or out. It made me feel normal to have company, people in the house admiring art or colors, the simplicity of style or a new front porch, my new dog or old roses. I like to share it. I am a slow cooker, as Ani told our Indiana neighbor, Mrs. Beck, but I'm an okay cooker. Many of my friends are excellent cooks, adept at culinary delights from Julia Child to Mark Bittman. But I can throw together a spicy cioppino, bake a great chocolate cake, and host a dinner that lasts long into the night.

I learned from my mother never to apologize for food I make. It's good practice. In the right company, I tell of our first dinner party in Wisconsin, when Ed and I were very young. I dropped the rice cooker on the floor minutes before guests arrived. I scooped the steaming starch back in the cooker with a rice paddle, replaced the lid, and served it thirty minutes later. The floor was clean.

MY FRIEND JOSETTE CALLED THIS WEEK TO ASK IF I would like to meet her houseguest from Swaziland, Thuli Makama, who is in town working with the environmental law group on the University of Oregon campus.

Josette and Thuli arrive at my house for dinner, and we exchange introductions in the kitchen before we carry a glass of wine to the garden house. I often go to the little cedar-clad dwelling with visitors, first-time guests or someone honored for a birthday, new baby, anniversary, or retirement. Tonight's honored guest is Thuli from Swaziland.

In the garden house, we read poems to represent, how-ever loosely, the occasion. I pass out books of poetry, includ-ing Garrison Keillor's anthology *Good Poems* and a volume of selected Mary Oliver. Guests thumb through the books to find a poem they like. Men often say they're no good at this, but when they land on a poem to read, it's just right.

Everyone notices the scent of Douglas fir when they enter the garden house. They ask about the art deco light fixtures and admire the window that swings open onto the garden like a French country house. Tonight, Josette says, "How did you do this?"

"I had a good builder who got my vision. I collected discarded cedar and fir from a salvager—short pieces that typically go in the landfill. Everything else came from Hippo Hardware in Portland," I say. "Hippo is the best—four floors of reclaimed items from multipaned windows to clawfoot tubs and locks with skeleton keys. You could spend a day there just touching cool things."

After Ed left, the garden house was the right project to capture my imagination—design, gather, finish, create something warm and beautiful to share and welcome diverse people on varied occasions.

On this night to honor Thuli, recent winner of the prestigious Goldman Environmental Prize for the con-tinent of Africa, I learn about her three-year battle to ensure public voice in environmental decisions in Swa-ziland, a tiny, beautiful country nestled between South Africa and Mozambique. Before she arrived, I found Thuli's homeland on a map.

"The environment is all the life our people have—for shelter, food, medicine, and cultural practices." Thuli and colleagues had long watched tourists and safari companies reap all the benefits of the land. Turning this around caught the attention of the Goldman family.

Thuli describes the reception in the East Room of the White House for the 2010 Goldman winners, one from each of the world's six geographic regions.

"President Obama entered the room and spoke directly to each of us, calling us by name and discussing our project at length. He had no notes," she says. Thuli's report gives me goose bumps. I love this president, and I like Thuli.

In the garden house, as evening turns to night, Josette and I each find a poem to read. I choose Julia Kasdorf's "What I Learned from My Mother." A few lines reinforce my own mother's wisdom about understanding loss.

> I learned that whatever we say means nothing,
> what anyone will remember is that we came....
> To every house you enter, you must offer
> healing: a chocolate cake you baked yourself,
> the blessing of your voice, your chaste touch.

> "What I Learned From My Mother" from *Sleeping Preacher*
> by Julia Kasdorf, copyright 1992. Reprinted by permission of
> the University of Pittsburgh Press.

I tell my guests about another bit of advice from my mother: If someone brings you a plate of something, be it snickerdoodles or celery sticks, don't return the plate full, for if you do, you've evened the score and robbed the giver of a gift to you. Let the gift be a gift.

Josette reads Mary Oliver's "Some Questions You Might Ask" and wonders if the soul is solid or maybe delicate and fragile. Every Oliver poem a reader chooses in this little house fits the moment, whether it's geese in formation, silence of snow, or a journey of the soul.

Thuli chooses "Another Spring" by Kenneth Rexroth, maybe because the moon on the river, the air full of blossoms, and the mountains remind her of home. Words slide off Thuli's tongue like liquid gold, the King's English set to music the color and flow of honey. I want more of Thuli's sound, so comforting I'll never forget it, but dinner is waiting in the house.

WHEN THULI PREPARES TO RETURN HOME A WEEK AFTER our dinner together, Josette asks what she'll remember about Oregon. Thuli doesn't hesitate. "Reading poetry before dinner in a little cottage."

I'll remember Thuli, two continents and an ocean away, and her project and poem. I wouldn't have missed it.

CHAPTER 21

I'm Not Fond of...

2013

M ike is smart and cute and rides a Bike Friday like mine. My experience on dating sites has been dismal, but Mike and I scheduled a second visit after coffee. I enjoy his sweet devotion. He likes my wild tights, sends me poems, and cooks salmon on a plank to perfection. He plays good music on a sterling sound system and introduced me to Diana Krall. A wood stove radiates warmth in his little house in the woods. I've been walking the narrow road to Mike's place for a few months.

One spring Sunday, on a bike ride not far from home along the Willamette River, Mike and I talked about taking a road trip together up the Columbia Gorge, cut deep by the cataclysmic Missoula floods and especially lush in the splendor of spring.

TODAY I'M STANDING WITH MIKE ON A BREEZY BLUFF above the Columbia River, watching the river roll along. The mere sight of the wide band of river that separates Washington and Oregon makes me launch into Woody Guthrie's "Roll on Columbia." Every time I survey this gorge with the mighty Columbia in its deepest recesses, I imagine Lewis and Clark coming over a rise from the east, after a tough route through the Bitterroot Mountains of northern Idaho, which they survived with help of the Nez Perce. Was the party spellbound by the spectacle before them as they took in the sweeping vista for the first time? I'm enchanted every time from every direction, the Columbia banked by basalt columns, emerald mesas rolling into prairies. The gorge is gorgeous any season. The explorers had to be dumbfounded, if that's a sentiment they experienced on their arduous journey, but they didn't know Woody's song.

It's the first trip Mike and I have taken together. We check into the historic Columbia Gorge Hotel, on a cliff above the river. The view over this steep bank of waterfalls and wildflowers tucked in layers of mossy rocks is grand, like the river. The swift current looks glassy and slow from above. A barge, with a load the size of Texas, glides downriver to the port of Portland.

We're perched on tall stools at a table on the hotel patio, late spring sun at our backs. The waiter brings a hummus tray with two Oregon draft beers, and I smile at the perfection of the table and the day. We're visiting over beer when Mike nonchalantly says, "I'm not fond of abortion."

Who is? I think of "fond" as a word that refers to babies or hockey or my fourth-grade teacher. I shouldn't be surprised—Mike watches *Judge Judy* on television. I have to respond.

I tell Mike about a *New York Times* article this week. The journalist and her husband chose to terminate her pregnancy at twenty-three weeks. The unborn baby had a rare and fatal birth defect, and had it gone full term, the baby would have lived a few short hours in excruciating pain. "The writer describes the decision as agonizing," I say, "but she was grateful she could make it."

Mike says, "That's rare."

"Maybe so, but for every case like this, ten more aren't rare." I add a news bit about Texas facing a crisis of unplanned babies, many poor, since Texas began defunding Planned Parenthood clinics. The loss of abortion providers might be the least of the problem. Many women depend on Planned Parenthood for contraception and health care and now have no place to go for that care.

I know Mike's political leanings. The first time he kissed me, he whispered a confession that he admired cranky conservative editorialist Charles Krauthammer. But Mike also canoes and cross-country skis, and he's devoted to his friends. One of his closest long-time friends is a kind and tolerant professor and brilliant musician whom I know. When I met Mike as a perfect stranger, I considered her a solid reference.

I swallow what I'm feeling. I'm not sure I can get beyond this. I know I can't ignore it. We finish our local beers and drive up the valley to see fruit orchards in bloom and Mt. Hood cloaked in snow. Summer solstice is a week away. The towering mountain, illumined by late-afternoon sun, appears within reach. I want to touch it. My heart is in my throat.

Back in Hood River, we walk Main Street and dip awkwardly into a few restaurants to check the menu or the ambience. We choose the one I remember as quiet, with soft lights and good food. Tonight it's loud with sports on a big screen. A candle flickers in a glass votive on the table.

If the restaurant isn't quiet, dinner is. Mike says, "We should talk so we don't look like old married people."

I return a meek smile. I don't have much to say. I don't have anything to say. Suddenly the chasm I thought I could bridge feels as wide as the gorge. When the dessert tray comes around, we shake our heads with "Thank you," push in our chairs, and return to the historic hotel above the river.

In our room with ornate woodwork and molded ceiling, my head rests on a king-size pillow with lace trim. Mike tells me he's not "fond of gay people." What? That word again—what a peculiar use of the term. Is he testing me on a road trip?

Mike knows my social and political commitments. Our first visit over coffee was shortly after the 2012 election. I told him I went to a movie rather than watch election returns that November Tuesday, nervous as I was that President Obama might lose to Mitt Romney on his second run. When the movie ended and credits scrolled on the screen, I hurried out the nearest exit, no interest in hanging around for a handful of people to pull out their phones and check election results.

I left the movie theater and drove to the grocery store without turning the radio to NPR. The store was largely empty, no indication of election results anywhere. I selected toothpaste and navel oranges to Vivaldi's "Four Seasons" on the sound system. The produce manager was talking on a cell phone as she stacked garlic. With an animated "goodbye," she dropped the phone in her apron pocket and looked across the onions at me, my shoulders hunched to my ears and my hands open.

"Four more years!" she announced.

I dropped my head in my hands and my hands in the lemons. "I am so glad," I said to the citrus-scented produce aisle. I don't buy nonfood frills at the grocery store, but I turned to a twirling rack of hats fashioned of repurposed fabric and plucked a purple one off the rack to try on. I liked it, dropped it in the basket, and chose a black-and-white herringbone hat for my daughter. At checkout, I had $3.89 in navel oranges, $3.79 in Arm & Hammer toothpaste, and $68 in caps.

"Great choices," the cashier confirmed.

I agreed and offered my thoughts on our nation's great choice for president. "I am so glad!" I told her.

When I walked in the door at home, the phone rang. "Aren't you so happy?? Have you been watching the results?" Ed said.

"Yes" and "No," I answered.

MIKE HAD LISTENED TO MY ELECTION NIGHT STORY WITH amusement, but back in the Columbia Gorge Hotel on a beautiful June evening, the election is distant past. Mike's comment about gay people is heavy on my heart. This time I'm surprised. I've thought about this a lot—values and moral compass, holding out hope when we skied a narrow trail up and around a mountain, or canoed a canal, my paddle dipping the water in time with his, that at least our attitudes about the world were in harmony. From my pillow, still hoping Mike's social orientation isn't as rigid and foreign as his political persuasion, I ask, "What if your darling new grandson Henry is a gay child?"

Mike answers without pause. "I'll tell him to try the other way first and not believe what they teach him in school."

My heart suddenly weighs four hundred pounds.

Try the other way? How would it work for me to try the other way? I don't ask. I don't want to know more. Tears brim and drop on my pillow as I stare at the ceiling. I love the light fixtures and crown molding where the walls meet the twelve-foot ceiling. I would like nothing more than to contemplate the history of this hotel room, not the gravity of Mike's comment. I can't explain this away, and I say no more. I hear freight trains hauling on the Washington side of the river all night long.

Before dawn, I climb out of bed as Mike sleeps, slip into yesterday's clothes and slip out the door undetected. I walk as far as I can walk along the cliff above the river. A barge, big and heavy as an iceberg, has no trouble navigating the water stirred up in waves by the wind this morning. I turn back toward the hotel, facing a stiff breeze and stiff differences I can't navigate and can't get over.

Mike and I find strong coffee at a bakery, read the newspaper over currant scones, and punctuate a stony silence with few words. I'm noticeably noncommittal. I'm not sure what to do about my sentiments. It's a long drive home today.

We leave the bakery and travel up the slate-gray river to cross the Columbia on the bridge at Biggs Junction. The wind batters our tall vehicle as we cross the gorge from Oregon to Washington, and I can't help but think of the driver and tractor-trailer truck that plunged off this very bridge in fierce winds some years ago. It's a horrible image.

Mike and I planned a stop at the Maryhill Museum of Art on a hill above the river. Over the years I've driven the Columbia Gorge highway, dozens of times to and from Montana, I've wanted to stop at Maryhill. I wish I wanted to stop today.

Sam Hill turned his castle on the hill into a museum for his wife and filled it with Rodin sculptures and Romanian art, all gifts from friends, including Queen Marie of Romania. The grounds are stacked in green rows of orchards and vineyards. Artifacts of Pacific Northwest natives fill reflective cases of polished glass. The whole place is stunning, but I don't exclaim. I don't want to engage Mike in conversation. No matter how cool Maryhill is, I feel cooler. What in Sam Hill am I doing here?

The drive home through central Oregon is long. I'm sleepy, warmed by the sunshine that flickers between ponderosa pine and juniper through the windshield and onto my shoulders, but I don't nap. Less than an hour from home, we talk about Mike's grown children. I commend him for the support he gives his disabled adult son, a day at a time. I know what I'm going to do, and well-deserved praise is the least I can offer.

As soon as Mike turns into my driveway, I lift my canvas bag from the back of his car and hastily thank him. He looks expectant, as if to say, "Should we have dinner tomorrow?" but I don't give him a chance. I thank him, say goodbye, and shut the heavy door of his Mercedes SUV.

The first time I rode in the silver SUV months ago, Mike said, "I always admired this Mercedes model that the military uses. I bought it as a reward after my divorce." He was hurting then and is probably hurting now. No shiny vehicle will fix that, and no savory suppers or smiling adoraton will fix the connection I'm missing.

I unpack and begin a note to Mike on a photo card of Oregon. I thank him for the trip and write, "This should come as no surprise…" I suggest he might want the Bialetti coffeemaker he gave me and note that he can find it in the garden house. I miss my late afternoon mailman but catch a postal van around the block and hand my envelope to the driver. Mike will pick it up tomorrow in his sturdy mailbox on the main road.

My daughter calls to ask how the short trip was. I tell her. I also tell her about the card I just posted.

"Mom, a letter is too easy. You owe him a telephone call."

She's right. My heart races as I dial the number I've memorized. Mike answers. I explain my feelings in the kindliest, swiftest way I know.

"I thought we had something special," he says, with both assurance and resignation.

"We did," I say. "Mike?"

"Yes?"

"We don't teach kids at school to be gay. We teach them to read, multiply, and be kind."

I hang up the phone and don't even cry. I know how to be alone, and this wasn't a relationship out of desperation. I really liked Mike, and I liked that he liked me and smiled when I walked down his road or when he arrived at my door. But arriving isn't enough. I can't get past "Go" with Mike and his social disposition. I feel relief. I will get over this.

I hop on my bike and pedal toward the river that rolls north to the Columbia.

CHAPTER 22

Ellie

2014

When I was a girl, my best friend's mother was named Eleanor. She was blond and more glamorous than other mothers of my seventh-grade friends. She wore mascara, and her eyes smiled when she talked. She laughed a lot. "Oh, Vir-GIN-ia," she'd say to her thirteen-year-old daughter in mock exasperation, with her head cocked and a ripple of laughter.

Now I have a best friend Eleanor—a tall, darling, freckly girl who teaches math and science to rowdy middle schoolers with a little sarcasm and a lot of humor. She moved to Maine, and I miss her.

Ani has a best friend Eleanor. She's both strong and fragile, an artist with a soft smile and a soft Iowa sound. Bree's best friend Eleanor is tall and lean and lovely and devoted to her black lab Hailey, who romps on the shores of Lake Washington.

Even my mother had a best friend Eleanor. Today I'm on my way to see Ellie, the last of two friends alive who loved both my parents. She's also an old friend of mine in both years and kinship. I've been thinking about her gifts—the handwoven blanket she made when our baby was born, our daughters dancing around the May Pole in her backyard, and the music that spills from her in many ways.

149

This will be the last time I see Ellie. She's been alone the month since her husband died, and at nearly ninety, she is moving away, close to a son and family. She'll ask about Ed and how I've been since he moved away. She probably doesn't remember it's been ten years I've lived alone.

I sign my name at the desk at Sheldon Park, Ellie's senior residence, and climb the stairs to her apartment. The pictures in the hall, like those in almost every hall like it, resemble motel art. How do I tell a senior establishment I would be delighted to recommend some fine art? I doubt I'll be consulted before it's time for me to move into such a residence.

Ellie is expecting me and greets me in a way I know well. "Hel-lo, Brenda. It's so nice of you to come." Music fills her voice. She's an organist and pianist. I remember a Sunday fifty years ago, when Ellie directed the children's choir in the church our families shared in Montana.

AS A TEENAGER, I SAT NEXT TO MY FATHER IN THE church pew every Sunday morning. He purposely sang five words behind in the hymn, making it impossible to share a hymnal. Just when I gathered my composure after laughing through the first verse of "Be Thou My Vision," my dad sang five words behind on the third verse. He also thumped the bottom of the collection plate to make it sound like he dropped in a pocketful of change.

In church that Sunday five decades ago, my father played into Ellie's good humor. She led the smallest children in a rousing rendition of "This Little Light of Mine" and turned to lead the giggly kids down the aisle after the last smiley verse. My father seized the moment. He leaned into the aisle and touched Ellie's hand. She bent down as Dad whispered,

"There's no one behind you." Alarmed, Ellie whipped around with a swish of her maroon choir robe. The cherub choir skipped to a stop. Ellie turned back to my father and lowered her brow in mock fury before she picked up where she left off and sashayed down the aisle with all cherubs in step.

Ellie had coffee visits with my mother and their friend Adele, in the days when friends dropped in for coffee in the kitchen, not a coffee shop with eight different expensive drinks, from malt to mocha, each in a paper cup. In the kitchen, friends had Folger's from a glass percolator on the stove, served in a mug, with a cookie from the cookie jar.

ELLIE SPEAKS OF MY PARENTS AGAIN TODAY. EVERY TIME I've seen her in the last forty years, she has spoken glowingly of them. I love that she still holds a warm place in her heart for them, both gone a long time. She reminds me how Barbara and Bill made her feel welcome when she moved with her young family to Montana and repeats memories of summer hikes and winter snowshoe trips.

I have known the melody that is Ellie in a few different places. As a teenager, I babysat for her family in Montana, where she trusted me with her children and two dozen peanut butter-chocolate squares in neat rows in an aluminum cake pan with a sliding cover. At my house we always had oatmeal-raisin cookies on hand, but these squares were a whole different story. I couldn't eat just one, but I didn't want my reputation to follow me into that pantry, where an empty row in the pan would be obvious.

In Wisconsin, Ellie knew my young husband and me in our first married years. Her husband Larry helped the two of us get our first job in Wisconsin in 1970. We were college graduates with bachelor's degrees in English, which didn't give us much purchasing power. We took a job as houseparents at a residential treatment center for emotionally disturbed children, where we didn't have much power of any kind with troubled teen boys.

Houseparenting was hard, and we spent many respite and renewal weekends in Madison. Ellie and Larry's big house was filled with sunshine and Beethoven. "Do you know the Ninth Symphony?" Ellie asked about the music on the record player. I didn't know Beethoven's Ninth, but I liked it.

Now Ellie and I have lived in the same Oregon town for twenty-five years. In her small apartment across town, she has boxed up a few things in the wake of Larry's death and before she moves near Peter in Bellingham, by the sea. There's not much to pack since the last big move out of their pink stucco home above the golf course. No grand piano, no floor loom, no snowshoes. Just some art and a few books.

"I'll be close to grandchildren for the first time in my life. My new apartment has a big picture window on the woods!" Ellie tells me. "Larry was my best friend. I miss him terribly, but this move will be good."

I know something about losing a partner and missing a best friend. Ed told me once, sitting in the glider in our backyard several months after he left, that I was his best friend, probably more so than before he left, absent the challenges.

Tomorrow Ellie's four children will arrive from four corners of the globe for their father's memorial service. I'm sorry I won't be there to see them and to remember their father. I leave early in the morning for Arizona's Canyon de Chelly, to hike in Navajo country.

Ellie has also reminded me over the years how difficult I was in ninth grade, sassy and unpleasant to my parents. Today she doesn't say a word about my behavior at thirteen, but she does ask about Ed. She's always been fond of him.

"He's fine. I see him now and then—we're friends."

"Oh, I'm glad," Ellie says. "I hope he treats you well."

"He does."

Ed remembers Ellie, including his first exposure to classical music and fine art. It was intimidating. He didn't know Beethoven's Ninth Symphony either. The difference between us is that he thought he should. Many years later, we would sing the first verse of Beethoven's "Ode to Joy" as a grace at the dinner table with our children. We liked the line about hearts unfolding like flowers.

"Do say hello to Ed for me," Ellie says. "I'm pleased you're friends."

Ed will ask about my visit, and we might speak of trips to Ellie and Larry's home those early years of our marriage. We stayed on the third floor of their colonial in a pretty Madison neighborhood following a Jose Feliciano concert or Marcel Marceau's mesmerizing mime. We had never seen anything like Marceau and mimicked him as Bip the Clown, feeling his way out of a glass box, in Ellie's kitchen.

Remembering will make me wistful, maybe Ed, too. The five years in Wisconsin were good years with good friends, music, and potlucks. We picked tomatoes out the back door in summer and cross-country skied out the same door in winter. Crosby, Stills, Nash & Young sang "Our House" on the stereo.

Our house was a very fine house, where friends gathered often for dinner, a full rice cooker the base of every meal. We sang along with guitars in the living room furnished with a burgundy velvet sofa and chair, orange crate end tables, and a heavy cable spool covered with an Indian bed-spread. We couldn't imagine ever wanting better furniture or choosing an expensive painting over an expressive poster.

ONLY A FEW PAINTINGS REMAIN ON THE WALLS IN ELLIE'S little apartment. This is real art. I admire the paintings that first hung in her stucco Montana home on a big shady corner. She has five paintings by Walter Hook, an acclaimed Montana artist. My favorite is an oil of Rattlesnake Creek, a roaring tributary my teenage friends and I forded in slippery canvas Keds, holding hands and squealing with summer. The swift current terrified us as we picked our way across slick rocks that glimmered in clear water, to the quiet shallows on the opposite bank.

Next to Walter Hook's *Rattlesnake Creek* are two paint-ings by Ken Hansen, another Montana artist. I have a Ken Hansen still life of apples with stems and scattered autumn leaves that Ed gave me one early anniversary. The last paint-ing I spot on the apartment wall is by Carrel Pray. We talk about the life and death of the artists.

"Ken died of cancer," Ellie says.

"Yes. But Adele is alive and well in Montana, right?" I ask. It has to be lonely to reach advanced age and lose your friends, one by one. Some days I'm lonely for my mom. Many days I'm lonely for my husband and friend. It takes time.

"Carrel and I were such good friends in Madison. Besides being a painter, she was a talented musician, you know."

I do know. Ed and I went to Madison Boy Choir con-certs, Carrel the exuberant director. We watched two dozen fresh-faced boys, eyes glued on the director, sing soprano before their voices betrayed them in a pubescent assault. The crystalline beauty of the boys' voices moved us to tears.

Ellie has only a few prized belongings to move next week—a handmade quilt, a small clay Madonna, and the paintings. She asks me to reach under the bed for a shoebox of silver bells, some tarnished and some as clear as their sound.

"Choose one you would like to have," Ellie says. The most wonderful of all is a school bell, tarnished sterling with a worn wooden handle. My first-grade teacher had a bell like it on her broad oak desk. My ten classmates in a one-room schoolhouse in northern Idaho took turns ringing in students from recess.

I would love to have the school bell, but it feels opportunistic to take it. One of Ellie's children might want that very bell. I thank her and take a small silver bell with a filigreed handle that rests flat in my palm.

Ellie and I hug goodbye at the door. I cry all the way to my car. I will miss her as a connection to my parents and the good years Ed and I shared in Wisconsin, including our cultural initiation in Madison.

I suddenly feel old and lost. I buy groceries for my hiking trip to Canyon de Chelly, a privilege only for those with a Navajo guide. We'll camp on our guide's tiny farm. I pack lentil Tasty Bites and chocolate with my tent and hiking shoes in one large suitcase.

"Think of it, Mom," my daughter says, when she calls to wish me a good trip, "you wouldn't be going on all these cool trips if you were still living with Dad." That's true. I would still be waiting for the time when he would have time.

Ed calls, as he always does the night before I leave on a trip. "Do you need me to do anything while you're away?"

"No, thanks."

He asks about Ellie.

"She's good, both steady and fragile."

I'm steady and fragile myself. I'm prepared for challenging hikes next week. I'm less prepared for the rush of emotions that sends me to tears. Often. Often on my way to or from somewhere, and almost always when I hang up the phone.

"Bye."

Bree and Ani—Indiana autumn on the front porch.

Brother Bruce, Brenda, and cousins GB and Susan.
Summertime on the Selway River.

*Ani honoring her grandmother on the Selway River.
Also pictured, Bree and her Uncle Bill
and Aunt Brooke.*

After lunch on a southern Utah hoodoo.

Brooke and Brenda hiking at Ghost Ranch, New Mexico.

Garden house, where sweet moments and poetry meet.

CHAPTER 23

Retirement Party

2014

A full year ago, all-time favorite teachers Ann and Mark retired from my elementary school. Ann, a quiet giant whose gentle way of speaking students' names made them feel responsible, and Mark, a friendly guy with a sense of humor who used the right measure of sarcasm with third graders.

For the school year's final assembly last year, I wrote a verse for the school song about each Ann and Mark, and six hundred young voices sang along to bid them farewell. At the conclusion of the assembly, some dramatic, yet earnest, third and fourth graders cried all the way to the school bus.

A few days after that dramatic assembly a year ago, class-rooms emptied of rowdy students and their stinky gear for the summer, and teachers scrambled to right the shambles of their rooms before the entire staff gathered for lunch. There we roasted Ann and Mark, thanked them for decades of service to students and families, and offered testimonials. The afternoon was orchestrated and spontaneous, tearful and hilarious. It was exactly right, and the two venerated teachers left school knowing their professional generosity was recognized, their personal relationships appreciated, and their presence would be sorely missed.

Ed called that evening.

"You're home," he said. He can't see through the phone line, but he knows I don't carry a cell phone. "How are you? How was your last day of school?"

I told him about sports day and kickball, the singing and sobbing students, the roast and the toast.

"I bet you had a lot to do with honoring those two teachers. They won't forget it," he said. Ed has always been my biggest advocate professionally and with friendships. "You have so many friends, people important to you. I have a couple."

"It's because women work at it," I say.

Today it's been a year since Mark and Ann retired, and now I'm the teacher emptying my classroom for the last time. I've sorted everything into a pile that cannot be recycled, a pile that can, and a stack of drawing paper for Granny Camp this summer.

Ed called my classroom this week to ask how the process was going.

"What should I do with all the journal articles I've saved and the checklist for this and rubric for that?" I asked.

"Do you want another job?"

"No."

"Then dump them," he said. "You can find anything you want on the internet."

I did dump things. Now I'm preparing notes for the person who assumes my job as a reading specialist next fall. I want the new teacher to have an easy transition to systems and success. I also want it to look like I knew what I was doing on the job, nudging students every day, with no time wasted. All thirty minutes in this room must be friendly, efficient instruction, a rare minute spent on color sheets or a child's report on the last kindle of kittens born under their bed.

I'm proprietary about this classroom operation. Students who can't read up-to-speed by third grade are likely to struggle in school. Adults who can't read are often destined to be second-class citizens. Worse, they're condemned to jail or prison, like some of my students' fathers and a few of their mothers.

I've been teaching four days a week for two-and-a-half decades. I didn't think I would ever retire. I love my job and my school. I have summers to hike, bike, kayak and pick blueberries and transplant raspberries. I share summer days with my children and their children, and always, by the end of August, I'm tired of myself and ready to go back to school. I'm the oldest person in my school, and every year for the last several, people have asked when I might retire. "Four more years," I say.

Suddenly one day, it hit me. *I'm sixty-five years old. If I have another twenty years, I'll be lucky. I better get started.* If I needed further confirmation, it came the next day. I'm not a yeller. I hollered to get the attention of my own children when they went careening down the street on a Big Wheel, but I didn't yell, and I don't yell at students.

That sunny day in April, my exceptionally boisterous group of twelve fourth graders was exceptionally chatty. "Be QUIET," I said, failing to use a better tool. At that moment, a parent walked in the door. Busted. It was time, before anyone said, "Isn't it about time she retired?"

My school principal announced in the next staff meeting that I would retire at the end of the school year. My teacher friends, sitting at round tables in the library after a long day, let out a communal gasp. Within seconds, they clapped. It was a sweet moment.

I LOVE MY SCHOOL'S MIX OF TEACHERS, MOST YOUNG and spirited and willing to turn inside out for our challenging population with many needs. Teachers come early and stay late. They meet with students and meet with parents. They use point cards and design reward currency with their names--Burgess Bucks and Combs Cash. They bring the class clown at the back of the room to the front, as an assistant. These teachers do anything to help kids succeed.

Our final school assembly earlier this week honored students who embody the "Superhero" theme by doing their personal best and helping others. We recognized them and sang the school song. The principal announced the retirement of Betty, an illustrious classified employee with twenty-five years of experience shepherding kids indoors and out, enforcing no food sharing in the lunchroom, and bellowing soccer rules on the playground.

The principal announced my retirement, and Betty and I moved to the gym floor, where students wrapped our shoulders in butcher paper Superhero capes. We sang the school song and students dismissed from the gym by rows.

TODAY IS OUR LAST DAY OF SCHOOL. IT'S MY LAST DAY of school forever. Sports day fills the morning. Each six-student team has six opportunities to line up and carry a trembling egg on a spoon across the field, fly a kite, shoot hoops, and more. Every year on sports day, I pitch a rubber gym ball to thirty or forty screaming students in short games of kickball. I also field and tag runners and give everyone a nickname. "Tina the Tiger is up to the plate." "Robbie Red Stripes is gonna kick it out of the park." Girls who don't want to participate wear flip-flops on sports day, but I talk them into kicking a punt. I fumble the ball, and they make it to first base. At the end of a morning of kickball, I'm hoarse. Tomorrow, I'll feel the pitching and fielding in my fanny.

By noon, the school building has emptied of students and parents. Teachers begin to thin out, put away, and pack up. Big blue rolling bins of recycled science projects and swollen writing journals stand overflowing in every hallway. I search for Chutes and Ladders pieces and put away games in the common area. I repair checkers boxes with duct tape, throw away broken crayons, and return to my classroom to clean up my own mess.

Piles remain on three tables—one for home, one for teachers, one for deciding. Then my desk. A drawer of paper clips and paper reinforcers and cheap pencils that won't sharpen. Ticonderoga is the only #2 pencil that will.

I have five hours to finish this job that keeps growing new heads, before the year-end potluck at Jen's house. I think I can do it. If a talkative teacher with a big heart stands in my doorway to talk, I'll listen, but I will keep moving. And I can't leave this room for any distraction.

I make a final sweep at 5 p.m. I gather the last Superhero tickets, old calendars, and student papers and pitch the whole lot into the blue bin, now stacked twice its height. I take my keys to the front office and sign out. Peggy, our school secretary, stands to give me a hug.

"You're coming to the potluck, aren't you?" I ask.

"No," Peggy says.

"Oh shucks," I say. "Are you leaving town?"

"No. I just can't do such sad things," she tells me.

I love Peggy. I'll miss her. We hug as we do the last day of every school year, and I carry my potluck dish to the car.

Jen's house in the country is a long way and not easy to find. Most teachers and staff are already there, surrounded by partners and families and resident dogs. The table is filled with shimmering spring salads of pea pods and baby lettuce, Albertsons supermarket roasted chicken, and chocolate cake. I find a place for my blueberry quinoa salad and join a tour of the beautiful house and property.

When the baked beans and brownies are gone, the principal calls everyone together.

"We have transfers next fall of two of our best. They helped build our school from the day we opened twelve years ago, and we will miss them."

The principal offers small gifts to these fine teachers and a third gift to the teacher who designed reward programs that helped highflyers manage the school year with only a few behavior referrals and fewer blowouts. Everyone appreciates the important work.

Sandy, our social chair, calls Betty and me forward to the wide steps of Jen's porch. She offers a token of appreciation for Betty's years of settling playground disputes and rounding up soccer balls.

Betty tearfully accepts her gift and returns to her husband in the crowd. Sandy turns to me. "Brenda is always on us to share poetry with our students, so we have a poem for her."

She reads Shel Silverstein's "I Cannot Go to School Today" replacing Peggy Ann's name in the poem with my name as the one who has measles and mumps. I offer an embarrassed smile and say, "Thank you." I take the poem framed in a decoupage of words clipped from a first-grade reader. A few voices call out, "Speech, speech."

"I am so proud of you," I say to my colleagues. "I'm proud of your dedication, your commitment to the idea that every child can learn." The words come easily. I love these friends and colleagues. "You don't just say it, you do it. For every kid, every day. I honor all of you for showing up for the tough kids and the easy ones. I love public schools, the best embodiment of democracy I know. Thank you for doing what you do tirelessly and well."

Standing in front are my education assistants, who teach kids to read as well as I do. They've worked with me for a dozen years and are dear to me. Yesterday, they gave me a card that announced their gift to the food bank in my name. They know me well. Three EAs in front are in tears.

In five seconds, Jen says, "Wiffle ball in five minutes." I return to a patio chair. A two-year-old runs past on a chase with a black lab.

Wiffle ball? Shouldn't someone say something about Betty and how we'll miss her? Betty, the most roastable education assistant we've ever known, with a rigid sense of justice and black and white judgment about playground rules. Betty loves students unflinchingly, and they love her. They know what to expect. *Not a word of affection for Betty?*

I want to say, "But wait, we're not finished."

The hum of voices and sounds of laughing children chasing children sail through the trees. I look at my feet. *And me—I'm easy to make fun of. I look like the wrath of God when I arrive by bike on a stormy morning. My heart has been here. It was a good run, and now it's over.*

Sandy, the social committee of one, did her part with a gift. Maybe she thought kindergarten designed something fun. Maybe kindergarten thought first grade had a retirement committee in the works, or first grade thought the social committee had more than one member to cook up a story. These are the same people who recently nominated me for A Champion in Education (ACE) award and whooped and hollered in the darkened civic theater when my name was announced, when I stumbled to the stage in my polka dot tights, mumbling, "You have to be kidding." The last time I had won something in a darkened theater, I was nine years old. It was the day before Easter, and the prize was a live bunny.

A few days ago, my friend Jenny, principal at a neighbor school, said, "I want to be part of any festivities in your honor this week." I'm glad Jenny is too busy passing out kudos at her own school this evening to come to the potluck. Our secretary Peggy could have been here, for it's not sad at all. Or it is.

A teacher asks about my first retirement plans. "I'm going to Washington, D.C. at 5 a.m. My first assignment is to potty train my grandson. It seems I'm good at it." She chuckles at the challenge.

I gather my stainless salad bowl with a few grains of quinoa at the bottom and parsley clinging to the sides. The blueberries are gone. I thank Jen for hosting the party and hug my education assistants.

My heart is so heavy that I hurry to my car and haul myself behind the wheel. I turn right out of the driveway, retrace the route backward, and point the car toward home. I left behind my favorite stainless serving spoon. It's different, a beautiful wide oval shape. I don't go back for it.

Ed will call when I walk in the door, to ask how my last day was. I won't tell him about the celebration. He would be crushed. He'll ask if I need a ride to the airport in the morning. I don't. He'll ask me to give his daughter and grandson a big hug.

I lie awake after midnight and think about my send-off after twelve years at the school I love. Was it me? Is everyone so busy they don't know what it means to wrap up a career? I will think about it in the middle of the night this week, tired as I'll be from chasing a two-year-old with a potty chair. I won't tell Ani about my feelings, but one day I'll tell Ed. He'll be sorry, really sorry. He'll say it wasn't me.

I MAKE A RETURN VISIT TO MY SCHOOL FIVE MONTHS later, on a November Friday. Peggy and the other two secretaries greet me at the entry with hugs and questions about my new life. I tell them I've come to say hello to friends and see photos of new babies.

It's a joy to see my education assistants and meet Jess, who's doing a bang-up job at my old job. She gets it, the part about kids mastering reading in time, and takes the responsibility seriously. I like her, and I'm grateful she's here.

Before I leave the building, the principal emerges through a door to the hall. She offers a big smile, her head tilted enthusiastically in a way characteristic of her greetings.

"How's it going?" she asks. "How's retirement?"

"I'm still new at it, but it's good."

I tell her something has been on my mind.

"What's that?"

"I hope no one will ever retire again without some kind of recognition, whether they've been at school two years or twenty," I say. "This is where people plant their heart and soul. We have to tell them it means something. It would have been a hoot to tell stories about Betty."

The principal doesn't skip a beat. "My sister arrived in town the evening of the potluck. She called me at the party to say she was on my front porch and couldn't get in. I don't know if I was even there when Sandy gave your gift."

You were there. You laughed at the Silverstein poem about the girl with mumps and measles. The girl was Brenda.

"It was a crazy day," she continues. "I had to meet my sister, and I was leaving in the morning for the leadership conference at Harvard. I always wanted to go to Harvard!"

CHAPTER 24

Hospice Training

2014

W hen I retired three months ago, friends warned me not to jump into a half-dozen volunteer jobs until I get my bearings. I haven't. I've had hospice volunteer training on the calendar for the same three months. I want to learn something new. The number of people without shelter grows every day. Families are separated by distance or bad blood. Some people have no connections. I don't want anyone to die alone. Holding witness with a person in the last weeks or moments of life seems like something I could do. I'll find out.

I live alone, but I won't die alone. My former husband has been out of my house ten years, but he reminds me he would do anything for me. I imagine that includes help me die.

On a recent evening, he called. "Bree told me you have tendonitis in your shoulder. What happened?"

"Too much tennis, not enough follow-through," I said. "I need lessons."

"Can I do anything or pick up something for you?" He's attentive and kind, but I don't need a thing.

_____

THE TWO-DAY VOLUNTEER TRAINING BEGINS TODAY. I leave home uncommonly early to bike to the hospice office. I don't know exactly where it is, and I don't want to be late. I too often slide into a dentist's chair or slip into a meeting at the last minute, after leaving home at the last minute, but not before I mow the lawn or wash a window or locate a stud in the wall to hang a coat rack. I imagine I'll either die of a heart attack on my way somewhere, hell bent and late, or I'll live to 105, my heart strong, powered by pedaling. I'm not sure which to wish for. Today's training may help me decide.

I bike through town and onto the path that follows the river, low and slow in September. The river laps gently at the shore and cuts into the bank here and there. A blue heron stands one-legged in a quiet spot in the water. Out beyond the heron, the river flows north to the Columbia.

I like this bike route I haven't been on before today. The season is changing, a few red leaves light the skyline on fire, birds fly in different directions. It's beautiful. My season is changing, now that I'm retired with no breathless school children who need me every morning and afternoon.

I cry as I roll along at a good clip, contemplating life that's more fragile than willows bending over the bank or the spindly legs of the blue heron, knee-deep in the river. I'm not unhappy behind the tears, just paying attention to this precious life I enjoy.

I arrive early and enter a windowless room in a second-floor suite of cluttered, carpeted offices. I aim for a cushy chair and pull it into place next to a man in a wool felt fedora and flip-flops who is busy on his iPhone. He introduces himself. "Hello, I'm Richard."

At 8:30 a.m., Ashanti introduces herself and spells her unusual name. "It means 'beloved one' in Swahili," she says. "What can I say? My parents were hippies." This is a comfortable woman in a long skirt, a sweater with long tails covering her large frame, and a bead necklace.

Ashanti greets the volunteer cohort and welcomes each person by name. She counts heads and finds only one person missing. "We'll wait just another minute."

An empty seat remains in the front row. At 8:40, Ashanti begins. "I want each of you to think of two things no one in the room would know about you."

I have time before the personal revelations get around to me in the back row, but I don't know what I'll disclose to this room of people I don't know and will probably never see again.

A few volunteers in front offer predictable responses, like the number of children they have. I might have guessed Margaret has two children, but I wouldn't have guessed teenage twins. I could have guessed Michele is a Michigander by listening to her, but I wouldn't have guessed her goal to read 100 books this year. She's on number 83. Nor would I have guessed that Eric, who sports a clean, lean look, plays Johnny Cash look-alike shows. He does sound like the Man in Black.

Peak is married to a furrier. "A furrier tans hides and finishes furs and mounts fur creatures," she says. Peak is cute, like her name. I wonder where her husband does the tanning and if he smells like a goat when he comes in the kitchen.

Becky is a soft woman with fair skin and looks nothing like a strong hiker. She logged ninety miles backpacking this summer. I'm impressed.

I've been thinking. My first "nobody knows" revelation will be easy. Who would guess I was a homecoming princess in college? I looked good at nineteen, but I wasn't tall and I wasn't a beauty. I'll never know how I was nominated. My friend Ruth, who *is* tall, was also a princess (what a silly name), and we laughed about being unlikely princesses. We held no illusions of becoming homecoming queen (an even sillier name), for we knew beautiful and shy Kathy would win that title.

Between reading Kant and Nietzsche, I sewed a red velvet sheath on the Singer Featherweight my mother sent to college with me. Someone pinned a giant white chrysanthemum, adorned with my school's initial P in black pipe cleaner, above my heart. I even rode in a parade and probably waved. I admit, it was fun.

One time, when I used the truth that I was a homecoming princess in the game Two Truths and a Lie, my husband asked later that evening, "Does it hurt your feelings that everyone at the table thought the homecoming princess was a lie?"

I laughed, and Ed didn't know what to make of me.

"What??" he asked.

"The notion that it would hurt my feelings is funnier than people not believing I was ever royalty," I said. "No, it didn't hurt my feelings."

Did my husband not know me as well as I thought?

Introductions in the hospice office include ordinary and fascinating things about volunteers. Ashanti reflects each volunteer's revelation, modeling what we'll do in a setting with a hospice patient. "Michele from Michigan has read 83 books this year, and Richard plays in a band called The Implication." We're learning to listen, not analyze.

At 9:01 a.m., Dudley enters the room looking relaxed and takes the empty seat in front. Ashanti welcomes him as he opens his three-ring binder and settles in. He pulls a pink china teacup out of his bag and rises to leave the room. I notice his bowed legs.

I wonder if Dudley is sick. He returns fourteen minutes later and stops to brew tea in the pink china cup. He waits for the tea to steep, pulls out the tea bag, and returns to the front row.

Dudley seats himself with an unselfconscious flourish. He's not looking for attention. He sits on his right leg, exposing the sole of a shoe with a clip that attaches to a bicycle pedal. Dudley has a soft, boyish look, with a hint of a lisp and a little curl at the back of his neck where his hair is graying. I wouldn't have guessed he's a serious biker.

By now, Richard, on my right, is chewing his second apple. This apple, like the first, is cut into eight pieces. I hear every crunch of the Honeycrisp. I don't look, but I think Richard is chewing with his mouth open. Crunch, crunch, swallow. Again.

After lunch, we regroup in the windowless room of fluorescent lights. Richard arrives in noisy flip-flops and takes pains to quarter another Honeycrisp and cut out the seeds. I hear the knife edge work through the firm white flesh, cutting quarters in half again. Soon Richard is chewing every bit of every apple fraction. He accompanies his exhaustive chewing with a few burps. I plug my right ear with a finger so I can hear Ashanti with my left. And to make a point.

Before Ashanti begins the instructional part of the afternoon, she asks how we're doing, how we're feeling. Around the room again, each person offers one word to describe a feeling about today's training. We start with Dudley, who mentions a job loss, sleeping poorly, and feeling melancholy. Ashanti doesn't stop him at one word. She asks why he signed up for training, and he says he wants to be a better person. "Dudley lost his job recently, it hasn't been easy, and he hopes to be a better person through hospice training and work," Ashanti says.

I suppose I also hope to be a better person. Did I sign up for hospice training to be with someone who really is alone or to get over being alone myself? Maybe, but I've had ten years to get used to living alone, and it's okay. I admit to still missing my former husband at home. I liked being married.

I'm ready to get over myself in general. I think about peeling away my straight-backed judgment of Richard sitting to my right, but Richard is now munching on a third large, crisp, juicy apple, cut in many pieces. It's driving me to distraction.

Ashanti resumes instruction from the three-inch volunteer manual in a three-ring binder. Richard pauses from the forbidden fruit to flip through fifty or sixty pages of his binder, one page at a time, and now he is full-on burping. I want to scream, "Richard!!" He raises his hand to say something about restarting again.

This training is nothing if not thorough. I land on the page of the manual on nondiscrimination. Hospice personnel, and presumably all amiable volunteers, are not to discriminate against patients or each other in any of the predictable ways: Race, color, religion, age, gender, sexual orientation, disability or disease.

The text takes me down a notch, but it doesn't say anything about a person who is annoying. I swallow and try to sit up straighter in my chair.

At the end of our first day of training, Ashanti asks our assessment of the experience. I offer a clinical but honest response about the good organization, the comprehensive training, and the exceptional delivery.

Dudley says, "The certified nursing assistant who presented this afternoon was lively. She has passion for her job. She was icing on the cake. I'll have a story to tell at Toastmasters next week." If Dudley had been here early this morning, he might have told us he was a Toastmaster. I never would have guessed.

On the second day of training, I'm early again, after another perfect autumn ride on the river path. Richard isn't here yet. In case he brings apples today, I move my binder to another table, sacrificing the comfortable chair. Maybe it appears that I moved to the edge of the room to stand if I go into an after-lunch slump. I do get sleepy in meetings, but this one has been so interesting, my eyes haven't drifted to a droop.

Ashanti asks the group to go around the opposite direction and tell what we did for self-care last evening. Talking about self-care makes me shrink into myself, but I like Ashanti. I respect her approach. She's an excellent trainer. There must be a reason for this.

Michele started book number 84. Richard "went to a fantastic concert to hear one of the nation's best mandolin players, right here in town." Raquel cooked a nice dinner. Ashanti played with her kids (she has six biological children and foster children under nine), and Maria Jose, of the beautiful name, talks at length about her son, an accomplished DJ in town.

I say, "I messed around in the garden last night." I love the garden—morning, noon, and night. I'm mildly obsessed, even in moonlight.

The training this morning moves faster than yesterday, and soon it's time for lunch. Yesterday's lunch from Baja Fresh was very fresh and green. Tortillas with a host of healthy things to load on top. I helped myself to seconds and thirds of greens and salsa in different colors. Today, however, we have four varieties of pizza from a chain. I eat a slice of vegetarian pizza and wish I hadn't. It tastes like wet cardboard and tin cans. I wonder how they stay open with the competition of really good pizza ovens in town.

Dudley brought his lunch and doesn't eat pizza wedges from the cardboard box with the lift-top lid. He's eating a large green salad, and his fork clanks the straight sides of the glass bowl. I'm surprised to hear him say, between bites, that he recently joined AARP. I thought he was younger.

Hospice training wraps up with TB tests and evaluations. Dudley takes as long as I do to complete the evaluation. He asks if he can skip the TB test, for he recently had a skin test.

Ashanti is as patient and calm as she's been for two full days. "You would have to bring in those test results."

"Is it really necessary to have the second TB test, twelve to twenty-seven days from now?" Dudley asks.

"Yes, it's essential to the validity of the test," Ashanti explains.

I don't know where Dudley picked up a pink china cup or why he disappeared for several minutes at a time, but I think he suffers anxiety. The TB test might cause more.

I close my binder and pack my bag. I like hospice because it helps people face final days, along with a companion. How did I end up here, aside from not wanting anyone to die alone? What sparked my interest in death and dying? I'm not afraid of death. I'm not afraid of life. I live alone in a house, but I don't *live* alone. I have health care, attentive daughters, and a former husband who wants to know if something happens to me or if I have tendonitis. He'll be there when I'm ready to die, if he hasn't moved on to the next world before I do.

I listen to Dudley's earnest ideas of how he might volunteer, and my initial impression of his childlike manner begins to fade. Dudley is a Toastmaster. He puts himself out there and gives two- to three-minute talks at meetings.

If I'm assigned a hospice patient next week, I want to be good at it. I heard Dudley say he does too. He's more ready to commit than I am, and he has experienced loss and appears to face down anxiety. If Dudley accompanies hospice patients, he will understand their fear, offer a calming presence, make tea in a pink china cup, and listen.

I could learn from Dudley. I won't join Toastmasters, but I could read poems or songs or comic strips to someone in the final weeks of life.

I want to get over my biases and myself, because I have to live with me. This is the first September in decades that I'm not returning to school, and I won't have students as distraction. I'll have to find another way to get over myself.

I could cut Richard slack over that aggravating chewing, considering the hospice nondiscrimination policy, but it's hard. However, I can get over his out-there manner, the over-the-top earnestness that makes me back away. I can practice listening without analyzing, as Ashanti does.

I hear Richard offer cheerful goodbyes. He's a "howdy-do" guy. He will be the person someone needs in that final week of life and death. He will hold a patient's hand and feel the pulse of her last days. She will know Richard gets it, the loss.

I HAVE THINGS TO LEARN AND MORE TO PRACTICE. THE tears I've spent pedaling aren't complicated. I've never been broken. I missed my husband before he left ten years ago, and I missed him after he left. *It woulda been nice…*took up space in my mind. *What about retirement and grand-children?* took up more.

Thich Nhat Hanh writes that we suffer from wanting permanence in our lives. The global spiritual leader probably knows the Welsh word *hiraeth*: *longing, yearning...or earnest desire for the past.*

Bree was right. It takes the time it takes to get over being sad, and you never get over loving some people. It's okay. Long after he left, Ed told me he would always love me. After watching Dolly Parton sing "I Will Always Love You" on a country music special, he said, "I cried at the television."

That's me. I cry at concerts and at home. I cry at *Story-Corps* on NPR every Friday morning, when a pair of people, related or not, tells a tandem story that reveals their tenacity or recalls their mutual tragedy. I cry at world news. I cry when Pachelbel's Canon in D comes on the radio. I cried when Hank Aaron broke the homerun record in 1974.

I pop up the kickstand and roll upriver toward home. Something beautiful or broken on the way is bound to make me cry.

CHAPTER 25

Christmas at Home

2014

One year ago, our family celebrated Christmas in Seattle at Bree's house, where Ani landed from Washington, D.C., with her husband and two-year-old son. Ed and I drove north together. It made sense, both of us going to the same place at the same time. The family time was familiar and fun, with a tree, a star, six adults, three children, and a dog. Our daughters made light of their parents and their foibles, but the temporary nature of the time weighed on me. Ed would return to his partner, who would return from a ski trip. I would return to my empty house.

When I did walk in the door at home after Christmas in Seattle, my house felt hollow, except for the dog, a wagging, welcome fellow. Winter had settled in, dark and cold. It took a while for the furnace to warm the house, and I cried like I often do in silent, solo moments.

———

A YEAR LATER AND A COUPLE WEEKS INTO DECEMBER, Bree calls late in the evening. "Are you still okay with everyone coming for Christmas? Dad too?"

"Yes, it's fine. I've done enough things with your father in the last ten years. I can handle it." Our daughters are grateful their agreeable parents can be together to enjoy family dinners, weddings, and holidays with them, in the same place at the same time.

This year everyone is back at my house for Christmas, this time with four children, including an infant, and the adults responsible for them. Ani's family traveled from Washington, D.C. again, managing full flights and tight squeezes. I wish they lived near, but I don't say it out loud.

At my house, Christmas morning means gooey cinnamon rolls, good music, and complaints all around that I'm too slow to open my gifts. Later in the day, Ani's husband, a tireless chef who could make a culinary delight out of cardboard, prepares an outstanding vegetarian dinner. Some years I yearn for a turkey leg with cranberry sauce on the side, but I don't say that out loud either. The thought of a turkey on a platter gags the vegetarians, and I don't want the culinary artist to think I'm ungrateful for his holiday dishes, which are nothing but delectable.

Every year, Ed writes each daughter a Christmas poem to accent the moment in time. A poem for Ani, the December she returned home from a college semester in Nepal:

> The Mountain requires vigil
> and deep prayer,
> not the trample of foreign feet on its back,
> or the splintered bones of its children
> stitched through its cold skin.
>
> You were there
> bold, upright
> at its feet.
> Not to pray, not at first,

but to stand in vigil,
to gain comfort….

And a poem for Bree, after a college year in Ecuador:

Before summer breaks anew through old growth,
You will have walked…
In a different place far away,
into cold ruins of another age,
ancient people under stone.
Before summer fades into old light,
You will walk again,
and the rise in your step
will be enough
for the long walk
to another place.
Call it your own,
and there,
a warm light.

Driving to Seattle with Ed one year ago, I remembered the poem he wrote for me on a Christmas two decades ago. He recalled W. H. Auden's famous poem "Funeral Blues" and referred to me as his north, south, east, and west. I didn't ask Ed, behind the wheel on the drive north, if he remembered thinking of me as a reliable compass.

I STARTED THE CINNAMON ROLLS LAST NIGHT, SO I wouldn't be so slow in taking my turn to open a gift. It's Christmas morning, and the yeasty dough rose above the bowl's brim in a warm spot overnight. I'm rolling it in a wide sheet when the earliest riser, four-year-old Kiele, creeps downstairs. She helps me cover the glistening dough with cinnamon and raisins. Soon everyone is up, and children are in a swirl of paper and gifts. When the flurry is finished, I serve the rolls, warm and slathered in butter, while Ed charms each daughter with his poem for the season, full of his heart. The poems, folded in legal envelopes and tucked on a branch of the tree, are spotted first and saved for last. The typewritten words are evocative and beautiful and make the reader cry, this year and every year.

I REMEMBER ANOTHER CHRISTMAS POEM FROM MORE than twenty years ago.

> For Brenda
> "Where have you been?"
>
> [Saddled next to me,
> Eyes full of mercy,
> Tongue red with history,
> Lost in forest to trees uncovered?
>
> My story is a long one,
> too short for song
> too cryptic for history.
>
> Your story sings sweetly,
> too crisp for words,
> a picture on straight edges]
>
> "Here, right here."

I was right there. Call it support, shoulder, or saddle, I was there all thirty-three years. I miss being there and belonging.

Along with happy grandchildren, poems, and cinnamon rolls, everything is right as rain on Christmas day. But in the end, I have everything but the boy. Or man. I feel a little hollow again, with all the familiarity in the world but no partnership. I'm missing more than turkey and cranberries.

I don't want to be sad anymore. Does all this familiar contact with Ed make it worse? As the year turns to a new year, I sit down at my desk to write him a letter.

"Feel free to share this letter with your partner. No secrets," I begin. Secrets aren't fair. "Please don't call to talk about the kids or invite me to dinner or ask how I am. I've tried this every way to Sunday in the years since you left." This being connected but not really. I'm even willing to put a hold on our precious connection over daughters for now. The contact with their father is nice in the moment—we are good friends. But it's lousy when he leaves. My few divorced friends chose to be divorced, and they're happy for their independence. I want to embrace being alone.

Was separation hard because we grew up together in college, during a seminal time in American history? Add to that the history of two daughters we love equally. But everyone who gets divorced has history, and often as not, half of it is good.

Finally, I admit in the letter, a day after the new year, "Almost ten years out, I'm still tearing-up in fifteen seconds and crying in thirty. I don't want to feel this way anymore. I would like to get over it, and maybe, just maybe, this will help. Please don't call."

I don't know if absence of contact will help, but I'll try. I mail the letter.

CHAPTER 26

New Year

2015

A few days into the new year, after everyone returned home from our Christmas together, I'm folding gift wrap and cleaning the garage. I have a child's bike to hang on a hook anchored in the ceiling, and I need a tall man's reach. Ed has offered help many times.

"Would you like me to do anything while you're away?" he asks before I leave on a trip to Patagonia or Portland. I've never asked for help. I prepared our joint taxes, spilling tears on the Form 1040 the same month he left home. I rearranged the garage and organized the tool chest that first spring. I can manage almost everything at my house on the corner, from pruning holly trees to polishing skylights. I don't do gutters. I promised my children I wouldn't hang off the edge of the roof.

It's late afternoon when the phone rings. I pick it up in the garage and secure it between my ear and shoulder as I sweep dog fluff and dry leaves off the concrete floor.

This time, Ed doesn't ask how I am. He says, "I just read your letter."

Oh, that. "Okay."

His voice is thin at the other end. "So, I'm supposed to do nothing and not care if you get hurt or something happens?" I can hear the single-page letter rattle in his hand.

Something happens? A lot has happened in the last ten years. I'm weary of what hasn't happened. I haven't erased the "If only…" loop in my head. If only we had gone to a counselor before we were in crisis. If only we spent Sundays together. If only I had asked for more. What if we had hiked or biked or gone to more concerts?

It's curious that Ed thinks first of me getting hurt. Since he left, I've only had two mishaps. I fell off my bike on a patch of ice one winter morning on my way to school and crashed on a spring morning when a raccoon ran out of the rushes, through tall, lush grass, and straight into my bike. I arrived at school with wonky handlebars and a bit shaken after being broadsided by a four-legged bandit. The common mammal seemed uncommonly large. I emailed my daughters to report the collision.

"I was sure I'd be in a tangle under the bike with that raccoon," I wrote, "but the masked mammal vanished. I have a skinned knee but no abrasion on my Mandy pants. They look like new."

Title Nine, a women's active wear company, features beautiful, fit female athlete models in its catalog. The distinguished women are climbing Half Dome, docking a sailboat, or mountain biking around the world, each wearing a product with a woman's first name, like rugged "Melissa" pants. My tough Title Nine pants, however, didn't come with the name Mandy. I made it up.

Beyond a couple spills on my bike, nothing's been hurt but my heart in recent years. To be fair, it was my young husband who tenderly tended me at twenty-four, when I flew off a sixteen-hands horse at a good gallop. Duchess knew I was green and took off with me, then without me. I was out cold on a dirt road. My husband first feared I was dead and then that I might die. When it was clear I wouldn't, he worried I would be out of commission a long time and out of my mind forever.

I don't know if I knew Richard Nixon was president when I arrived at the hospital, or if I counted backward by sevens, but I did answer the doctor when he asked my name. It was the wrong name, but it was a name.

When I came back to myself, I had dizzy spells and I couldn't smell. The dizzy spells went away after a very long time. My sense of smell stayed away. Forever.

STILL ON THE PHONE IN MY DUSTY GARAGE, I STAND THE broom on end and tell Ed, "If I get hurt, I'm sure you'll hear about it," knowing my dutiful daughters are in a regular circle of communication with each other, their father, and me.

Gripping the broom, I want to say into the silent receiver, "I wish you had cared for me the night you stood at the foot of our bed and told me you were moving to an apartment, when I thought I would die from pain, my heart falling out of my chest, leaving a gaping hole," but I don't. Tears spilled into the pillow that awful night, when I finally fell asleep two hours before my alarm buzzed for school.

Neither do I tell Ed, before we finish our spare conversation, that my psychologist cousin Margy said, "The poor fool!" when I told her Ed left in midlife misery. "I've been through divorce of one husband and death of another," she said. "I tell you, death was easier. It's final, and there's no blame."

My dog sits in watch in the garage, wondering what's next. He knows something is up, or maybe it's down, and stays close. Margy takes her standard poodle, Jesse, to the office, where he sits sentry in an upholstered chair in the corner, staring a hole in the stony silence between husband and wife. Margy has helped clients manage everything from swinging threesomes with ropes and handcuffs to custody of the family dog. She knows the love-and-loss story in every chapter and verse. "Why would I retire," she says, "when my work is so darned interesting?"

Waiting on the hushed phone in the dusty garage, I wonder if only we had seen a counselor like Margy in the middle of our marriage, we might have found our problems interesting, not impossible.

I think about how I will end this telephone conversation with Ed. *Thanks for caring. I could have used your devoted attention ten years ago.* That ship sailed before Ed left home. I don't offer my thoughts, but if I had, Ed would have answered, "You're right."

Sweeping two piles into a dustpan with the phone wedged between my ear and shoulder, I tell him, "I shouldn't be this sad after all these years. It's not right, and I'm tired of myself this way. I'd like to get over it. Visiting over coffee is nice, but watching you leave is too often like tearing off a Band-Aid."

Before we finish, Ed sounds tearful on the phone at his house on the river. "Okay, if that's the way you want it." He always honors what I want. He's sorry I'm sad.

"It is," I assure him, though I'm not sure this approach will work any better than the last. "Bye."

I scoot the bent-up steel dustpan that was in this garage when we moved here twenty-five years ago, toward the last pile of debris. The awful scraping on the concrete floor covers the noise in my head. "Get over yourself."

My tears are brief. I don't know any women who have been left, and I don't know any who have felt this sad for this long. I'm satisfied with my decision.

I pass the dog with all the fluff. "Okay, buddy. Wanna come inside?" He may not have the soul of our yellow lab, now long gone, but he's a good companion. In the kitchen, he sits on his haunches and watches as I pull kale and onions and wild salmon out of the refrigerator.

"It's time to get this show on the road," I say. My show, my moving on from tears, my dinner. Tinder cocks his head. I tell him that people survive horrible divorces, and mine wasn't. It just happened, but it was a blinding surprise. Not me. Not ever.

Losing a partner but not really losing him puts me in the permanent in-between. How do I get over family that is part of my life, but not really? I don't think I feel sorry for myself, but why all the tears? What's keeping me from getting over whatever "it" is? Embarrassment at being left in middle age? Attachment? Disappointment at devoting all those years to my husband's academic career in hopes of devoted attention in return? Or simply wanting to be in a partnership with the person I love? *Hiraeth: longing or nostalgia. A deep and irrational bond felt with a time, era, place, or person.*

Tinder stays near and looks up now and then. It's simple to him. He gets it and probably knows what "it" is. We're in this together.

Tomorrow morning I'll bike to the Y just after sunrise. I'll work my muscles and bones with good people, some who make me laugh. I'll head for home as the winter morning brightens, ready for my spinning tires to deliver me from the emancipation I didn't want to the liberation I do.

CHAPTER 27

Soft Horizons

2015

In late winter, the gardens on the big corner lot of Soft Horizons Fibre are a brown and seedy remnant of their summer splendor. The corner is beautiful, despite the bent and drippy perennials, waiting for warm soil and sunshine. Early spring shoots push through the ground. The wrap-around porch of this popular knit shop near the University of Oregon campus suggests "come in," no matter the season. Today one knitter after another crosses the porch to turn the brass knob of the squeaky front door. Some are shopping, some are hoping for help on a project they started in winter and want to finish before all attention is drawn outside to spring gardens, when knitting needles are set aside and hands begin to work the soft earth.

I'm here to get help, though I can scarcely call myself a knitter. I've made a few straight-as-an arrow scarves or mufflers over the years. I don't follow a pattern—I just stop. After finishing my first knitted wool hat, I cannot figure out how to sew on my three-year-old grandson's name. I tried YouTube but found only a demo on how to applique a felt field hockey number onto a sweater and how to knit "hug me" into a cutesy valentine pillow.

Inside Soft Horizons, I move to a small room of wool yarns stacked in handsome displays and wait. I twirl the

heather brown wool cap in my hand and search for a contrasting color to embroider the name. I pull a skein of blue
wool out of its stack, then a tangerine and a green as delicate
as spring. No wonder people love to knit. Everything in the
room is touchable and delicious. It's so cozy here that you
could forget a pesky trouble. The fibers in gem tones set the
mood, and no one selling or shopping or hoping to get help
is pushy or impatient. Shoppers hold up two or three colors
together and finger the fibers. Women wait or watch or work
on a project. It's dreamy. Why haven't I been here before?

A tiny woman enters the small room where I sit. The
tone in the room changes when she speaks to anyone or no
one, her voice high and intense. It sounds like she is near
tears, but I look her way, and she's not.

"I've been vandalized twice in the last six months by the
Aryan Nation, up in Sweet Home. It's a bunch of neo-Nazis.
They wrecked these sweaters, and I need them fixed. They're
handmade from Cambodia. I was there twenty years ago."
The woman talks as she pulls sweaters from a bag and slides
them onto an oak table in the middle of the room. She tugs
at her coat, removes her hat, and tosses both on a chair.

I sense her torment. I've never been vandalized or thought
I was. I've never been pushed around or thought I was.

The agitated woman moves to a display of handmade
bags on a hat rack. She touches a large black-and-gold
brocade travel bag.

"This is half-price. That's good." She giggles at the price
tag. "It's $100! My sister would like it, but maybe I'll get this
one instead." She handles a small zipper bag that fits inside
a purse. "I'll have to come back on Thursday when I have
some money." She turns back to the sweaters in a heap on
the table. Her anxiety is palpable.

A Soft Horizons clerk pushes back a curtain and enters from a back room. "Can I be of help?" she asks. The woman tells the clerk about being vandalized.

"I have two biracial children and a Chinese daughter. Those Nazis have attacked me twice before. There's been an investigation. It's supposed to be in grand jury, but the sheriff put a hold on it." She tells the clerk about her prized sweaters. Her strawberry blond hair, gray at the hairline, separates in sweaty strands on her rosy scalp.

This woman may have been targeted by white supremacists because she has three children of color. Supremacist violence and hatred are hidden and not hidden in this blue and green state. I wish it weren't so. The election and reelection of an African American president has brought white supremacists out of the woodwork.

I'm getting warm. I prepare to be here awhile and slip off my coat and scarf.

The clerk gently handles both crocheted sweaters and lays them flat on the table. One in a black lacey pattern has several big holes that are not part of the pattern.

"We can't fix them, but I can give you telephone numbers of people who can," the clerk tells her.

"Oh, you can't fix them here?" the woman asks, her voice full of urgent disappointment.

"No, I'm sorry. We don't do any repairs in the shop. I'll give you the numbers to call. Until then, I recommend you go all the way around the sweaters and put a clamp or safety pin on each area that's torn, so it doesn't continue to ravel."

The clerk plucks a class schedule off a shelf. "I'll write the phone numbers on here for you. One woman prefers to call you. If you give me your number, I'll tell her about the sweaters."

"It's 541-…Well, my phone's been hacked. I'm getting a new phone on Thursday. I suppose the number will be the same, but tell her not to call before Thursday. 541-276-1521. That's Sweet Home, so she'll have to dial 1 first."

"And what's your name?" the clerk asks.

"Myrna. M-Y-R-N-A. Myrna. M-Y-R-N-A."

"Okay, Myrna. Here you go. I hope this helps." She passes Myrna a paper with names and numbers of fiber artists who may help stop the sweaters from fraying further.

Myrna picks up a skein of gold yarn from a basket on the floor. "Is this cotton yarn? It's pretty."

"No," the clerk answers. "It's silk."

"Oh, I love silk. It's warm but not hot. Two of my three silk scarves were stolen. My son was in Afghanistan and brought them home to me. I can't get any more. They were real wide. I used mine as a blanket on Amtrak, not too hot or too cold," Myrna says.

"Yes, silk is good that way," the clerk says.

"They have lots of silk in China. My daughter lives there. She wants me to come visit, but it's too hot where she lives in southwest China. I'll have to wait 'til it cools off," Myrna says.

I wonder how long it's been since Myrna has seen this daughter or if she's been to China. She knows the climate. Do her children call her or come home? Will Myrna have money on Thursday to buy a new phone and the small bag for her sister? Does her sister return Myrna's affections?

The room doesn't have a mirror, but if it did, I could stare privilege in the face. I suddenly feel small and lucky. Born in the right place to the right parents, I went to good schools, had a safe marriage and healthy children. I've had solid jobs with a host of rewards, including health care and plenty of support. I've had losses, but losses or not, my life has been easy. I want Myrna's life to be easier.

William Stafford, former distinguished Oregon poet laureate and prolific writer, was celebrated last year all around Oregon, in honor of the one-hundredth anniversay of his birth. I remember a Stafford poem as I wait in this shop filled with fiber and women who love it and serve one another.

The Way It Is

There's a thread you follow. It goes among
things that change. But it doesn't change.
People wonder about what you are pursuing.
You have to explain about the thread.
But it is hard for others to see.
While you hold it you can't get lost.
Tragedies happen; people get hurt
or die; and you suffer and get old.
Nothing you do can stop time's unfolding.
You don't ever let go of the thread.

—William Stafford

I think Myrna is trying to hold on. She collects her coat and hat and moves toward the door to leave the shop. She stops to look in a basket of braided skeins of worsted wool, each one rich and tempting to the touch. She picks up a yellow yarn she likes.

"I have a six-year-old student. She wears a yellow sundress with no sleeves. It's very pretty, and it looks like sunshine," she tells two women at the cash register on her way out.

I wonder what Myrna might teach—and where. Maybe the sundress with the look of sunshine has a thread for Myrna to hold onto.

I had a good teaching career. I'm retired with a pension. I can be in this warm yarn shop midday, midweek. I wear privilege well because I'm accustomed to it.

Myrna continues to handle loose balls of yarn piled in a wide wicker basket. She turns back to the clerk. "What's your name?"

"Margaret."

"My godmother is named Margaret. It's a good name. It's a really good name."

"Thank you," the clerk says.

Myrna is still talking as she turns the brass doorknob, embossed in a pattern. The door squeaks, and Myrna calls over her shoulder as she walks out to the porch, "Goodbye, Margaret."

Margaret returns the goodbye and hurries to the table where I wait.

"I'm sorry you had to wait," she says.

"It's fine. You were patient and kind," I whisper.

"Thank you," says Margaret, no stranger to people who drop in with a story.

"And no one at the counter pushed Myrna out the door or rolled their eyes when she left."

This could be my story, but it isn't. I can get over hardships. I have everything I need, two daughters who are steady-as-you-go and a former husband who would help me out of any mess. Myrna's struggles started piling up a long time ago. Soft Horizons was respite from the storm today.

Margaret sits down beside me and picks up the heathery wool hat I knitted for my grandson. She tells me to double a contrasting yarn—the soft green I have in my hand would be nice, in a blunt needle. "Pull the yarn through the V in the knit stitch and make a chain stitch, like so. Then push it back through here."

"Oh, thank you. *That's* how you do it. It's so easy!" I take the hat from Margaret and pull the yarn through to practice my first letter, "K."

I leave by the same door as Myrna and thank the women she thanked. I hop on my bike and pedal home to my simple challenge—follow the thread and stitch Kaleo's name in spring green.

Crocuses in the same color are bursting out of the earth.

CHAPTER 28

City Bus to Maryland

2015

I would love to be better at tennis. I'm fair, and no one signs up to play tennis with a fair player. An instructor at the rec center is doing her best to bolster my skills.

Ed and I often played tennis with friends in Wisconsin, but that was forty years ago. It was the outdoor court in a public park where I first learned to swear under my breath when I missed a good shot. I wasn't a hothead player, but I really wanted to hit a good one, and the near misses were so near. Or not near enough.

When Bree was born, my friend Linda and I took our babies to the tennis court in their bucket carseats and volleyed around them until they wailed with infant hunger. Linda and I were a good match with our wood rackets, and the babies were a good match, born two days apart. Those tennis rallies were also a long time ago.

I RARELY SIT DOWN AND I DON'T WATCH TELEVISION, SO I don't hang around my house without something to do. I choose any task outside before inside, rain or shine. I should have been a farmer—my capacity for outdoor work is endless.

Spring in Oregon is long and lush, beginning with daffodils and narcissus nodding cheerfully in February, moving through weeks of dogwood and rhododendron in riotous bloom, and ending with roses fit for a rose festival in a fresh burst of blossom every morning. I spend most spring days in the garden. I love it there—the dew drops on new growth, the soft earth, the long list of things to do. I like to share the garden with neighbors.

Eager to forget myself, I added tennis to hiking, biking, and gardening when Ed left ten years ago. I didn't carry on with grief, but I ruminated long on what I was missing. I needed to keep moving.

I met a nice man on the tennis court. He played tennis with me but had no patience for my shrieking on the outdoor court when I made an error.

"It doesn't improve your game," he said.

At least I didn't swear. He liked me, and I liked him more, but a woman across the Pacific was waiting to marry him, and he was waiting to marry her. So we played tennis, enjoyed a draft beer now and then, and had a few dinners together over a few months. We thought alike, which allowed easy conversation, especially welcome after I faded on the fellow whose social values got in the way. Way in the way. Two friends suggested, as we played Rummikub one night at a cabin in the mountains, that I might have one man for day and the other for night. I laughed.

IN THE REC CENTER, AFTER ANOTHER GROUP TENNIS lesson with the formidable instructor, I zip my modern metal racket in its cover and prepare to leave. I'm bound to improve—more instruction, more practice.

I pedal fast to catch the bus on a busy industrial street, lift my bike onto a rack on number 91, and pull a spring-loaded arm over the front tire. With my bike helmet still clipped under my chin, I'm ready to hop off at the transfer station and roll downriver toward home. I look odd but harmless in the highly visible green helmet, a tennis racket and canvas bag over and under my arm. The city bus usually sports a motley crew of passengers.

Out the bus window, I read a signboard towering above an auto body shop. "Mother's Da poker relay canceled Sunday." The "y" is missing, as well as the context. I'm curious about a poker relay. Do poker players tag team in honor of their mothers? Or do mothers play poker with other mothers? I wonder why it was canceled.

At the next stop, a young man, lean and messy, climbs on the bus with a backpack and blue Tupperware tub jammed full. He returns to the sidewalk to collect more gear, a bag and snowboard. Once on the bus, he props the snowboard against a vinyl seat. It slides to the floor.

"Will this bus take me to the Greyhound station?" he asks.

The bus driver is pretty, kind, and patient.

"This bus doesn't go to the Greyhound station, but you can buy a day pass for $3.50. You'll catch another bus that will drop you off close to Greyhound," she explains.

The lean young man flips through his thin leather wallet, soft as flannel, and pulls out a five-dollar bill.

"I'm sorry, I don't have change," the driver says.

The man turns to passengers to ask if anyone has change for a five. I have only a twenty-dollar bill, zipped in a pocket on my racket cover in case of emergency. I've zipped a large or small bill into every bag and purse and jacket I own—just in case. My children should check all my pockets when I die.

This might qualify as an emergency.

A large man in a green "Oregon Duck" T-shirt sits behind me. Both his heavy breathing and bulging belly spill onto my shoulder as he rises to reach in his pocket.

"I can give you change," he offers.

"Thanks, Bro," the young man says, moving toward the Duck. The two men take time sorting change and counting bills. The driver watches in the rearview mirror, never suggesting her patience is running thin. Once the young man makes the exchange, he moves forward, lines up dollar bills, and feeds them one-by-one into the fare meter. He adds two quarters. The bus driver hands him a day pass and tells him the right bus to take, but the information passes over him. He doesn't know he's in one town and will cross over the river to another.

"Where are you headed?" a man with a scruffy beard and cockeyed glasses asks the young passenger.

"Greyhound," he answers.

"Where ya goin' on Greyhound?"

"Maryland." He smiles, hitches up loose pants, and checks a button on his shirt.

Maryland. Maybe the traveler is going to Baltimore, not a great place for young African American males this month or any month. The country has been embroiled in weeks of protest and riots in the wake of another Black man's death at the hands of police. Freddie Gray was arrested and handcuffed by Baltimore police for possessing a knife that was legal. He died a violent death in the back of a police van. Freddie Gray was twenty-five, about the age of the traveler headed to Maryland.

The older man on the bus explains to "Maryland" where to find the Greyhound station in the town across the river.

Maryland grins and says "Uptown!" I think he means "thanks for the tip" and isn't referring to the geographic location of the station, which is uptown.

Maryland is darling. He is some mother's son. His broad smile reveals beautiful teeth. Perhaps he hasn't been on the road or on the street as long as his clothes and belongings suggest. Does he have family to help him get over whatever this transience is? I hope he's heading home and has someone to welcome him. I hope he belongs somewhere.

Maryland rearranges himself and his things on the city bus and props the snowboard across the aisle.

"Where do you plan to snowboard?" I ask. I rarely chat with bus riders, but I'm curious about this friendly fellow. I want his cross-country Greyhound trip to go well, but I have doubts. I think about the twenty dollars I'm hanging onto and all the bills in all the other pockets of mine.

"I don't know, but you can't just pass up a free snowboard," Maryland says.

Maybe not, but a loose snowboard under the arm is some bother on a bus trip from the Pacific Northwest to the Mid-Atlantic, especially if the board wants to roll away and is the third or fourth piece of cargo to keep track of.

The driver offers Maryland more direction on bus numbers and destination as he scoots his board and bag toward the exit. Once the bus is empty, the driver climbs down and folds the door closed.

I pull my bike off the rack and wheel toward her.

"I can't get over how patient and kind you are. I bet you see a lot."

"Oh, it's just what we do," she says.

"I know, but you're very good at it."

I would like to be good at lots of things, from tennis to tolerance. Today I can't get over Maryland or Freddie Gray. The police could learn something from bus drivers.

I watch Maryland search for the next bus. I set out to bike home along the river, a kindly bus driver and a cheerful traveler with a big smile on my mind. Maybe Maryland will be home for Mother's Day, to a place where he belongs. I know about belonging.

CHAPTER 29

Mother's Day

2015

I haven't seen Ed since we shared Christmas with our children and theirs, when I remembered too well my old dream of being grandparents together. It was a few days after that and a few days into the new year when I wrote Ed the letter asking him not to call with friendly offerings. I was still feeling too sad too often, even after nine years, soon ten.

I haven't been a wreck all those years, or any of them. I don't wrench in grief or take to my bed. I never have. I take trips and bake chocolate-lover's cake for a potluck. I see neighbors every day and set plants and lawn chairs on the street to give away. I ski and hike. And I ride my Bike Friday everyday, everywhere. I'm as normal as the day is long, but a cloud of sadness has perched on my shoulder. I'd rather be living the Emily Dickinson line, *"Hope" is the thing with feathers / That perches in the soul.* If only the cloud on my shoulder had feathers.

I admit that for several solid months, maybe even years, after my husband left, I hoped he would come back. I also admit *You Can't Go Home Again*, as Thomas Wolfe writes.

After Christmas, I thought absence of contact might help me get over absence of husband. That was January. Now it's May. I don't telephone my former husband, but yesterday I called to thank him for the yellow rhododendron I found on the front porch and already planted in soft spring dirt. "The rhodie is in full bloom! It's beautiful, and I planted it right where it belongs," I said. "A big Doug fir branch broke in the ice storm this winter, opening a window onto Tom's driveway. Now I have a screen. Thanks!"

Ed was eager, as always, to do something nice for me. I never say "ex-husband," or worse, "my ex." "Ex" means out, and that former husband is not out of my life. I don't say "ex" because it often sounds angry. *Ex-* is the prefix that forms a regulatory product and a derogatory term for formerly incarcerated.

When we were married, I occasionally introduced Ed as my "first husband" in friendly company. It was funny at the time. I thought he would always be mine and it would always be funny. Yesterday, that first husband came to my house when I was out biking along the river and left a sunny yellow rhodie.

As luck would have it, at the moment he was driving past a Lions Club rhododendron sale earlier in the day, Ani called him from three time zones away.

"Hi, Dad. I didn't get my Mother's Day card in the mail on time. Could you get Mom something from me—maybe a rhodie?"

"Of course," her father said. He would stand on his head if Ani asked. He ended the phone call, turned off the road to support the Lions Club, selected a robust rhodie, and delivered it to my house within an hour. Sitting next to the rhododendron on the porch was a pint of Black Dog Honey, a product of Ed's new life that has absolutely nothing to do with me. He has a garden, blueberries, and dogs. The Black Dog Honey, from Ed's new husbandry, has a shiny label, with a photograph of his partner's black lab, Bugaroo. The last time we worked a garden together was forty years ago, when we blanched corn and "put up" tomatoes in a steamy Wisconsin kitchen with four friends up to their elbows in salsa.

"Thanks again," I said at the end of my thank-you call about the sunny perennial.

"Would you like to go to breakfast tomorrow for Mother's Day?" Ed asked.

"Sure," I said.

Mother's Day is for children to honor their mother, but this year, down one card, I agree to breakfast with the father. I'm still feeling the cheerful color of my new perennial, and I'm ready for Mother's Day breakfast. It's been four months since Ed and I have spoken, and I have a story to tell about my spring break trip with our granddaughters.

I love Mother's Day. I have only two children. They are good girls, appreciative young women, especially now that they have families. They've always expressed gratitude as the language of the heart. They write exquisite, soulful cards for Mother's Day and my birthday. I save the cards to open with a cup of coffee in the morning or a glass of wine in the evening. The message makes me dissolve in tears every time. Then my daughters call, as does their father, to wish me a good day.

Years ago, when we had children at home, I enjoyed the entire day dedicated to mothers (inspired by a forgotten historic figure, a peace activist mother who cared for wounded soldiers) in the garden, with no indoor demands. Digging in the dirt came after church on Mother's Day, the day when ninth graders are confirmed. Teens love Wednesday night confirmation class so much they don't miss a session all year long. They talk with a skilled adult about God and sex and rock and roll. They confirm it all on Mother's Day, when the minister offers a few lines about each celebrant that speak of their promise and commitment to one another and the world. The remarks never fail to hit the mark on this auspicious day, and they never fail to make me cry. *How could these young people do anything but believe in their worth and take their responsibility to the world seriously?* It's a beautiful thing to witness, fifteen-year-olds commended and commanded to be their best selves.

I bike through town early Sunday morning, glorious in sun- and rain-drenched blossoms, to Via Dolce, a pop-up bakery in a pizzeria. Ed greets me in the entry.

"Happy Mother's Day," he says with a smile.

"Thanks," I say. The restaurant interior is light and spacious. Chalky pastel murals on three walls invite pastry or pizza patrons to step into Old Italy.

The lovely young woman who commands Via Dolce greets us from behind a counter with the warmth of Italy. I feel like I know her from the mouth-watering email invitations to Via Dolce on special Sundays. She props a three-year-old almond-eyed child on one hip while she takes orders at the counter.

The array of tarts and frittatas, zeppole and cannoli is dazzling.

"How do you do all this?" I ask.

"I start making everything on Wednesday and begin baking in these big pizza ovens at 4:00 in the morning," she tells me, already five hours into her workday.

"Would you like those frittatas heated?" She sets the toddler on the floor to run to her grandmother and reaches for my lemon tart, covered in gleaming blueberries. I consider asking for the raspberry-covered tart instead, with crimson berries upright on creamy lemon curd. The truth is, I could eat both.

Ed and I find a table near the window and watch two grandparents walk the curly-headed three-year-old from the bakery counter to their table and back again.

"Tell me about your trip with Azra and Kiele," Ed says. It's fun to share stories and act like we belong here, together on Mother's Day, celebrating what we did well together and being grandparents. I would rather be the grandparents at the next table, getting ready to shuttle the cute three-year-old to the home they share.

I would like to say to the grandfather across the table from me, "Remember that wide reading chair? I would have read *On the Night You Were Born* to Azra and later Kiele, and you would have followed with *James and the Giant Peach*. Better yet, you would have told them stories in sequels, like you told Bree and Ani."

Instead, I tell Ed about taking the girls to the Dungeness Spit on the Olympic Peninsula in Washington State during spring break last month.

"The kids played for hours in the sun and sand behind a giant drift log that made the perfect wind break on the beach. Kiele assigned me the role of 'nice mother,' but she told me not to be 'too nice.' When the tide came in, we packed up buckets and shovels and walked a mile through the woods back to the parking lot."

"No complaints about the long walk?" he asks.

"No, Kiele was into surfing postures and the 'hang loose' wave the entire way," I tell Pop Pop, waving my thumb and pinkie finger.

I'm having fun reporting this good trip, and he's interested. He thinks the children are as smart and darling as

I do. "We stopped at the National Wildlife Refuge booth, where the volunteer naturalists intrigued them with sea lion and otter skulls and stuffed shorebirds. The naturalists were impressed with their understanding of marine life."

"I would be impressed too," Ed says.

I tell him about giving the girls a No-Tangle Tuesday Trim in the sunshine outside our cottage with a yonder view of Puget Sound. I tell him about the movies they chose from the cottage library. The old *Peter Pan* film was so racist in its portrayal of a head-dressed Indian singing "What Makes the Red Man Red?" that I lunged at the TV and switched it off before I told the girls why.

"Did our kids ever watch that movie?" Ed asks.

"Impossible. We would have done the same thing. The racism is so blatant. I should have suggested the cottage owner pull the video from the library. I wish I had thought of it."

"We popped Kiele's choice, *Charlie and the Chocolate Factory*, into the video player," I tell Ed. "Later I read that this Roald Dahl book is considered everything from great allegory to sure racism." I need more experience with the screen. The last Disney film I saw was *Lady and the Tramp* in 1956.

I cross the pizzeria for dark Italian coffee refills and stop at the counter for biscotti. I set coffee mugs and crisp biscotti on our table and pick up another story about the trip.

"I drove seventeen winding miles from Port Angeles up the mountain to Hurricane Ridge, where we had a 180-degree view of the Olympics, as far as the eye can see. It's spectacular. Kiele did more surfing in the snow, with bent knees and the wave. Always the wave."

I tell Ed that back in Port Angeles, I spotted a green sign for the public library and asked the girls if we should go there.

"'YEESS,' they screamed. They cheered like we were off to the circus. Inside the library, we learned about a poetry project between Olympic National Park and the city library.

"The next morning, we hiked four trails in Olympic Park, each one with poems posted along the trail. It was wonderful."

I knew Ed, a poet himself, would love this. I tell him about the poems from Emily Brontë to Shel Silverstein and local S'Klallam tribe member Duane Niatum, each etched on a green national park sign, sturdy and beautiful with a leaf motif. The seven-year-old read and photographed every poem.

"She could read all the text?" he asks. "Wow."

"She could and she did, with some eloquence. One favorite was Niatum's poem "Spider," where the spider invites the reader to spin with him.

"Kiele was tuckered out and done with hiking after the second trail of poems. Finished. She still takes naps, so she fell asleep in the car. Azra and I waited patiently at the next trailhead for her to wake up, and when she did, she still wanted no part of hiking."

"'No more hikes, Granny,' she said, and I was out of ideas."

"So what did you do? I know it's impossible to talk her into anything," Ed says.

"I shamelessly bribed her with Paul Newman mints in a polar bear tin. 'Would you carry these mints to the waterfall for me?' Bingo, it worked."

I want to tell Pop Pop, "You would have loved it."

He would say, "You're right."

This is what we should be doing with our time.

We are.

It's a nice Mother's Day. Phone calls, cards, yesterday's blooming rhodie, breakfast with dark coffee. Today, I think

less about what I'm missing and more about an easy relationship with a nice man who supports and cares for his
family, including me. It beats the alternative—no relationship at all with the father of our children and grandfather
of their children. Or worse, a bitter divide that everyone
has to step around.

My life is full of things I don't want to get over, all the
beauty that makes life worth living. Kids on a trail of poems,
choral music bouncing off the rafters, sunsets in triple layers
at my back, all the people and places and poetics that keep
me from feeling lost when Ed visits and leaves. Balance. I
may shed tears, but I'm not lost.

"I can't get over how great it was," I'll say about the sim-
mering sunset or college choir or trail of poems.

I BALANCE A BAG OF VIA DOLCE BISCOTTI IN THE GRIP
of my handlebars and cruise along the bike lane sprinkled
in dogwood petals, thick and soft as velvet, that cling to
my bike tires.

At church, I remember the day each daughter was confirmed—the dress she wore, the way the morning sun cast
light on the church pews near the aisle, the elegance of the
moment. I wish I had a record of Reverend Flint's words
that honored Bree and later Ani. The affirmation of their
confirmation more than twenty years ago might carry them
through a rough patch one day, when they really need it.

I count on words—poems from Rumi to Jane Hirshfield,
old hymns and popular songs, my daughters' heart-filled
cards and thoughtful phone calls. Crying at the words is
sweet solace. It's what I do.

CHAPTER 30

Boot Camp to Backpack

2015

"Knees 1, 2; inner 1, 2; outer 1, 2. All right. Now repeater knees 1, 2, 3. Are you warmed up yet?" Shannon asks the boot camp class of a dozen women and one nice man named Ted, age seventy-five.

We never say much in response to Shannon's questions. It's early on a cold November morning, and we're just beginning to sweat.

"Are we warmed up yet??" Shannon adds herself to the friendly question.

"Yes!" This time, three of us answer at once.

I joined the YMCA ten years ago, when I first began living alone, and filled evenings with tennis after twenty-five years of not playing the game. My first night on the court, other players had a good laugh at my wood tennis racket. The next day, I went to the sports store for a lightweight metal racket.

Now I bike to the Y most mornings of the week. The facility's low-brow flavor and the community appeal to me, from children's sports, where eager and anxious parents aren't allowed to exercise their egos by scolding their own child or booing others, to older adults hooked on pickle ball and fitness classes that build strong bones and hearts.

The halls, classes, and weight rooms at the YMCA tumble with young and old people, women out of work, men in wheelchairs, kids tagging along with moms when school is not in session. Posters line the walls in glossy encouragement to "live your life" or "get moving." I never stop moving, but it's good for me to take a breath and remember this is a good life, and I'm living it pretty well.

The Y's mission to support youth development, healthy living, and social responsibility is evident everywhere. Students arrive in late afternoon from the nearby middle school and the sprawling high school across the street to play pool or ping-pong or finish homework with friends. Kids who don't fit anywhere else can find a home at the YMCA.

The Y facility is old and cramped and inadequate, but people in a variety of fitness shapes and variegated fitness tights are welcome and happy here. Truly Veg, the café tucked in a small space, serves lunch. Even the high school kids, who survive on expensive coffee drinks or soda pop, acquire a taste for seasoned greens sprinkled with sunflower seeds. Y members squeeze into a small meeting room to learn about memory care, baby care, or budgeting.

At the Y, someone notices if another someone is absent too many Mondays. Gail asks Chris about her latest theater production. Terese tells us about the World Cup when she returns from Brazil. "It was hot and steamy and crowded and wonderful." Terese impressed her children in Rio de Janeiro with her competent Portuguese.

Today the forty-something boot camp instructor welcomes us. Shannon points to her shaved head and explains, "I did this to support a young friend who has cancer and started chemo last week. I told my husband I look like my little brother." She laughs. Shannon is youthful and pretty in a distinct way. She sports close-cropped hair well.

"Make it your workout," Shannon instructs. When we're into it, on the fourth series of jumping jacks, burpees, lunges, and push-ups, Shannon says, sympathetically, "I kn-o-ow." Before we're done, we've pumped fifty-five push-ups.

After a long series of stepping sideways with a wide green band around my ankles, I ask if anyone has ever died stretching quads and hip flexors. Owww.

"Use perfect form. Stay with it. Push yourself to the edge. Listen to your body. You can always adapt if you need to," Shannon says.

The first time I came to Shannon's boot camp two years ago, she offered a practical message about taking care of yourself.

"I'm leaving with my family tomorrow for Yellowstone National Park—a long drive and lots of hiking," she said. "You want to be in good shape and health. It's a gift to your husband to stay in shape so you can keep up on the trail. It's important to keep up your health too."

Shannon's message sounded moralistic or something. Maybe archaic. It struck me the wrong way. If I *had* a husband, I could hike circles around him.

I admit, it would be nice to have a husband to say, "Shake a leg," when I leave for the Y early on a foggy morning. Or to plan a hike or trip with me. I do love Yellowstone. I cross-country skied one February in Yellowstone—past Old Faithful and bison, around wolf tracks in the snow, and nine miles downhill from the Continental Divide. It was heaven, and Ed might have loved it, but I couldn't have talked him into taking the time.

Hiraeth: an earnest longing or desire, or sense of regret. Longing for a home that no longer exists. I may be wistful at times, but I've cut the tape of "What if?"

I got over begrudging Shannon her suggestion simply because I didn't have a husband to go to Yellowstone with me. She has our health at heart when she asks, "Does it burn? Don't pace yourself—keep pushing. But remember to listen to your body." Lest anyone die from overdoing it.

Shannon works another thirty-two repeater knees and sixteen plié squats into our routine and asks if we had a good Thanksgiving. A few people answer a breathless "Yes" between sumo squats.

"How was your Thanksgiving in Texas?" I ask, sitting as far back as I can sit in a squat.

"It was good, but I missed the Y and injured myself running on concrete. I also ate too much," Shannon admits. "My husband is a farmer, right? We have an organic farm, so I took a dozen perfect potatoes to his parents' house in Texas for Thanksgiving dinner. Organic potatoes—really good."

"And heavy," I add.

"Yes. On Thanksgiving morning, I carried those heavy potatoes from my suitcase to the kitchen and set them on the counter. My mother-in-law watched me unload them and said, 'Shannon, honey, we won't need those. We prefer frozen b'tatas.'"

Shannon tells us more between high and low lunges. "For Thanksgiving dinner, we had shredded frozen-potato casserole with corn flake topping."

"Made with mushroom soup?" I ask.

"No, no. That was in the green bean casserole," Shannon says. "And Aunt Sylvia brought the salad." Shannon raises an eyebrow and adds, "It was green."

"What was it?" someone asks.

"That's what my son said. 'What is that?'"

Shannon continues. "Pistachio Jell-o pudding with Cool

Whip. My son was the only one at the table who didn't ask for seconds. People love this stuff." Feeling guilty at generating amusement over her Texas relatives, Shannon adds, "I laugh, but these are good people. I love my in-laws, and they're very good to me."

Back to butt kickers and high knees and a solid minute of jumping jacks, I feel like the jacks could kill me. Then we move into the serious part of boot camp. One minute on, ten seconds off. We can all do it. Ted's knees don't come as high as some, but they're up there.

A few of us over sixty are rolled and dimpled, but we're tough. No one ever congratulates us "for our age."

Hannah is new today, aiming to get in shape after having a baby six months ago. She says she's overweight by twenty pounds and doesn't like it.

"I was so toned before I had my second chih-ld," Hannah tells us with a southern accent I can't place. She slows down to take a break in the middle of twenty burpees, followed by twenty mountain climbers. After class, Shannon tells her, "You did great. Come back!"

As we leave the Y, I welcome the new young woman. "Hannah has always been a favorite name," I tell her.

"You're so fit," Hannah says with a pretty smile. She's new to this variety of women in boot camp. We're all fit.

HANNAH'S COMMENT REMINDS ME OF A BACKPACKING trip last summer, when I hiked with three friends high into the Eagle Cap Wilderness in the Wallowa Mountains of northeastern Oregon. Four younger women, swinging ponytails pulled through the open space at the back of their cute caps, met us on the trail as they hiked out of the Eagle Cap. They stopped to ask if we were heading to Mirror Lake for the day.

"We're camping at Mirror Lake for the week," we answered.

"Where's your gear?" one hiker asked, seeing nothing but daypacks on our backs. My friend Lana explained that Effie, on up the trail, turns seventy this year. Effie's gift to herself was packing into the wilderness with a mule team. She invited us to come along.

"It's glam backpacking," I told the younger women surrounding us on the trail. "Back-country experience with camp chairs, roasted red pepper dip, and wine in the cooler."

This is living.

"Were those your mules we just passed?" one woman asked, flipping her ponytail as she nodded uphill.

"Yes, the mules were ours."

"How much are you allowed to pack in?" another asked.

"Fifty pounds each," Lana said, "but our packer let us get by with a little more."

"Wes mantied up our gear in canvas tarps so fast it made you dizzy," I said. "Then he slung those big canvas bundles on either side of a mule's broad back." Wes was so swift at flinging rope that he made the job look like gift wrapping. Wes was quiet the entire time he loaded three broad mules, single-handed."

The four hikers with heavy packs looked at each other and agreed this is the way to enjoy their annual trip next summer. "Mules or llamas," one said.

One woman, blond streaks mingling with gray at her hairline, turned to say more. Attractive in cap and over-sized sunglasses, she looked my way. "You're such an inspiration."

I couldn't be more than ten years your senior, cookie.

On our way down the trail, we laughed at the perky blond with eyes trained on me as her hiking inspiration. Am I sensitive about looking my age? Is it because I'm single at sixty-six? I can keep up with the best of them on the trail, but wrinkles are beginning to give away my age. I attribute the wrinkles to growing up in dry country and too many scorching sunburns to count, not to aging!

I LIKE THE YMCA MORE ALL THE TIME. WE DON'T HAVE to inspire. It's enough to just be. Everyone, no matter age or limits or injuries, is doing a great job. Everyone belongs and no one counts wrinkles.

My reflexes are sound. I hop on my bike to pedal home from Shannon's boot camp, but not before I pull down a visor to protect the tender skin on my face.

CHAPTER 31

Ducks Travel

2015

I thought the Seven Wonders of the World were sacro-sanct, wondered at by mortals forever. The Taj Mahal, Machu Picchu, the Great Wall of China—those wonders. I assumed the Grand Canyon was one of the seven, the North American addition to the forever list, especially because it has been around forever.

Now, I learn the invariable list includes the Seven Ancient Wonders of the World, only one of which remains today, the Great Pyramid of Giza, on the west bank of the Nile River. The Seven New Wonders of the World change every year or so, based on international vote. If the Grand Canyon isn't on this year's list, it should be.

Ani and I just spent ten glowing October days at the South Rim of this astonishing American wonder. October is a good month almost anywhere, but here, on the edge of a chasm, it was radiant. Ani was engaged in a course with the National Park Service, and I was engaged with her one-year-old Kainoa, all smiles and motion.

The grandfather of this little boy in my care called three times during the week to ask about our good time. He doesn't like to lose touch, and I expect the brief calls.

"How's it going with Kainoa?" Ed asked on my third day in northern Arizona.

"It's going great. He's easy, and this is one amazing place to be, especially for several days in autumn," I exclaimed, breathless from either the splendor of the wonder of the world or from chasing a one-year-old at seven thousand feet.

"I forgot the magnificence of the Grand Canyon from our visit forty years ago. I can't get over it. Magnificent doesn't touch it. I've run out of adjectives."

"I bet," he said. "I'm jealous." This grandfather wished he was here with this baby who shares his name, not to mention to peer deep into the six-thousand-foot canyon of colors and layers, to witness a feature of our lives that hadn't changed over forty years. I would be jealous if I was the one calling for a report on a baby and a world wonder.

"Remember the helicopter ride we took over the canyon as a promo for something—a condominium or investment of some sort that we had no intention of making?"

"I do," Ed said. "I was blown away."

"You would be again. Maybe more. Remember the end of the flight, when I told the pilot, as we climbed out of the helicopter, I didn't think it was a good idea to fly over that wondrous canyon? It wasn't fair to him. I felt bad that we were opportunists and jumped on a free offer, young and naïve or not. We shouldn't have done it, even then, take advantage of an environmental intrusion on a glorious place."

"You're right," Ed said, "but we were young."

"Yes, but we weren't stupid."

In ten days at the rim of the canyon, Kainoa and I put dozens of miles on a stroller with wonky front wheels that finally lined up on the Trail of Time. The National Park Service interpretive path features a brass marker every meter to represent a million years. Chunky rock samples line the trail, taken from young limestone layers (a mere

252 million years old) and sedimentary layers of ruby sandstone and dark layers of granite from Elves Chasm Gneiss (close to 2 billion years old). The samples encourage the casual visitor to ponder the magnitude of geologic time. At the end of the trail, a sign reads, "Grand Canyon's rocks are incredibly old." There I turned the buggy around each day. We strolled back in time a billion years and rolled our way to lunch and a nap.

Ten days at the rim of the sun- and rain-streaked wonder of the world were the best they could be. Ani and I had a hard time pulling ourselves off the rim and the view on history in layers. The geology is complex. Our time was not—eat, sleep, stroll, marvel.

———

NOW IN THE EARLY MORNING HOURS AT THE FLAGSTAFF airport, we're delayed by a raging thunderstorm. We've been chasing the baby, on his hands and knees, up and down the airport lobby stairs and in and out the automatic doors since 6 a.m. We finally board the plane and bounce Kainoa from knee-to-knee and lap-to-lap in the confines of a prop jet. We're still waiting. The thunderstorm isn't unusual for this extreme topography, but a small plane can easily be grounded by a storm. The friendly flight attendant explains the storm route to Phoenix.

"We'll fly north into the weather before we turn south to Phoenix. We need extra lift, so we'll have to reduce our weight. I'm sorry anyone has to get off, but that's the way it is in these mountains." She asks passengers who checked in last at the counter to be first to check out of the little plane. Ani and I arrived at the airport in pitch dark and chased the one-year-old into dawn. We're safe.

Two distance hikers, draped in rain gear still dripping from last night, volunteer to get off the plane, reducing cargo weight by four hundred pounds. They've been hiking and camping in the Grand Canyon for days. They're good sports and announce they'll camp one more night.

Another forty-five minutes pass before the jet propellers begin to whir. Ani and I look at each other wide-eyed, in hopes the whirring blades will lift us off the ground, into the storm and out of it. Kainoa is pacified by the rain-streaked window and the engine's hum.

We land in Phoenix without a minute to spare for Ani to make her connection home to Washington, D.C.

"Run to the gate with Kainoa. I'll get the stroller," I say. To the aggravation of a grounds crewman who waves me away from the rolling luggage cart, I grab the stroller and run like mad up the stairs to Ani's gate. The gate agent is watching for me and hurries my way to snatch the stroller. Ani waves and disappears with the baby I didn't have a chance to kiss goodbye.

I'm grateful Ani made her flight and doesn't have to while away hours chasing her livewire son up and down the B concourse. I return her wave, turn to go my way, and burst into tears.

I find a good cup of coffee at Phoenix Sky Harbor and locate my gate. The gate agent is on the loudspeaker. "The captain has announced that if you cheered for the Oregon Ducks last night, you won't be allowed to board this plane. You'll have to catch another flight." The dressed-in-green Oregon Ducks, standing three-deep in line, detect the humor in the agent's announcement. I've been out-of-range for ten days and don't know anything about current football standings, Oregon's or anyone's. I never know much about football.

"Did the Ducks play Arizona last night?" I ask the young woman next to me. She's flying to Portland with the rest of this crowd. Maybe she knows.

"They played Arizona State," she answers kindly, before she dials the phone to inform her husband she'll be late on account of weather. It's nice, updating the person who's expecting you.

As the storm passes over Phoenix and the plane is cleared for takeoff, eager passengers line up to board. I'm in no hurry to sit down and wait. I enter the plane with the final boarding group.

As I arrive at seat 13A, a pair of Duck fans moves into the aisle to allow me passage to the window seat. Even though the gentleman steps aside, I brush his kelly green sweatshirt, emblazoned in glossy gold D-U-C-K-S and stretched over his ample belly. I take my seat and take out my book.

The Duck fan on the aisle, retired, relaxed, and not flummoxed by an airport dash or the weather delay, asks his partner if she needs anything.

"No, I'm fine."

"Nothing out of the bag up above before we take off?" he asks.

"No, I have my book. Thank you." She pulls a bookmark out of Nora Roberts' *The Liar* and puts a finger in the fat paperback to hold her place. She slips off her slip-on Keds, stamped in green and yellow OREGON letters. Four little shamrock tattoos peek out of her blue jean capris on her ankle. Maybe the shamrocks represent her children. Or grandchildren.

My town is home to Oregon Ducks football, but I've never worn a Ducks color. The green is too green, and the yellow is too garish. Nike offers Duck wear in more agreeable tones, but I don't buy it in pink or mint green either.

"Was it a good game?" I ask my seatmate.

"It was, at the end. It was a triple overtime," she tells me. This woman knows plays and what happens after the third overtime and which player made the decisive move. I'm impressed by her zest for the game.

"Did the third overtime take it out of you?" I ask.

The woman agrees it was exciting. Her partner looks her way. "We spent a lot of money in two days, but it was worth it, don't you think?"

Once the plane lifts off, it tosses in the weather. My stomach drops. We talk more football.

A short time into the flight, *The Liar* seems to take the reserves out of the woman. She pulls down the tray table to rest her head on her arms. The big green "O" of her beaded green and yellow earrings folds accordion style on her shoulder.

The gentleman next to her puts his hand on her back and resumes reading the inflight magazine. He orders Scotch from the flight attendant. I order ginger ale and cranberry juice.

"A can of each, or do you want them mixed?" the attendant asks.

"Mixed." I should have asked for a can of each. I meant to say "no thanks" to the pretzel mix, but it's already in my hand.

The woman next to me snores softly, and her partner on the aisle adjusts the belt on his snug khaki shorts before he opens the pretzels. He's wearing a large ornate class ring on his right hand. The stone is emerald green, maybe a real emerald. He must be an Oregon alum.

The descent into Portland wakes the woman. The man says something sweet to her, and she agrees it was a nice nap, though her arms are kinked. She looks over me at the scene below, the city of Portland. "It's always nice to see the green here," she says, "no matter what time of year it is."

"I like it too," I say. "Is this your home?"

"Now it is," she answers. "I moved up from Medford."

"And the rain doesn't bother you after that dry climate with all the blue sky?" I ask.

"No, this is home now." Her partner takes her left hand in his as they wait out the bumpy landing.

It's sweet, their devotion. Some to football, more to the Ducks, even more to each other. I don't put myself in the woman's shoes. I don't wear canvas Keds with Duck emblems or dangly earrings, and I don't fancy football. But I'm sweet on tenderness, the unembarrassed loving someone enough to take up her hand. The woman is happy in Portland.

When I arrive home, the dog welcomes me and spins in spirited circles. I talk to him like an old friend who belongs in this house, because he is and he does. Just as I get the last of my suitcase put away, Ed calls.

"How was your trip home?"

"It was good." I tell him about thunderstorms, a bouncing baby, and a tight flight. I mention the lighthearted raft of Ducks at the gate.

"I bet. It was a big game with Arizona State last night," Ed says. He loves football.

I don't tell him about the committed pair of Ducks who sat next to me. I don't tell anyone that I envy the adoration they unabashedly displayed.

CHAPTER 32

OK Cupid

2016

B oot camp at the YMCA is hard, but I wouldn't miss it. Shannon moved away, and this boot camp is with Shelly, another good teacher. I've just finished squats and sprints, and I'm unlocking my bike when my phone rings. I scramble to find a tiny flip phone at the bottom of my bag, beneath a bundle of gym clothes wrapped in a wet towel.

"Hello?" No one ever calls me on this phone. It must be "searchingforsoul" from OK Cupid.

"Hi, this is Ron. I realize I didn't get your name."

"No, you didn't. Are you on your way to Wandering Goat?" I ask, without offering my name. I never give my name before I meet someone, reluctant to reveal anything before I even meet the fellow. I think this might be my last coffee date.

"Yes, I'll be there real soon," Ron says.

"Okay, I'm setting out now. It will take me about twenty minutes," I tell him.

A few weeks ago, I quit paying for the old-people-meet-old-people online dating site. I'm embarrassed to admit the number of months SeniorPeopleMeet milked my money with no reward—or even results. Online searchers for soul-mates paint themselves in broad strokes, from sexual persuasion to religious affiliation or body type, but my limited experience is that men aren't always honest. Women may not be honest either. I wouldn't know. Online dating is like homework, without the "job well done" part. Many times I've thought, as the man I'm scheduled to meet walks in the coffee shop door, *A few extra pounds?* or *Loves outdoors?*

One fellow who reached out to me gave me a smile or a nod or whatever a searcher does online. He sported a photo in his profile of a favorite pastime, pushing his cat in a stroller along the river path. I was polite with a thank you and the admission that I just don't do cats.

Of the two coffee dates I was interested in revisiting, one had no interest in me and said as much when the coffee ran dry. The other asked, "Can I see you again?" I said yes, because I liked him. Mike is the fellow who lived nearby and cross-country skied, which was appealing, for it was winter. He had all the right aesthetic touches, but I learned my hunch was right. I could never marry a person whose social sensibilities, followed by political allegiances, made me wince. Nor pair up with one.

Today I'm meeting "searchingforsoul" from OK Cupid. It's a free site, bringing me as much luck as the old folks site. The meet-up location is Ron's choice. He likes the vibe and easy parking. He turned down my first recommendation, because he was worried about parking.

The weather gets wilder as I ride toward Wandering Goat, and a sheet of rain slants sideways and strikes me from the west. By the time I ride six blocks, the rain has blown through me, one side to the other.

I park my bike at a loopy rack outside the coffee shop. My bag, already soggy with gym clothes, is dripping rain as I sling it over my shoulder and enter the cavernous coffee shop. I scan the room for anyone who could be a sixty-six-year-old man fresh off the OK Cupid screen and locate an empty table on a small raised area in the corner that might be a stage. I drape my raincoat on the back of a chair and balance on one foot to slip off my rain pants. I take a chair and wait for Ron behind a young man marking Bible passages with a yellow highlighter. He's wearing large headphones. He won't hear my conversation with Ron.

It's easy to spot pairs on a meet-up. The man leans forward and talks. The woman sits upright and laughs. I'm a little uneasy, pretty sure the upcoming meeting won't be any more significant than the last.

A freight train rumbles past the coffee shop for eight long minutes. I assume Ron is caught behind the safety arms on the other side, but long after the caboose at last pulls up the rear, Ron doesn't emerge from the backed-up traffic. After another several minutes, he pulls open the glass door of Wandering Goat with a smile, recognizing me instantly as a fellow cupid. His glasses are fogged from the weather. He reaches a hand toward me and says, "You must be Sierra. I bet that's from the Sierra Mountains. They're nice. You got here fast—I thought I was fast."

"I haven't ordered coffee yet. Would you like some?" I aim to be friendly, knowing this is not "the one." Ron has a big smile, cascading locks, and a rumpled shirt. We move between tables of wet young people dressed mostly in black—hoods, sweatshirts, tattoos. I order house coffee and a bagel covered in seeds. I don't even think about caraway or poppy seeds lodging in my teeth.

Ron orders a latte and offers to pay for my coffee.

"No, but thank you. I'll pay. You had to drive a distance to get here." My "everything" seeded bagel takes a few minutes to cycle through the old-fashioned toaster with a rotating track and drop onto the counter. This toaster is quite the conversation piece. A bearded fellow my age remembers one like it at summer camp. A thirty-something says his grandmother in New York City has the same toaster. I butter my bagel while it's warm and ask the man behind the counter if they have jam.

"No, the only sweet we have is honey." I feel slightly juvenile, like Frances in *Bread and Jam for Frances*, who likes nothing but bread and jam. I do love jam, especially Oregon marionberry.

Back at our table on the raised area that Ron says is a small stage, I move my wet clothes and pull out a chair. It's going to be a long hour, but I start with the usual questions. What brought you to Oregon? Do you have children? Do they live nearby? Are you retired?

The fog has lifted on Ron's glasses, but they're tinted and remain dim amber. "I moved to Oregon to get out of Bay Area superficiality." He nods toward sound and lighting equipment in the nook next to us. "I build sound systems." Ron tells me he moves music to free radio, or something like that, and he tells me he's the best in the area in that field.

Ron's ex-wife took all his money. "I earned that money from building sound systems for stars and other high rollers," he says. "She took it all." The amount was either $1 million or $10 million—I didn't hear the figure clearly.

"All of it?" I ask.

"All of it. My wife had to raise the kids, so what could I say to the judge?"

"Gosh." I'm serious in my response.

"I had an accident and then a health crisis. Then there were pain pills to get through the day. I had no money. I had to get out of southern California."

Ron tells me about the misdiagnoses of his back pain by California doctors. "I couldn't find any relief til I found this specialist in Oregon." He adds that surgery saved him from himself and from the pills and finally vindicated him to his wife. "Until the surgery, my ex-wife thought I was a fraud and a drug addict."

I ask about his children.

"I won't even go there about my daughter. She's all about drama. Takes after her mother," Ron says.

"Does she live in California? Do you see her?" I ask.

"She lives with her mother, and I don't see her. It's okay, because I don't care to." He smiles meekly, sensing that I think this is sad. "It is what it is," he says and shrugs a shoulder.

I can't imagine being out of touch with one of my children. It's hard enough not being connected to their father.

"I'm proud of my son," Ron says. "He works with a lot of big stars and might be the only person in the field who is better at sound technology than I am. He's in very high demand. My daughter is a different story. I don't know what she's doing right now. She's not in college."

I eat the buttered, seedy bagel in front of Ron. My coffee cup nearly empty, I slow down, wanting the coffee and bagel to come out even. I feel like Frances again.

Ron is pale and gangly. I don't think he's an outdoors guy, either before or after his serious surgery, but I don't ask. He tells me he's an empath. "I don't tell many people," he says, "because it doesn't always go well. People don't understand." His OK Cupid profile lists "empath" as one of his attributes, followed by "people don't always understand."

I have no experience with an empath. I looked it up: *a person with the paranormal ability to apprehend the mental emotional state of another.* Did I agree to this meet-up out of curiosity?

To stretch the conversation to fifty minutes, I pursue empath. I pepper Ron with questions because I'm interested and have no desire to talk about myself. We won't meet again. I check my watch.

"Do you have to go somewhere?" Ron asks.

"Yes, I have a dental appointment at 12:15. It will take me a good twenty minutes to get there." I don't really have a dental appointment, but it's not unlikely. Last week, I had two root canal flare-ups and appointments. People say, "I'd rather have a root canal than do this or that."

Ron and I continue the exchange as I begin to layer my wet clothes. I bus my dishes to the bin in the middle of Wandering Goat, and Ron asks if he will see me again.

I call back over my shoulder with a smile to be kind, not coy. "Maybe."

I shouldn't have said that. I won't see him again, and I'm not brave.

"Maybe, huh?" Ron asks. I don't feel good about any of this.

I thank Ron for meeting me and tell him it was interesting. We say goodbye outside. He looks really tall folding himself into his old tan Toyota Camry. I wave as I pedal past Ron at the wheel.

I don't want to do this anymore. It's not an attractive me, feigning interest to be polite and then slipping away. I'm ready to get over thinking I need a partner for the rest of my life. Not a man off a screen, anyway. Odds aren't with me in this online game, and I'm okay alone—better than OK with cupid.

I love company, and I loved being a companion. I liked when my husband stood relaxed in the kitchen and called me "Babe." I leaned into him and we talked, even if we didn't talk much, or enough.

I don't want to be a companion to just anybody. If I want company in my house, I could rent a room to that graduate student I keep thinking about who doesn't have much stuff and doesn't have any baggage.

There's a break in the rain. I pedal home past the turn-off to the dentist.

CHAPTER 33

Sunday Morning Breakfast

2016

In the twenty-five years since our family worked at a soup kitchen, before it was better named the Dining Room, food insecurity has grown worse, despite many local efforts to address food scarcity.

My parents didn't talk about suffering. They just saw a need and did something. Suffering was less obvious when I was growing up, before the optimistic, or mistaken, release of tens of thousands of mentally ill patients to community, before veterans returned from five tragic wars, and before decades of wage stagnation.

Misery isn't pretty, and if I don't hide from it, I often walk around it. I don't feel guilty, but I recognize I'm often better at donating money and supplies than my efforts in the hard places. Several people from my church work the free breakfast at First Christian Church every fourth Sunday, and some gather fresh produce from their gardens to scramble into eggs every Sunday, not just the fourth.

As I told my young children, one way to stop focusing on yourself, your happiness and your good time, is to do something for somebody else. I would say the same thing today. The world isn't devoted to making me happy.

I'm on my way to First Christian Church to serve
the fourth Sunday breakfast for the first time. The sun splits
a gentle spring rain into iridescent spray. I lock my bicycle
to a rack at the church entrance and tuck a bundle of men's
socks under a grocery bag in the basket. Later I'll deliver
the wool socks to CAHOOTS, the crisis asistance team
that helps out on the streets. A shiny white CAHOOTS
van, staffed with a highly trained mental health worker and
a medic, motors around town to intervene in street crises
with able and sensitive attention. CAHOOTS offers finger
foods to people in trouble on the street. Socks are second
only to food as currency when someone needs help—or
kindness and Kind Bars. Food and dry socks calm anxiety
while talented workers mitigate the crisis.

The alley entrance to the church basement is a sea of
bicycles, trailers, dogs, and people. Dozens of people, mostly
men, are inching in line down the steps to the fellowship
hall for breakfast.

"Excuse me." I move past the disheveled line of early risers.
The moment I enter the large hall filled with people eating
egg-and-vegetable scramble, a woman screams at a man
leaving the hall. He calls her a bitch of some sort, and she
raises both arms, pinky fingers and thumbs extended, and
says, "Yeah, you got it. I'm the biggest, best bitch you ever saw."

My young friend Emily comes from the kitchen in an
apron over a short skirt and leggings. Her long blond hair is
pulled into a knot. Emily manages the scene every Sunday
for this free breakfast. Her eyes are on the situation, and
the fuss de-escalates as quickly as it flared, once the object
of the woman's ire is gone. Emily turns back to get more
melamine plates for the breakfast line. Everything about
Emily is lovely--her six-foot frame, her spirit, her know-

how. As a college student who works at least two jobs, she would say she thrives on this kind of work.

I hang my coat in a closet, tie an apron around my waist, and find the hand-washing sink. No one gives me a big hurrah welcome, because they've been here for an hour or more and were here last month or last week. Dozens of cheerful spirits fill the kitchen and move about the dining room. With obvious experience, Marsha asks if I need a job. I do. I begin to pour orange juice.

The busy and able movements of volunteers contrast with the hard luck in this room. People like Emily who staff the dining hall are saints. They set the tone and offer the most dignified experience possible for people who have rare occasion to enjoy dignity. The servers offer choices, many colorful options, and the diners take a seat in a pleasant dining room. It's in my bones to care, and today it's my turn. I'm glad to be in this hard place.

While I pour small glasses of juice, Marsha's husband fills tall glasses of milk. As milk runs out, Lee pulls full gallons from the refrigerator. We run out of cups and glasses and wait for replacements, warm from the industrial dishwasher.

Diners come to the table with a steaming plate piled with eggs, sausage, diced potatoes, and ketchup, lots of ketchup. With a free hand, they stack a bowl of cereal on a mound of potatoes and grab a glass of milk. With spare fingers, they clutch a glass or two of orange juice. Some return to the table for coffee or cocoa mix. Today half-and-half is on the table. It won't last long.

Marsha is striking with gray hair, handsome red lipstick, and a beautiful smile. She remembers that Naomi can't drink milk. "I'm sorry we don't have soy or almond milk today," she says.

"That's okay." Naomi takes her granola dry.

At fifteen minutes from closing, there is no end in sight to the line that snakes through the dining room and down the hall. Rodney approaches the table, spinning and talking to himself. His body jerks uncontrollably, and he struggles with a plate of eggs as he picks up a bowl of cereal. His pants are grimy, and milk streams from the cereal bowl down his pant leg, onto the floor. Marsha tries to alert him. Rodney clutches his plate with black fingernails and moves on.

Dean comes through the line with a phone to his ear. Certain he's talking to someone on the other end, I soon realize he's not. He talks into the phone until he reaches our table and tucks the phone in a pocket. When he finishes breakfast, Dean talks on the phone all the way down the hall to the bathroom and back again. He gathers a bundle of plastic bags filled with dry foods collected from somewhere and prepares to leave.

Diners exclaim about the terrific food as they pass through the line. "This is the best breakfast in town—it'll hold me for a while!" Only a few people talk to each other. Most are surprisingly solitary and spend their time eating.

A well-spoken woman of about fifty is an exception. She chats at length with a person at her table. This interested talker is a white woman with dreadlocks twice the size of her head. The dreads look like a mop with perfectly consistent strings, thick as rope. I look for a seam, wondering if this is a wig. The hair doesn't seem natural for this tiny person.

A mother hustles through the breakfast line and asks her teenage son, "How ya doin'? You still rollin' okay? You good there?"

The son stiffens under this grilling but gives in to the mother's grasp around his shoulders. "I'm fine," he assures her. His brown eyes are big as saucers, no evidence of a pupil. His mother ruffles the stringy brown hair that falls across his face. She follows him to a table.

Deborah takes up one end of a table with her breakfast and her stuff. She doesn't remove her sunglasses or pink fleece coat and polka dot hat. Deborah is uncomfortably large, and after an hour, she rises with difficulty to leave the table. She pushes a wire cart of belongings and pulls a blue suitcase. Leaning on the cart filled with one stuffed plastic bag on top of another, Deborah makes her way across the dining hall. I wonder how she'll climb the steps to the outside. Maybe there's an elevator.

Nan comes by the drink table to talk to Marsha. Her ponytail is neatly fixed sideways. She carries on a conversation about the weather and the day and looks more put together than most people dining this morning. These folks are shuffling and shifting from bridges to cars to the back of city parks every day. Health workers say it only takes a week to a few months of living on the street for the street to "take" people and put them in a permanent state of post-traumatic stress. For teenagers, the fourteenth night on the street is the critical one. After that, it's hard to get young people back from the "family" they find there.

Another tiny woman arrives just before the kitchen runs out of eggs and shuts down. She is covered in hoods and rags and hair. I can scarcely see her face and must get very close to hear what she's saying.

"Yes, granola. No milk," she whispers. I only guess at the rest. Her face, like many in the room, is red and ruddy. It's hidden. Her eyes are mere slits. I carry her breakfast and follow as she zigzags between tables and relaxed bodies until she spots her things—a bandana and two paper bags filled with something.

As I wipe tables with soap and rinse and disinfectant, the woman who arrived late is the only one still eating in this big room. She asks for more syrup for her pancakes, and I tell her it's put away. Later I'm sorry I didn't look for it. I assumed it was locked up with other food, but maybe it wasn't.

Paul, a worker as tall and lean as Emily, plays the piano while he waits to stack tables on a trolley. His music is upbeat and spills over onto the good hearts and strong shoulders of everyone who is cleaning up and sweeping up.

I finish sanitizing the last table. Nan lingers.

"Do you know when Palm Sunday service is at this church?" she asks.

"I don't, but I know their regular service is posted on the sign out front."

"Oh, yes, and Palm Sunday isn't until next week. That's good—it gives people more time to give up something for Lent. I think it's important, but I didn't give up anything this year. It's good for us to sacrifice just a little to really feel what Jesus gave up for us and our sins. He suffered so much on the cross—we should feel it a bit."

I think about the cross and that burden Nan speaks of. Why is there so much suffering? Why don't these people have food to eat or a place to call home? No answer makes the grime of this Sunday any easier.

"Most people don't know a thing about Lent," Nan continues, "but some people give up something for forty days, like Jesus in the wilderness for forty days. That's an awfully long time. I think giving up something for a week is just about right."

I can't imagine what this woman could give up. What does she have or do in excess? I can name fifteen things for myself, from water to chocolate, and I didn't consider giving up anything for Lent.

I find Emily before I leave. "You and your volunteers have this breakfast down to a science," I say.

Emily is a master at this, but she takes little credit. "You can see I have lots of help."

Emily has a contagious smile.

I collect a load of recycling to carry to the alley. At the bike rack, the woman with dreadlocks sits upright in a sleeping bag against the building. She looks up with a kindly smile. "What have you brought for us?"

"I don't have anything. I just came to get my bike," I say.

"Oh, I thought you were someone with donations, but now I see who you are. You probably noticed that only a few people in there are totally wacko crazy—or crazier than I am. A lotta them don't take the right drugs or take drugs that aren't good for them. That's a problem, and they end up in big trouble." She's wearing bifocals, barely visible under the dreadlocks.

The wool socks that were hidden under a grocery bag in my bike basket are gone, but the envelope of emergency cash is still there. I tell the woman goodbye. "Have a nice day."

"You have a good day, too, honey," she calls after me.

But for the grace of God, there go I. I came from a good zip code and most everything has come easily to me. I can't take credit for pulling myself up by my bootstraps, because I never had to pull. What people need in the church dining hall isn't simple. All the poverty or mental illness or gritty need that spills out of the basement and up the steps into the alley doesn't come from a bad choice or two. A wrong turn or bad luck, a health problem or divorce, dropping out of school or losing a job may all tumble into a cascade of crises. And then a cross with the law, maybe jail. Trespassing? Sleeping in a public place? Dumpster diving?

I can't get over the people in that church basement—people with staggering need that's hard to watch and people who show up every week to do what needs to be done. My pastor Melanie imagines what Jesus said to his disciples: "You want to follow me? Take up your cross and come. Find your place here, not running from misery, but knowing that walking with Jesus means you walk into the misery companioned." I'll be back to the basement breakfast. I hope sooner than later.

In the meantime, I'll remember Emily. "There's no place I'd rather work than here," she says. Emily would never let all those people who carry full plates to the table bear their crosses alone.

I set out on my bike to buy more socks for CAHOOTS. *Get over yourself.* I'm doing it.

CHAPTER 34

Dinner on the Road

2016

I've long considered the wolf more than a dressed-up villain in a fairy tale, but I've never studied this giant of the natural world. In the Wallowa Mountains of northeastern Oregon, I looked for wolf tracks, hoped for a wolf sighting, and made wolf calls. It was a regular Wolf Rendezvous. Oregon Wild protects public land and wildlife, even where it's hard, like cattle country, and sponsors the wolf meet-up every year. I signed up.

I didn't see the noble predator this week, and I didn't make a convincing wolf call, but our leader did. I pictured wolves near and far standing on hind legs, listening for more. Wolves are elusive creatures, which is a good thing, but it would be a thrill to see one loping on the prairie or waiting for a jackrabbit in the meadow.

I spent three days in the Wallowa Mountains, near Enterprise and Joseph, birthplace of Nez Perce Chief Joseph, and not far from Homestead and Halfway. With eight Oregon Wild supporters, I learned the importance of the long-reviled predator wolf to the health of our ecosystem.

The first morning of the rendezvous, I climbed out of my tent and into the van with other wolf enthusiasts. No one told me I had two distinct rosy dots on my cheeks, where I had forgotten to smudge the lipstick I dabbed there to achieve a robust, outdoorsy look. I didn't know that radiant rounds the size of half-dollars remained until noon, when I caught sight of myself, not a wolf, in the van's side mirror. I looked like Little Red Riding Hood's real grandmother. I laughed, other women laughed, and I set out with my new eco friends to track a wolf and find wildflowers on the Zumwalt Prairie, a waving sea of green on the edge of Hells Canyon.

I've been on the road alone only one other time in the many years I've lived alone. On my drive home from wolf watching in the Wallowas, I stop for the night in a pretty little town in the middle of Oregon wine country. The verdant hills, mapped in heaving rows of climbing vines and blossoms, are in spring-green splendor. Before long, vintners will squeeze or mash grapes into fine pinot noir. Filbert orchards, in the neighboring acreage, stretch in endless diagonals over the next rise.

Next door to my boutique hotel with a bathroom down the hall and a view of the Coast Range is Nick's Café. "Café" belies the simple elegance of this restaurant, but "Italian," in the subtitle, takes it a step further. People drive from the city to dine at Nick's.

Nick's heavy glass door shutters out the cold, and I shudder with the chill I brought inside. A young man greets me. "It will take just a moment to get the table ready," he says and offers a choice of two tables.

I ask for the small table farthest from the door. While the gentleman prepares the table with a clean white cloth and napkins pressed to points, I go to my car parked in front for a scarf and wool socks.

My server arrives at the table with a smile. She doesn't tell me her name or that she'll be taking care of me this evening. She offers a wine list. "Here you go, M'lady. Many of the wines on our list are locally grown and produced."

"Is the local Chardonnay good?" I ask.

"Well, it's not oaky or buttery and doesn't have a smooth finish," she says. I don't know what an oaky or buttery taste is in a wine, but a review that begins with "Well" and lists what the wine isn't, speaks volumes. "Nor is it fruity," she adds, which I do understand. I move along on the list to a fruity Italian wine. "Good choice," she says.

At a two-person table in a tight spot between two couples, I'm comfortably distant from the drafty doorway. Before my wine arrives, I pull out a college paperback of Hemingway's memoir *A Moveable Feast*. On the tan, pulpy pages, Hemingway recounts two years in Paris in the early 1920s. There he dedicated himself to writing, became friends with Gertrude Stein, looked for James Joyce, and found Ezra Pound, whom he considered a great poet and a gentle and generous man. "Hem" taught Ezra to box and ate cheap food and drank fine champagne with F. Scott Fitzgerald. He was struck by Scott's good looks and called him "pretty."

My book group chose *A Moveable Feast* in spirit with Annette, who leaves this week for a trip to Paris. I turn the page and sip my Italian wine, which is fruity and delicious, like my server said.

On my right is a tall couple sitting upright, especially the woman, long and lean and smartly dressed in a black-and-white turtleneck with stylish earrings stacked in sterling circles. Her husband, on my side of the table on the bench seat, is dressed in plaid flannel and wears glasses attached to Chubbs or Chums. I can never remember what the cord is called that keeps reading glasses from falling in your soup or sunglasses from falling in the river. Perhaps the serious-looking husband went fishing today.

This couple hasn't spoken since I arrived, but they appear to be enjoying starters of olives and bread. Hungry for something salty with my fruity Italian white, I'm tempted to order the olive medley. At six dollars, with white bread, I don't.

Nick's Café is busy tonight, a Monday. It must be this way every night of the week. At a table off to my left, a family is celebrating an aunt's birthday. The aunt just came from the beauty parlor with a new bob and strawberry blond stripes. Her husband sits next to her, and the husband's sister and two children are around the table.

My former husband would reasonably ask how I make the assumptions I do (like who's who at a table), and he might think I am nosy. Bree and Ani and I have sorted large restaurant parties into mother and mother-in-law, children and stepchildren, and established who is fond of whom or who isn't. My girls' father could never figure it out.

"How do you know all that?" he would ask. "And why do you care?"

"We don't really care," we said. "It's just interesting. And fun."

THIS EVENING, I'M CAREFUL NOT TO GAWK. I LIKE THE big family, especially Donnie, the teenager who acts happy to be here in this restaurant, sharing his aunt's birthday. While his little sister busies herself with a game on a smart phone, Donnie leans forward on elbows to speak to his aunt. "I really like your new hairdo." The aunt doesn't hear him, and I want her to. In a few moments, she says, "What was that?" Donnie repeats his expression of affection. This is fun.

The woman at the table on my right doesn't move off her upright position as she speaks to her husband about a business deal. No hushed tones or restraint. She doesn't mind being watched or heard.

"It's like a business deal," she asserts. "Think of it as a business deal. Do what you want."

If Ed was with me now, opposite me at this two-person table, he would have to take notice of the married pair. It's impossible not to.

After several minutes, the husband speaks. "You've said that ten times." I sense irritation. The wife maintains her position, tells him with certainty that if he really wants something, he has to go after it. She doesn't lean forward to plead or invite his understanding or agreement. She appears to know the pulse of power. She fingers her wine glass and fixes a gaze on her husband. I try not to look. She doesn't take her eyes off him. I think she wants him to acknowledge her *just do it* message.

I can't imagine being as bold or sure of myself as this wife—at home or on the road. I'm strong, but I wouldn't embarrass my husband in public. This wife must be accustomed to getting what she wants. Tonight, she's persevering. Or bulldozing.

At the same time the table next to me is radiating heat, Hemingway's good friend in Paris, Gertrude Stein, has lost her shine. Hemingway often stopped at Gertrude's home at 27 rue de Fleurus to talk writers and manuscripts. His last visit took an odd turn that repelled him, just when I was getting to appreciate Gertrude's odd nature.

My fresh Oregon tuna spaghetti arrives, and I put down *A Moveable Feast*. I'm in a hot spot in the middle of a chapter, but I can't twirl spaghetti and read at the same time. It didn't occur to me the fresh tuna spaghetti wouldn't be served with Nick's famous Italian tomato sauce. I order the signature sauce to eat with a pile of noodles in the middle of my plate. "Here you go, M'lady," the amiable server says, as she places a small pitcher of red sauce on the table. She is taking care of me.

The tall, attractive wife has just finished a gelato dessert and catches her server and mine with an outstretched hand.

"We're ready for our check. I want to make sure I'm not charged for the second glass of Chardonnay I ordered that never came," she reports.

"I'm sorry about that," the server says. "I would be happy to bring you a complimentary glass of wine."

"No, thank you, I've had enough." Enough of everything. I imagine her husband has also had enough and is relieved she's not dragging out the evening with a second glass of Chardonnay.

I open *A Moveable Feast* again. Hemingway is in Paris with his wife, Hadley, who supports him with both her inheritance and enthusiasm for his writing. Within a few years, Hemingway will take up with Pauline, a *Vogue* fashion journalist, and marry her a month after his divorce from Hadley. Ouch. Hemingway invites Pauline, a talented writer herself, to critique his work.

For almost two decades, I read every professional letter or article my husband wrote. He trusted me to edit for clarity and brevity and limit the number of times he used "indulge" with a professor, provost, or president. He's a good writer, and I liked editing. I was quick and good at it. It was something I could do to support his work while I worked part time. You could say it was a business deal.

When Ed left home, or me, and one of my few talents, I was out that job, editing. I didn't worry about him being too wordy. I tried to delete heartbreak from my own page, and that job was plenty.

Hadley saw Hemingway only one or two times after their divorce, but they exchanged many letters. Ed and I have seen each other many times each year since divorce, but we haven't exchanged letters, which seems too intimate. Occasionally, Ed asks me to read something he wrote, maybe a sympathy card or reference letter, to see what I think. I almost always strike out "indulge."

Later in *A Moveable Feast,* and somewhere on his path with the next two wives, Hemingway blames Pauline for being a homewrecker who befriended Hadley to gain access to him. Hemingway is less appealing right now than his fallen friend Gertrude Stein, but reading is becoming impossible. The conversations and clamor in the restaurant make concentration a challenge, and the print on the pulpy pages is getting harder to read.

The commanding wife at the next table catches my glance.

"It's great to be out, isn't it?" she says.

Out? "Yes, it's lovely to be out on a beautiful June evening, having dinner at Nick's," I answer, a little too quickly.

"You get to sit here and listen to all these conversations, including ours."

I check myself. I didn't stare or strain to listen—I was reading Hemingway.

Next, the wife says, "You could be me."

No, I could be Hadley.

Did the now-familiar woman mean I could be her, sitting at a small table with a husband who wasn't invested in the business of marriage? Or did she mean, "I could be you," sitting alone in a nice Italian restaurant in a pretty little town? Flying solo might look inviting, considering the taciturn manner of the husband in the plaid shirt, who for some reason isn't into business.

Then the pretty and serious wife says, with a gesture across the table, "He could die of a heart attack, or I could die." She smiles self-consciously. "Or I could be divorced." *Okay.*

I could be dining with Hemingway, but I'm all ears. I don't look at the husband, who must be as eager as a fish on the line to be released and out of here. Does this wife, short hair in cute upturned waves, neat red lipstick, even now, after dinner, want me to tell my story in an abbreviated chapter, before she puts on her wrap and sashays out the door? Or is she comforting me, the lone woman with nothing but a book as companion?

I don't know why, but I say, "I'm a lot older than you." Am I trying to assure the handsome woman that neither she nor her husband looks to be on the brink of a heart attack?

She touches gentle wrinkles at the corner of her eye. Red nail polish matches her good lipstick. "I dye my hair." She nods toward her husband and continues, "And he's younger than I am." It occurs to me this woman has enjoyed being the center of attention—at least mine, if not her husband's.

My dessert of four profiteroles arrives, and I busy myself with the first tiny puff pastry. The couple stands to leave. The formidable wife wraps a shawl around her shoulders and collects a handbag from under the table. She stands behind her chair, her gaze on me this time. She's waiting to be noticed.

"You look fabulous, by the way," she says. Is this a concession to my being alone or to my age? That I don't color my hair and it's not gray? That I have wrinkles in my cheeks, but I look okay anyway? She all but says, "you poor thing."

She lifts one side of her mouth in a knowing expression and looks at me for another moment. Is there something she wants me to know? I smile and resist looking away. Like everything that's transpired in this dining room tonight, this is interesting. I don't want to miss a beat.

Would this woman at the center of the room like to be me, the lone observer on a night out with interesting people all around, living out the human condition in all its mess and beauty? Would she like to give up the marriage business and be independent? I doubt it.

I could tell the woman about being alone, how long it's taken me to get over loss and onto advantages. I'm there, and that's why I'm here. I'm not the center of anyone's attention.

I could tell her about the Wolf Rendezvous and the benefits of wolves in the wild. I would add that wolves mate for life.

The tall wife wraps her sweater shawl tighter before she takes the lead out the door, her husband following. I watch by the light of the streetlamp as the two move down the sidewalk, no suggestion that marriage is a winner in this evening drama. Husband and wife each huddle alone against the cold. The vision of them doesn't move me to tears.

Alone on the road has suited me fine tonight. I'm already better at it. I open *A Moveable Feast* back to Hem and his literary friends, some with peculiar marriages. I treat their creative genius to another glass of wine.

CHAPTER 35

Brave, Brave, Brave

2017

The first Episcopal church I ever visited was in San Francisco in 1967, the Summer of Love. I lived upstairs in Good Samaritan Episcopal with eight other college volunteers, all working one service project or another that spilled out of Good Sam and up Potrero Hill. I ate too much Creole food served in large portions by a generous New Orleans cook. I spent time off with my housemates in Golden Gate Park or clinging to a cable car that lurched up and down city streets to Ghirardelli Square. Haight Ashbury was at its Flower Power peak. I looked the part in jeans patched with flowers on the knees. No amount of summer or love, however, could warm my bones against Bay Area fog. I took the city bus downtown to buy a wool sweater on a discount rack at a department store.

TODAY IS MY SECOND VISIT TO AN EPISCOPAL CHURCH. When all the leaves are gone in winter, the Church of the Resurrection glows downhill onto my street. The stained glass window on the east wall sheds light on naked trees during cold, naked months. Resurrection is a welcoming neighbor, host to unhoused people inside and out.

Three weeks into 2017, it's a bone-chilling Saturday under oppressive fog that won't lift. I walk a block from home to the church, passing a humble labyrinth of mossy rocks and stacked sticks. I walked the narrow path in and out of this labyrinth, tucked in the shade of oak trees, many times before my yellow Labrador died eight years ago.

I was first alone the few years before Fenn died. When we walked the labyrinth together, I sang, "Holy, holy, holy. My heart, my heart adores you. My heart is glad to say the words, you are holy, God," in joy and sorrow, mostly sorrow. My heart was just getting accustomed to love and loss, Fenn my canine companion. I cried all the way into the labyrinth, paused for a moment at the center, and cried most of the way out. The dedicated lab cocked his head, nudged closer to my knee, and followed my lead.

Now, a dozen years after my teary walks in the Episcopalian woods, I come less often to the labyrinth, but I'm glad it's here. I love its simplicity in sticks and stones and its certainty, with a beginning, a sure path to follow, and a center in the ancient pattern as universal as time itself.

The occasion today at this neighborhood church is the ordination of two priests. Anne, a relative of a relative of mine, invited me to her ordination. She said the service would be two hours. I've never been to a two-hour service of any kind. What if I don't have the stamina?

The usher directs me to sanctuary left for Anne's friends and family. I search awkwardly for an empty seat and pull up an armchair on the side. I hope I won't be so comfortable as to drift off in the third quarter, maybe eighty minutes into the ceremony.

The church is packed. Visiting priests in white robes and bright red sashes float down the aisle singing a processional

before they split off to sit in a bank of pews in support
of Anne or Iain, the other ordinand. The vaulted ceiling
reverberates with these seasoned voices and a choir in the
balcony. I like this. The gathering song is fitting—"Let
Us Build A House Where Love Can Dwell." Today, the
forty-fifth president of the United States, inaugurated
yesterday, closed the nation's borders to people from
seven largely Muslim countries, claiming their threat
of terror. Foreign travelers are stacking up in airports.
Fulbright Scholars, neurosurgeons, and babes-in-arms
are pushed back home.

The song swells to the rafters in the Episcopal church
of wood and glass. Beautiful in all five verses, I don't want
it to end. Someone somewhere is harmonizing, and the
whole scene gives me shivers. I've always wished I could
sing, really sing. I once dreamed a friend said, "You do have
a nice voice," as if surprised. Today, I join the congregation
in the gathering song about opening doors to the stranger
in a place of peace and justice. The ironies of this day are
impossible to miss.

*Give me your tired, your poor, your huddled masses
yearning to breathe free...* America, land of the free and
home of the brave.

Red is the color of Episcopalian ordination. I wish I'd
known. I might have worn my red velvet scarf. A mother
and two young children sitting behind me are dressed in
red—a curly toddler in red plaid and his sister in an ornate
red dress a friend brought from China, the mother explains.

Two red satin banners frame the chancel, each embroi-
dered in a white dove with an olive branch in its beak.
Today, America needs an olive branch. At the center of
the chancel, a large bouquet of red roses sits on a table

dressed in more red satin. Hidden in the roses are daffodils, already. It's only January.

The Episcopal bishop of Oregon, topped in a baby-blue satin hat, welcomes us. The hat looks silly, but I see it's seriously bedecked in jewels and symbols in shimmering thread. Holding a scepter, the bishop looks comfortable as the master of pomp and prayer. The pastel mosaic of his vestment mimics the brilliant stained glass window behind him.

A smog inversion finally lifts in the valley, and sunshine makes a slow, low entrance. I'm grateful for warmth and the distraction from a White House already carrying out mean-spirited promises, only one day into the term. My daughters are each in a women's march today, protesting in Washington, D.C. and Seattle, Washington. I'm proud of them.

The last two months have been like times when I've wished for a different outcome to an historic film or footage. Chief Joseph and the band of Nez Perce surrendered to federal troops in Montana, only forty miles from safety at the Canadian border. The *Titanic* sideswiped an iceberg at twenty-three knots on its virgin voyage. A sniper assassinated President Kennedy in a Dallas motorcade. The space shuttle *Challenger*, one too many frozen O-rings, exploded after takeoff. Every time I witness one of these events on film, I hope this time will be different, disaster will be averted. For all seventy-three days since the 2016 presidential election, I've hoped that what was coming January 20 was a bad dream, that President Obama would just stay on where he belonged.

The sky breaks open in time to cast color on the song-filled sanctuary. It's a good thing I'm a believer. If I weren't, I would be more distraught than I am about the new president and what he's doing and might do. I don't believe God has a reason for everything, and I'm certain God is weeping today. I'm glad for the company.

The clear red at the center of the stained glass window cascades into more red, then yellow and a succession of rainbow colors. The bishop of Oregon stands before this backdrop to present the ordinands. "Does anyone present know of any impediment or crime that would keep me from proceeding today?" Not a sound in our midst. No rustle of red sashes, no gray heads turn, no children chatter. The red plaid toddler with a great vocabulary has fallen asleep on his mother's shoulder.

I know about impediments and crimes promised at the highest office in the land.

In the quiet that follows the bishop's query, he says, "Anne and Iain, will you be loyal to Christ and obey the bishop?" The two solemnly declare they are willing and ready. They exercise commitment and sacrifice. Anne is chaplain at the Oregon State Hospital.

I worked many years with struggling students, but now I'm retired and don't have a hard job or any job. I have a new commitment to democracy, which is a big job. Without belief in God and democracy both, I'd be lost this week.

A layperson in a purple paisley dress stands at a pulpit and reads from the letter of Paul to the Ephesians. Paul reminds us to speak the truth in love. Everything I hear today makes my heart race. Our president doesn't speak truth to anything, least of all love. What will become of Americans under a state-sponsored bully who enjoys pushing people to a fight?

We stand for the next hymn. These Episcopalians can sing, and I would gladly listen long into the night. I imagine there are hearts in this room as heavy as mine. The songs soothe my soul.

A woman with a swinging bob walks to the center of the chancel, wearing a white robe tied with a red silk rope that wraps twice around her waist. She introduces herself as Kammy, "short for Katherine Mary."

"I'm from Sewanee School of Theology in Tennessee, not the Suwannee River that flows into Florida, my home state. I met Anne when she was a student at the Sewanee School. This week I met Iain on the telephone. We talked about his hopes and dreams in ministry. I am privileged to be here today."

Kammy reflects on yesterday's drive from Portland to Eugene, crossing the river that "rhymes with damn it." People in the front row laugh and offer "Willamette." It's that river.

"My job at Sewanee School is to weave the Bible into life, into practice in the world. The stuff we gather to do as a church is real," Kammy reminds everyone in the open amber room studded in red. I am comfortable in this house of progressive Christians.

Members of this church know real. Every winter night the temperature dips to thirty degrees, Church of the Resurrection hosts a warming center for homeless adults who've been pushed out of somewhere. Volunteers pass casseroles and dinner rolls and bedrolls. The church is host to a group of tiny houses on wheels in the parking lot. I pass the homes on my way to the labyrinth. The men who live in them work a vegetable garden in summer. Today, pumpkins languish in the finished garden, soggy and mis-shapen from freezing and thawing. Dark green kale grows tall and narrow and rumply.

Kammy continues her homily without notes. "We are gathered in by a God who gives us a place to find our joy and way in life. Reconciliation and hope are real." We all need hope this week and this month and this year.

"Bryan Stevenson, author of the *New York Times* bestseller *Just Mercy*, reminds me that we do the work we're called to do by God," Kammy says. "Bryan is a Harvard Law graduate and founder of the Equal Justice Initiative in Montgomery, Alabama. He works to end mass incarceration—and so much more." *Where is she going with this?* In her soft Florida sound, Kammy, here to honor two ordinands for their future work in the name of God, tells more of Stevenson's story.

"Johnnie Carr, the woman who organized the 1955 Montgomery Bus Boycott, occasionally invited Bryan to her Montgomery home to visit. Every now and then, Carr called to tell Bryan that her friend Rosa Parks was in town. Would he like to come over and listen? Bryan always said he would. One time, after Bryan listened to the two women talk for a couple hours, Rosa Parks turned to him and said, 'Now what is this Equal Justice Initiative? Just what are you trying to do?'

"Bryan told Ms. Parks that the EJI is challenging injustice and helping people who've been wrongly convicted. 'We're trying to end life-without-parole for children,' Stevenson told Rosa Parks and Johnnie Carr."

The full house of Episcopalians is now listening as intently as Bryan did in the Montgomery parlor. I don't care how much time has gone by. I'm in.

"When Bryan Stevenson finished telling about the Equal Justice Initiative, Rosa Parks turned to him," Kammy says, "rocked back and forth, and said, 'Mmm, mmm, mmm.

That's going to make you tired, tired, tired.' Then Johnnie Carr leaned forward, raised a finger toward Bryan, and said, 'That's why you have to be brave, brave, brave.'"

Kammy closes with, "God's love reaches across all divides. We must all be brave—and bold, nurtured as we are by God's grace."

People traveled today from bombed-out Damascus and war-torn Yemen and elsewhere around the globe. They were brave and bold to leave the home they loved. Midway across the Atlantic, some learned that as of today, America would not welcome them. I hope they can feel God's grace, somehow, somewhere.

Mother Teresa believed that peace is lost when we forget we belong to one another. Kammy Young and Mother Teresa both know God knows no borders. We belong to strangers in Honduras and Amsterdam and Syria. The apostle Paul, read by the woman in purple paisley, was converted on the road to Damascus. Damascus, Syria, founded in the third millennium B.C., the center of four civilizations. Damascus, the "pearl of the East." Nearby towns have been bombed and blasted into bits, refugees fleeing for their lives, spilling across the Mediterranean.

No one wants to leave home. Today, Syrians are rejected at U.S. airports. "Go back where you came from." Where they came from is an ancient homeland, too much of it reduced to rubble. We have forgotten we belong to one another.

As testament to Kammy's message and a celebration of Anne and Iain, everyone in this overflowing Episcopal church is invited to break bread together, to belong to one another. The silver chalice is wine. The pottery chalice is grape juice.

I hope I remember which is which. A taste of wine to warm my bones sounds divine. I prepare to go forward and kneel at the rail, until I see that not only the ordinands drink from the chalice, but everyone does. Everyone. A server wipes the chalice with a towel after each person takes a sip, but it's not enough for me. At my church, we dip a cube of bread in grape juice. It's more antiseptic than intimate, but I've skirted the flu all season. I don't want it now. God is too busy to protect me this week. I hang back in my armchair. I may be the only person here who doesn't take communion.

The bishop cloaks Anne and Iain in broad red vestments and commissions them to conduct God's work. A few more hymns and chants move through the sanctuary, which is golden as the sun sinks lower. We end the service in song, some harmonizing, beseeching God out there and in here, to lead us to justice with mercy. Done. Less than ninety minutes.

The sanctuary empties. Anne's family and friends congratulate her, and I introduce myself. We haven't met in person, and Anne is gracious. She expresses gratitude for this day and invites me to the reception downstairs.

Children return to the table filled with cakes and cashews and chocolates. I enjoy a piece of white layer cake with Anne's name scrolled across the top in cranberry red. I enjoy it so much I return for a second piece before I slip out the door.

Minutes before the sun disappears behind the hill, splinters of sunshine pierce the clouds. I pass the church's garden behind an uneven fence meant to fend off turkeys and deer. A few pumpkins fold into the earth in a moldy mess. A handmade sign hangs on the garden gate: "Food for People, Not Profit."

Ed will call this evening to ask how I'm doing the first day of a menacing administration or if I've heard from either daughter at the Women's March. On the short walk home, I imagine the time I would have walked into Ed's office to tell him about this remarkable event or talk about the sorrow the country is in for. Even better, he would have sat next to me in the rosy glow of the sanctuary that echoed in commitment and song.

I hope I have the courage to defend democracy in coming years. I've been going it alone for awhile, doing what I do, facing off tears. Maybe it was brave, maybe it was just letting go of *hiraeth: the feeling or longing for home that no longer exists or never was.*

Now, when I walk the labyrinth at the pretty little Episcopal church, or a labyrinth anywhere, I may spill tears, not for what I'm missing, but for what's missing in our collective soul when we forget we belong to each other, or when police shoot a black child holding a pellet gun and families are torn apart at the border, children kept conveniently in cages.

Defending democracy won't be easy. I must be brave, brave, brave.

CHAPTER 36

Poems and Pint-sized Kids

2018

Zach texted the moment he saw light in my office early yesterday. "Deana down with flu, Ari too. I teach this morning—can't miss another day. Can you help with younger kids til noon?" I felt for him. Outside, the light of day hadn't even begun to creep over the hill. Zach had probably been awake since the first light of yesterday.

My young neighbors have suffered colds and flu this winter. Zach and Deana have three children under seven. Last week, when the kids finally slept through the night and didn't wake in fits of coughing, Deana still woke every two hours, ready with a spoon and bottle of Robitussin, and raced to a child's bedside.

Deana was sure she had escaped the awful flu that's claimed days, weeks, and lives of people across the country, but the nasty bug finally flattened her, along with six-year-old Ari. Zach couldn't cancel one more university class.

At 6:20 a.m., I crossed the street to pluck Sabrina and Jack from their early morning living room, one child in footie pajamas with squatty goblins, the other in zippered fleece appliqued in trucks and buses. I set the kids in their rubber boots, and we walked hand-in-hand across the street, dark with winter, to my house. We left Ari, too sick to come along, wrapped in a blanket on the couch.

I fed agreeable Sabrina and Jack a breakfast of oatmeal, one with raisins in, one with raisins on the side. When they had eaten all the oatmeal they were going to eat, I offered apples and a version of Cheerios.

"What's that?" Jack asked in his soft little deliberate voice. I showed him my multigrain Os. Jack and his sister ate dozens.

That was yesterday, and this morning things haven't improved for the family balancing everything they have to balance. Deana is still in bed, Ari is still on the couch, and Zach has another early class. When Zach calls before dawn, I cross the street to retrieve the two younger children. On the walk back to my house, Jack asks if he can have "more of those O things." Sabrina says "moh" and something about the doggie.

The kids are eating Os and molding colored clay into worms and bracelets when I look past them, through the dining room window, at a woman reading the poem in the poetry box on my fence post. She's there a long time before she begins to walk away, then turns back. She takes a photograph of "To the New Year," a W. S. Merwin poem I placed in the box in early January. She waves at me over the fence and turns down the sidewalk, heading for my front door.

I open the door as the woman comes up the driveway. "Would you like a copy of the poem?" I ask. I've sent this poem to a few friends with January birthdays. I have extras.

"Oh, yes. It's so beautiful—it touches the natural, some supernatural, while grounded on the earth. It even has a spiritual dimension," she says.

She's right. Merwin writes of the new year arriving with quiet and light and the voice of a dove. I invite this person I haven't seen before to come inside while I get the poem from my office. She begins to remove her shoes inside the door.

"You don't have to take off your shoes. I don't."

"Are you sure? I'm on my way home from walking my daughter to school. I need to get home for my oatmeal. I'm Italian—we're all about food. My name is Jennifer." She extends a hand toward me.

"That's an interesting name for an Italian girl," I say as I offer my hand in return. Jennifer tells me her mother didn't want her to be Concessa or Francesca. Appearances suggest she was born sometime during the dozen years that Jennifer was the most popular girls name in the U.S. My East Indian neighbors named their children Susie and John, perhaps a concession to assimilation.

Jennifer moves to the kitchen. "Is this okay? It looks like you're busy." She pulls up a stool next to Sabrina and Jack, still eating Os at the breakfast bar.

"I am," I answer, "but I don't have to leave until 11."

"You have little ones here," Jennifer says, her broad smile opening to beautiful, gleaming white teeth.

"Yes, their mom is very sick with the flu," I say.

Jennifer asks the children their names and ages. Jack is quiet and serious and whispers his name as he tries to raise three fingers, two from opposite ends of his hand. Jennifer's pretty eyes get big under hexagonal glasses. "Are you three??" she asks with enthusiasm. "Or is that three and a half??"

I answer for him. "He'll be four in March." I don't know why I jumped in. Jack is shy, but he was working the fingers and can answer for himself. Jennifer turns her attention to Sabrina.

"And how old are you?? Can you show me the fingers?" Sabrina is almost two. She's smart, but she doesn't do fingers, and she says "moh" for the Os and indicates she wants to see the doggie, who is snug against my leg and not visible over the breakfast bar.

Jack offers me a blue ring of clay with bits of purple gems perched on top.

"Oh, I like the colors together. It's pretty," Jennifer says. "Would you like to know where I live?" Sabrina doesn't understand the question or care, and Jack, ever respectful, nods gently.

"I live up at the end of a very steep street on the other side of the hill." The kids are still eating Os. Jennifer continues, "You go out your street and turn right, then left. When you turn left again, you go all the way to the end of the steep street, where it dead ends. That's where my house is."

Sabrina and Jack are lost on right and left turns and a dead end. Jennifer continues, "We have a lot of property with many pine trees."

People who aren't from the Northwest often call any evergreen a pine. I hear flat vowels in Jennifer's speech. "Are you from the Midwest?" I ask.

"No, I grew up in Maine. I'm a Mainer. My husband was looking at graduate schools and came out to Oregon and fell in love. Sometimes you just know what's right. We've lived here thirteen years but just five in the house up the street. Our first house was in a neighborhood that was wrong for us. Don't ever let your partner buy a house without you."

I don't tell Jennifer I don't have a partner. I doubt I'll have another partner or another house. I think of the two houses I bought alone in two days in two towns I didn't know, when my partner took two new university jobs two different times. One house had a breezeway to the back door and a covered porch with a bench swing at the front door.

The other was in a friendly neighborhood that welcomed us with a barbecue.

"Have you been here longer than five years?" Jennifer asks.

"Yes, almost thirty," I tell her.

"That makes sense. When my daughter and I walk down to read the poem in your box, she always notices your yard. One time she said, 'Mom, I know it's a woman who lives here, because she pays attention to detail.' I had to agree with her," Jennifer continues. "I told her this woman obviously works hard in her yard."

I do work hard in my yard. It's both requisite and recreation. I prune and plant to perfection. If I get carried away, everything grows back in the Pacific Northwest.

Jennifer peppers me with questions. I must leave the house in less than an hour. I consider offering her a cup of coffee, but I'm afraid I'll have to hustle her out the door with the kids when their sitter arrives.

Sabrina asks for help getting down from the breakfast bar, and Jack follows. They find the toys they played with yesterday. In a few minutes, Jack returns to the kitchen, quiet tears streaming down his cheeks. "Bwenda, Sabwina destwoyed my puzzle."

"She didn't mean to." Jack cries easily but stops just as easily. "She's kind of a bulldozer and doesn't notice where she's going. Let's get you and the puzzle out of the way." I slide the half-completed Bob the Builder puzzle to a corner of the room. Sabrina has no malice and no sense of direction. Jack is delicate. I love these kids.

Jennifer tells me she teaches science to college kids at the local Christian university. I know the school's evangelical persuasion, and I tell her I'm glad she's there teaching science.

"I tell my students to look at evolution as science and then open Genesis. It doesn't have to be one or the other." She assures the students and me. "We don't know everything."

"I love to walk and would like to walk to church," Jennifer says. "The Episcopal church in the neighborhood would be perfect, but I don't know anything about it."

"It's a progressive church," I say, about the little church where she turns left to go home. "They do a lot of good community work."

"Right. I've seen the sign out on the street when the Warming Center is open, but it's only for adults. I go to the Faith Center, and we host the shelter for homeless families in winter."

Many churches provide night shelter for families who have nowhere to go, short first- and last-month's rent and maybe a job. Shelter guests, as we call the overnighters at my church, are often long on medical bills and short on luck. They may have burned every family bridge or never had a family with a bridge.

The local St. Vincent de Paul, directed by a living saint and operated by a legion of saint understudies, supplies room dividers and bedding to families in whatever form they come through the door. Churches provide warm space, craft projects for kids, and meals for a week or two. Hosting is hard work, but not nearly as hard as searching for shelter night after night.

Jennifer adds, with some gravity, "Someone told me the Crossfire Church on the corner on our walk to school is turning into a shelter. He said there would be drugs and beat-up cars filling the parking lot."

"Oh, no," I say. "That won't happen. St. Vincent de Paul bought Crossfire." The name Crossfire for a church has always bothered me. Nothing about it seems right. What would Jesus say? "It's been empty for a while," I continue. "St. Vinnie plans to turn it into a night shelter for the same families that churches host on winter nights. It will be much better than moving from church to church every week. You couldn't ask for a better property owner than St. Vinnie."

"Thank you for letting me know," Jennifer says. "I don't know where the guy got his information, but we were afraid our kids couldn't walk home from school anymore." She's relieved. "I read about another old church St. Vincent converted into a home for teen girls."

"Right, girls have to be in school to live in the Youth House," I say. "I'm going to the dedication today."

In the office, Sabrina has located the TV remote. Yesterday she reprogrammed the furnace thermostat and reset the clock radio. Now she hits the red power button and turns on *Sesame Street*. This television hasn't been on since August, and it's never aired *Sesame Street*. I let Bert and Ernie roll with Cookie Monster. In a few minutes, Jack comes to the kitchen again, this time afraid of bouncing creatures in the program that follows *Sesame Street*.

"It's okay," Jennifer assures him, peering at the television. "Daniel Tiger will be back. He's friendly."

"Am I keeping you from something?" Jennifer asks, shifting on the kitchen bar stool and adjusting her black wool beret. "I didn't even get dressed for the day. I just brushed my teeth and left the house. I've done all the talking. Next time, we'll have tea and spend time talking about you."

I check the clock. I can't be late to the dedication of the Youth House. A babysitter will be here any minute to pick up Sabrina and Jack. These kids have always had love and a bed and a place to belong, unlike girls at the Youth House.

Jennifer leaves as the babysitter drives up. I slide little feet into boots, grab jackets, and shuttle the children to Naomi's car. I thank Naomi and dash in the house to dash out the door.

I think about Jennifer on the way. Is she lonely or just a gregarious and friendly Italian neighbor? She has healthy children, a nice home up the street, and a winsome way.

The Youth House is a brilliant St. Vincent de Paul project—another rundown, vacant church converted into a home for thirteen teen girls who don't have a home but have managed, no matter how broken or lost or left behind, to stay in school. St. Vinnie volunteers fitted all thirteen rooms in a color theme of handmade quilts, each pinned with a loving note from the quilter about warmth and comfort, and a few perfect tchotchkes to match, from a polka dot lampshade to a stuffed panda.

I'm eager to see Stephanie and Susan honored, the angels who appointed every room, as well as Paul, the inspiration for the project. Last night, I helped the two women set up the cozy bedrooms, sweeping construction dust from under the "scratch and dent" beds and straightening quilts. I polished mirrors to reflect the girls' new visions of themselves.

This seems to be what I do best—hope and pray on projects inspired and executed by other people. The Merwin poem that Jennifer took home speaks of possible hopes in the new year. Each young woman in the Youth House will have her own something to get over or get beyond, but she must have hopes, or she wouldn't still be in school. The best landlord in town will watch over these young women and help them get over or get beyond a past that trails them.

I'm not over hope, but I'm over longing for something that won't be, the romantic walks on the beach with a life partner. It would be good to slow down, get over my hurry to somewhere. I can offer time to the family across the street or a woman admiring a poem. I can stretch myself a bit, maybe make dinner for girls at the Youth House.

The Youth House is packed with welcoming neighbors and supporters when I arrive. I can't see Stephanie, Susan, or Paul, but I hear the emcee honor them in glowing terms.

I hope each girl will feel secure between the walls of her beautiful room and feel the love hand stitched in her quilt. I'll write my own girls about this exquisite example of neighborhood nurture.

CHAPTER 37

Santerian at Hideaway

2018

I bike toward music that drifts my way from Hideaway Bakery. A summer Tuesday means pizza and music at the neighborhood hideaway. The upright bass is my favorite. I often come to sit with friends at long tables in the sun and enjoy savory pizza with beer as we lean back and tap our toes to the music. Tonight, I'm going to Tuesday pizza for the fun of it. I plan to meet no one.

Hideaway Bakery rolls out a big clay oven and sets up an outdoor kitchen every Tuesday all summer. People line up twenty-deep for pizza and beer. No one complains about the wait or the crowded tables. Neighbors visit and families meet up with other families. Pairs and clusters of people who haven't seen each other since graduate school or last soccer season enjoy an exchange before promising to meet for coffee or go rock climbing together.

I join the line inching its way to the outdoor kitchen and watch the handsome, curly-headed Italian owner/baker stoke the fire with chunks of just-split firewood that crackle once they catch a flame. Mazzi rolls a small round of dough, dusts floury hands on a white coat, and decorates a pizza in shiny gems of basil and caramelized onions and roasted carrots. He slides pizza from the counter onto a large wood palette, and from there onto the floor of the fiery oven.

The Chicago-style pizza with thick crust is stacked in toppings fresh from the garden. Each hand-tossed pizza pie sizzles a few minutes in the blazing clay oven and comes out bubbly, crust blackened around the edges. The pizzas are perfect. Two people can share one, but the truth is, I can always eat the whole pie. The salads are easier to share. Beetnick, Garden Greens, and Greek salads spill over the dinner plate with greens from a nearby farm.

I stand in line behind a young man wearing white pants, white top, and white turban. I smile to be pleasant. This fellow doesn't glow from a day of summer sun but emerges pale from the collar of a white shirt over a white T-shirt. He tears a piece of bread from a white loaf in a white paper sack and smiles at me to suggest he wants to visit. Before I pretend I don't notice his eagerness, he says, "Have you been here before?"

"Yes, I have," I say. "Are you a baker?"

"No, I get asked that a lot," he answers. "The clothes are for my religion."

Local Sikhs wear turbans and a variety of colors. This young man is not a Sikh.

"What religion?" I ask. I'm getting further into this than I planned.

"Santerian. I'm an elder."

I look as puzzled as I am. In the next breath, he tells me he's a musician and music teacher. "Do you know anyone who needs lessons?"

"I can't say I do," I say, "but it's possible I could come across someone who does. I'll take a card if you have one." I look at the guitar case propped against his leg. "Do you teach guitar?"

"No," the young man answers. "Piano. In people's homes. I have the guitar because I played at my home-care job today.

It was my last day." He pauses. I think he wants me to ask why it was his last day on the job.

"It was my last day because I got fired," he offers. "Yes, I do have a business card." He sets down the bag of bread and begins to riffle through a floppy white cloth bag, then through the guitar case. It takes a long time to do all that rummaging. He comes up empty handed. "I guess I ran out. Do you have a piece of paper?" he asks.

I have no paper but a twenty-dollar bill in my pocket. The musician goes from the line to the cashier to ask for a sticky note. He writes his name, phone number, and email address— first, middle, and last name at gmail.com. No spaces.

Next, Kenton asks what I'm thought to be.

"Pardon me?" I ask.

"People think I'm a baker. What do people think you might be?"

"I don't know that anyone thinks I'm anything," I say. *Who even considers this question?* "Maybe some people think I'm a teacher because I was. I'm retired."

"Oh, wow. You have so much of my respect. Wow. Teachers are so important. I really honor you, totally honor you," Kenton says.

Teachers are important, but that's more carrying on than I'm accustomed to over my civil service. Is his response excessive?

"We're all citizens of the solar system first," he informs me. He ticks off a few attributes of this citizenry, like awareness of other beings and planets. You can't argue with that. Next the citizen tells me he's an alchemist, and because I don't want to explore alchemy in the pizza line, I'll look it up when I get home. Between my line mate being a citizen of the solar system, a Santerian elder, and an alchemist, I can't picture a Venn diagram. However, I entertain the possibility that the three circles overlap and intertwine somewhere.

I'm now only five people from the counter. I'm ready. I think I'll order what I usually order. The Santerian dressed in white asks, "Are you meeting anyone tonight?"

Dang. I don't want to be stuck at a table with this fellow, but I can't lie. It'll be obvious soon enough that I'm here alone, not meeting a soul. I scan the outdoor tables for a familiar face. I was rather looking forward to the freedom of my first Hideaway Tuesday alone.

He follows with, "Can I sit with you?" before I have a chance to lie that I am meeting someone or admit that I'm not. The combo of upright bass, banjo, and a couple guitars plays lively bluegrass. I'd like to enjoy the music and not try to talk over it.

"Yes," I answer with little enthusiasm. Actually, no enthusiasm.

The alchemist tells me he's heard Hideaway gives free pizza samples on Tuesdays.

"I don't think so. They might give away day-old baked goods inside the bakery, but I doubt they give away pizza."

Kenton disappears into the bakery and doesn't return until I'm seated in the sun, number 31 in front of me and strangers at the other end of the table. He's again empty-handed, except for his guitar case. He pulls up a green plastic chair next to me. "Can I join you?" he asks.

"Okay."

A waitress in a short, sleeveless dress and cowboy boots to her calves announces "Roasted Vegetable" as she sets the pizza on the table and takes away 31. I want to follow the number and the young woman in the cute dress and boots.

The hungry citizen of the solar system tells me more. "I was in Los Angeles for a while, researching drugs." I don't ask about the research. "That was after I got fired from Arc. You know what that is? Association for Retarded Children?"

"I do know."

"Firing from Arc was all political," he says with a genial smile.

I don't want to know more. I lift a piece of pizza off the tray and prepare to take my first bite off the point, where a piece of glossy winter squash dangles, ready to fall off. Instead, I put the whole shiny slice on a small plate and pass it to my dining partner.

"Oh, thanks," he says and eats half in one bite. This small pizza is cut in six pieces. How will I divide it? I'm hungry. I don't consider sharing the cold glass of Agrarian Ale.

"I also went to Cuba for six days. There are so many chickens there. I met more Santerian elders." I slide a second wedge of pizza toward Kenton. He continues to make conversation with a string of loosely related topics. I'm curious about Cuba, swaying palms, good food, nice people, but I don't want to learn more about the island here and now. I turn my attention to bluegrass. Small children dance with each other and with their mothers.

"Are you going to eat those?" the still-hungry Santerian asks, his finger and thumb hovering over the pizza crusts at the edge of the tray. I lift a third piece of Roasted Vegetable pizza for myself and slide the tray his direction.

"Where have you traveled?" he asks.

I'm eating pizza, and the banjo is on a bright riff. "What's that?" I ask.

"Where have you traveled? Have you traveled internationally?" he asks in a loud voice, to be heard.

"Yes," I answer, quietly.

"What's your favorite country?" he continues.

I don't want to chat. I offer that I've enjoyed different places for different reasons. I'm feeling less charitable as the sun gets lower in the sky. I don't want to carry on about my privilege with this hungry fellow, telling him where I've run rivers or climbed mountains or helped a Salvadoran fisherman stack cinder blocks to build a health clinic.

My three pizza slices are gone. I drink the last of the pale ale, wipe all trace of cheese and tomato sauce from my face, and gather my dishes to leave. I scoot the plastic chair to the table with my foot.

"Goodbye. It was nice to meet you," I say. If not nice, it was interesting. If I were here with friends or a partner, it would have been nicer, more fun, but I would have missed this encounter. It has been interesting.

"I must get going," I add, which is true. I don't feel great about this, but I don't want to hang around. I'm out of conversation. This is a story for my daughters. "Good luck with your music."

I drop the pizza pan and pint glass in a plastic bin. I might have been more generous toward a fellow citizen of the solar system. He was hungry.

My bike is tucked in shrubs behind the music. I unlock it and wheel it away. On my ride home, I think *Centerian*, something to do with one hundred. I know how to spell alchemist. I'll research both. I have interesting things to learn.

CHAPTER 38

Can I Come by to Talk?

2019

I've been working in the yard for hours. It's hard to quit, but I check my watch and go inside to make a garden salad for dinner guests this evening. The phone rings.

The fourteen years since my divorce have drifted into a comfortable pace. I have caller ID now, and Ed's calls are customarily brief, with a purpose. Our visits over coffee aren't laced with sorrow, and I'm not wearing the naked emotions of years ago. They're not gone, for I don't forget much, but "what about…" and "I thought…" no longer send me to tears in the quiet of my kitchen.

Hiraeth: a Welsh word for longing or nostalgia, an earnest longing or desire, or a sense of regret. Wikipedia continues: *a deep and irrational bond felt with a time, era, place, or person.*

I wouldn't go so far as to say my bond was irrational, but it was earnest longing—for us, a future together that would be generous and include our family breakfast table. The longing is gone, and we'll always return to breakfast. Or dinner.

I answer the phone.

"Oh, hi, Brenda. Can I come by a little later to talk to you?"

"Sure, I'm home all afternoon." I'll be cooking.

Talk to me? He usually asks if I have time for coffee or dinner.

Today he didn't ask if I have time. He just wants to "come by." Is he dropping something off? Last time he "came by with something," it was Ani, a surprise from Washington, D.C., for my seventieth birthday.

"Good. I'll see you in about half an hour," he says.

———————————

I'M LOOKING FORWARD TO GUESTS TONIGHT. I LIKE TO invite guests for dinner, or entertain, as one might say who sets an antique mahogany Duncan Phyfe dining table in a formal dining room over a Persian rug. Some women entertain their husband's business partners for drinks in the living room, wall-to-wall carpet vacuumed in one direction, and dinner in the dining room. But today, women are just as likely to entertain their own board of directors for both drinks and dinner on the patio.

My parents didn't entertain, but they had "company" for coffee, supper, pinochle, or a Tom and Jerry at Christmas. Shag carpet in the dining room that was also the living room, didn't vacuum in any direction.

My cousin hosts politicians, art collectors, board members, and large groups of friends and family in lovely, unruffled ways. She comes the closest of anyone I know to entertaining. A Duncan Phyfe table would look silly in her modern house of glass and steel, de Kooning paintings, and Chihuly sculptures of translucent glass in undulating sea forms. I would take a guess her favorite lunch guest was First Lady Michelle Obama.

Susan's western-themed country house doesn't have a Duncan Phyfe either. It does have a sand painting on one wall and Andy Warhol western paintings in a three-by-three grid on another. The tenth painting in the western Cowboys and Indians series is in a bedroom. One summer, Brooke and Ani grabbed a cowboy hat off a William Morris antler sculpture and snapped a photo in front of Warhol's *Annie Oakley*, positioned near the *Indian Head Nickel* and *Teddy Roosevelt*.

Susan's husband laughed the heartiest of all when the cousins arrived at the country house with dogs and tents and coolers of melting ice. He called us the Hokums. One evening as we drove down the lane to Susan's city house, past sculptor Richard Serra's two-story steel panels that grow out of the earth in curvaceous movement with the lawn, four-year-old Kiele, sitting tall in her booster seat, announced, "It's junky down here." Serra measures his works in tons, and Kiele surely thought the two-hundred ton rusted steel plates were hiding a scrapyard of rusted and busted cars and trucks.

Junky or not, it's fun to be at any Susan house for any meal. She doesn't have to entertain us. "I like to serve delicious, beautifully presented food that other people make," Susan says. I love her honesty. I love her. We grew up together.

Entertaining is a curious term. If I host guests, I usually feed them. Entertaining might include jokes, a magic show, or a ten-year-old playing the violin. I love to have people in my home—my sister, my cousins, my kids and their kids, old friends, new friends. I wasn't meant to live alone. I could fix it by offering a room to a fun, stimulating person who's low on rent. I'm averse to walking around someone else's stuff, but the stuff they're made of could be interesting. It's never too late to look into it, but then I think of the ways I've come to appreciate living alone.

One of the four friends coming to dinner tonight had a birthday this week. I love birthdays. We'll go to the garden house and select a few poems with metaphors about geese returning or frogs singing, to launch the birthday celebrant into the next year.

ED ARRIVES AS I SLIDE A CHOCOLATE CAKE INTO THE oven. The recipe I copied years ago from the back of a Hershey's Cocoa can calls for coffee and buttermilk. Buttermilk makes everything good. The recipe is hand-written on a green index card, soft as cloth, smudged with oil and cocoa, and marked with a red star next to "2 cups sugar." The matching star at the bottom of the faded green card reads, "Don't forget the sugar, idiot."

It's not poetry, but it seems to serve the purpose. I have forgotten the sugar in this cake no less than four times over the thirty years I've made it. The first time was for my third-grade daughter to take to a school potluck. You know when you open the oven after thirty minutes that something is wrong. The cake is one inch high and black.

When baked with all the sugar required, this chocolate cake serves as the healing offering poet Julia Kasdorf recommends, the one you bake for a grieving household. Today I remember to mix in the sugar and will offer the cake with my chaste touch for my friend's birthday.

I offer Ed decaf coffee and a cookie.

"That would be great," he says and asks about my trip next month to Utah, where I'll meet up with Ani for a week of hiking. I describe the places, among cliffs and canyons and hoodoos, and Ed says, "Wow, I'm jealous. I would love to spend a week with Ani."

Next, he says, "I want to ask your blessing on something."

Now I know why he's here. My heart skips a beat it apparently doesn't need.

Ed tells me that he and his partner of many years want to get married.

"Neither of us feels compelled to get married, but if I die, she can't claim my Social Security unless we've been married at least a year. Mine is significantly better, and hers might not kick in for a long time, you know, depending on when I die."

I do know. She's younger. Much.

"Of course. It only makes sense," I say, about the Social Security and marriage.

"I wouldn't want to do it, if it changed this," Ed says, sweeping his hand across the table.

"Changed what?" I ask.

"I wouldn't get married if we couldn't visit like this, to see you here or with the kids."

"No, that won't change."

Ed looks at his cup and looks at me. "Thank you for being so gracious. I'm not surprised."

He's teary. He must know what I'm thinking.

I'm a little choked up and teary myself. I can't deny I wanted to be this important, so important that he would spend the precious currency of time on me and with me.

He's said it before, but this afternoon Ed says again, as if to explain our marriage ending, "I was so insecure for so many years. It wasn't fair to you. I know it wasn't."

Today the time we spend together is valuable. I wouldn't have it any other way. Then there are those blueberries that weigh the woody branches to the ground, that Ed invites me to pick by the fistful. He tells me to bring friends with buckets.

I often marvel that Ed's partner, soon his wife, has never been resentful of the time he spends with his family or with me. It's rather generous. Last summer, Ani said, "Under better conditions, you would really like her."

I'm sure I would.

In the old days, when I occasionally introduced Ed as my first husband, it was a joke. Now he can introduce me as his first wife if we're ever together in company that needs to know who I am or where I am on the family tree. It's no joke.

On his way out the door, Ed says again, "Thank you. I really appreciate it."

I imagine he'll cry as he drives away.

I close the door and mix up frosting for the cake. I use butter, which makes everything else good. I won't entertain tonight, but I will encourage my friends to read a poem about feeding seeds of joy or about how the day arrives in the morn. One friend will ask for his wife's reading glasses, another will have a hard time choosing a poem, and two will read with lively intonation. The reading is soothing to the soul.

In the next few hours, Bree and Ani each call. "How are you doing, about Dad?"

"Fine," I say. "It only makes sense."

I return to the Stafford poem, "The Way It Is."

> There's a thread you follow. It goes among
> things that change. But it doesn't change....
> Nothing you do can stop time's unfolding.
> You don't ever let go of the thread.

CHAPTER 39

Soul in Santa Fe

2019

The first moment off the tiny plane at the Santa Fe airport, I remember why I love it here. The horizon is a long stretch across the high desert. To the north, the rugged Sangre de Cristo Mountains sport peaks fourteen thousand feet high in the wide-open sky. Every time I visit, I think I could live here.

Outside the small adobe terminal the color of cinnamon, the wind whips the American flag in noisy flaps against the azure sky. The flagpole is a perfect place to meet a Lyft driver to lift me ten miles into Santa Fe to my hotel. From there, I'll walk to a favorite gallery.

I pull up the Lyft app on my cell phone. My daughters would be proud. Google Maps wants to "activate my location," but I don't want Google following me around Santa Fe or anywhere. I decline.

I haven't made friends with my cell phone. I may never. "Just play around with your phone—you'll learn how to use it," my real friends say. I use it when I travel. I've even had a hard time saying "text," with an aversion to the trendiness of this convenient communication. I remain slow at texting, using two pointers, no thumbs. "App" is also strange to me. I know you don't want too many of them. My daughter downloaded the Lyft app for occasions like this at the Santa Fe Regional Airport.

A large "3003" is high and obvious on the terminal building. I type in 3003, and "Airport Road" pops up. Google Maps must have followed me after all.

"Excuse me," I say to a man who looks like he knows where we are. "Is this Airport Road?" I make a sweeping gesture across the parking lot and into the desert.

"Yes," he says, on the run.

I forward "3003 Airport Road" to Lyft, along with a note for the driver. "I'm under the American flag in front of the Santa Fe airport."

The return message informs me that Nafiz, in a blue Toyota Venza, is ten minutes out, then seven, then four, and finally, he has "arrived." Nafiz and the Toyota are nowhere in sight. I can see every car in the parking area of this little airport, and not one of them is blue or a Toyota. Not one person looks like a man named Nafiz.

Rides come for other passengers, but no Nafiz. In five minutes, I must cancel the ride and accept Lyft's five-dollar no-show penalty before I can proceed.

While I fiddle with my phone and app with mixed results, a young woman across the sidewalk struggles one-handed with her phone—not in operating it, for she's quick at that, but with securing a ride. She speaks into the phone and texts, then texts again, all the while sniffling. I wonder if she has an allergy or a terrible cold. It's October at seven thousand feet, and she looks cold in short, fringed white denim shorts. She sounds miserable. The sniffling doesn't stop. She needs a tissue.

I start over with Lyft to secure a ride into Santa Fe. The app spins circles and won't take new information. Google Maps doesn't offer to locate me now. I can't get a lift with Lyft, and I am fit to be tied with the app. I stop short of making a spectacle of myself by screaming at a cell phone, but no one is around to watch my repeat failures except the young woman I'm watching. She's too busy working at securing her own ride to notice me.

The young woman is having no better luck than I am, and she no doubt knows what she's doing. "I already did that," she insists into her phone. She presses more keys with a single thumb and adds, "How do I request? It won't work."

Nafiz's number appears on my cell phone screen. Relief. I call him directly.

"I was way over on Airport Road," Nafiz says. "I'll be there in ten minutes. You just wait."

I thought I was on Airport Road. I walk over to the young woman. "My driver is on the way. He can help you too."

She's crying. She doesn't have an allergy or a virus at all. The tears that don't dry instantly in the desert air make her snuffle.

"Are you sure?" she says.

"Of course." I've been annoyed by her constant sniffling, but she must have something to cry about. Now I'm just perturbed with my cell phone.

A security person appears on the sidewalk where we stand. I ask the question about the road.

"The airport changed locations from Airport Road to Aviation Way about thirty years ago," he says. "We're on Aviation Way right here."

I could suggest a new sign with the correct road name, maybe somewhere near the American flag. Even better, remove the large historic 3003, since the number no longer applies.

Ride share companies pick up travelers at the little Santa Fe Regional Airport, but taxis don't. Any good taxi would know where the airport is. It's just something taxis know.

"I'm Brenda," I say to the pretty young woman in white shorts, her hair tied in a knot for travel. "What's your name?"

"Amanda."

"Where are you going?" I ask.

"To a healing center. I don't know the name. I'm going for thirty days. I miss my family all the way back in North Carolina. I've never been out of the state before."

This girl is not only desperately homesick, but the high desert landscape is as foreign to her as moonscape and doesn't look like healing territory. It was warm when Amanda left home this morning, and she may have been cloaked in a blanket of humidity when she left Raleigh.

Nafiz arrives as promised. He assures Amanda he will get her where she's going. He's fuming at the Lyft app himself and makes a point of turning it off. "It's not working today. That's why you couldn't re-enter your request. I went way out to Airport Road. I'll turn this off and we'll do twenty dollars cash. Okay?"

Of course it's okay.

Nafiz loads Amanda's bag, heavy with everything she will or won't need during the thirty-day stay in Santa Fe to heal her soul. I think her soul must hurt.

I load my wheelie bag. Nafiz is a kindly guy with a scruffy gray beard and a frumpy sweater over a portly frame.

I offer reassuring words to Amanda and tell her Santa Fe is a heavenly place. "You will get better here." Nafiz offers his own words of assurance and forgets about the app.

Amanda locates the name of the healing center on the drive into Santa Fe. Nafiz asks, in the gentle way of a kind father that doesn't seem invasive, "Why are you going there?" He doesn't wait for an answer. "Whatever the reason, you can do it." He speaks beautiful English with a lilt. Nafiz immigrated to Santa Fe from Jordan thirty years ago, about the time they moved the regional airport from Airport Road to Aviation Way.

"I've been really depressed, and I've been cutting," Amanda says, lifting her left arm for me to see. I hadn't noticed bandages that cover secrets.

"How old are you?" I ask.

"I'm thirty-three. I've been in therapy all my life," she says.

I'm surprised. Amanda looks twenty-three, not thirty-three, and not worn from years of battling depression.

The trip into Santa Fe takes a while. I have time for more questions.

"Has your family been helpful?"

"No, ma'am. I worked in the family business. It was toxic. They told me to leave."

"That's probably a good thing," I say, not knowing what I'm talking about. "It's good you're here." I'm confident about that. The air and sunshine in this pueblo country of red rock and limestone, the wild and scenic Rio Grande River, and the nice people—maybe all of it will converge to heal Amanda. I hope the healing center takes patients or guests or clients, whatever they call those who arrive in some kind of trouble, to the plaza in the middle of Santa Fe. The historic Spanish plaza, with a touch of Old West, is lined with native artisans sitting on a stool or cross-legged on Navajo blankets, selling silver and turquoise bracelets and pendants carved or etched with delicate symbols of life and growth. Amanda might talk with a kind Navajo grandmother who detects her longing and offers wisdom from her soft-spoken soul. Perhaps Amanda will choose a Hopi bracelet with silver overlay symbols of rain and strength. Maybe she'll find a turquoise pendant to take home, to remind her of the mountains and hands that shaped the stone.

I look at Amanda's left hand for a wedding ring. An elaborate engagement ring, sprinkled with tiny diamonds, sits between two plain bands, one silver and one gold.

"How about your husband?" I ask. "Has he been helpful?"

"He's really good. He cried so hard when I left."

I don't know if thirty days will help Amanda with cutting and depression, but I tell her it will.

"You're young and lovely," I say, "with skills and a whole life ahead of you." I offer Amanda, who hasn't asked for my thoughts or advice, the same message in a variety of ways. Over the next few miles, I search for the right words to express "You can do it."

Nafiz inspires confidence. "You can do it. You can do what you need to do."

Amanda thanks her two new companions. "You've been very kind."

The highway lined in desert gives way to streets lined in agave and pampas grass, the long feathery plumes yielding to the breeze in a deep bend. We're not far from my hotel.

At the Sage Inn, I touch Amanda's shoulder before I climb out of the Toyota Venza. "You're a strong girl, and you will be okay. I'll think of you every day I'm in New Mexico."

"Thank you, thank you so much. You've both been angels," Amanda says through tears.

New tears will send Amanda into a new sniffle on the drive to the healing center south of Santa Fe. I cry myself, considering what this fragile girl faces. I'll write my daughters about Amanda.

Tomorrow, my sister and cousin and I will drive northwest of Santa Fe to the Arts and Writing Festival at Ghost

Ranch, twenty-two thousand acres of pinnacles and pinion pine, canyons and cactus—inspiration for dozens of Western movies, dozens more Georgia O'Keefe paintings, and home to Tewa people, who make the ranch hum. We will talk about ghosts and walk the labyrinth. We'll hike canyon and mesa and marvel at cliffs in relief against the desert sky, dramatic in pink and purple, morning and evening.

Brooke will paint, Glenda will weave in the Tewa tradition, and I will write, probably about Amanda and Nafiz, an unlikely pair. We will study with people much like ourselves, mostly privileged, mostly white, and mostly women who have come to draw and paint, weave and write in exquisite expression about this troubled yet beautiful world. My classmates will be interesting, and each will have survived something. Unless they write about their loss, I will never know if any one of them has overcome cutting or another obstacle.

What I do know is that everybody has something, big or small, life-defining or not, to get beyond or get over. Amanda's challenge makes mine, being left alone, look simple. It wasn't simple, but it is behind me. I hope Amanda finds comfort at the healing center and puts cutting behind her. I know it's complicated. I'm lucky, and I want Amanda to be lucky too, to get a break from suffering.

The break in a marriage covenant of trust unleashes a sense of betrayal and grief. Closure is but a myth. The give-and-take I enjoy now with my former husband isn't what I planned, but there's a fiber that hasn't raveled out, after all.

There's no app for that.

CHAPTER 40

Flexing Muscles

2020

I visited my sister in Mexico for a few days in February. I love Brooke's inside-outside house on a hill above Mexico's Pacific coast, a palapa of thatched palms at the peak, small black stones inlaid in small intervals climbing steep concrete steps, and crashing waves in the distance, music to the ears when all the village has turned off for the night. I admire my shy sister's facility with Spanish and her friendships with Aurora, of Casa Aurora's humble five-star rooms, and Anul, the aesthetic house builder with soul. We went to a different cocina each night of my visit, to sip salty margaritas and eat seafood dripping in salt water. We relaxed for an evening of dining, except for the band of a dozen tubas in the park next door that we wished on its way so we could hear the upright bass ensemble trying to outplay the tubas with mere strings.

Aware as I was that a visit from a sister-in-law can be like rotten fish after four days, I aimed to leave before I stank. I also wanted to get home in time to mentor a seventh grader at the middle school up the street. With a dozen other students and mentors, Dezi and I have lunch together on Wednesday as we mold playdough, practice times tables, or play Rummikub.

In the Puerto Vallarta airport, fresh news of COVID-19 playing on CNN, I was suddenly afraid to touch anything. I ate a sandwich tucked in cellophane and returned to the restroom three times to wash my hands. Masks weren't mentioned yet, and I didn't have one anyway.

———————————

IN THE MONTHS SINCE I RETURNED FROM CHACALA, a hamlet from yesteryear on a quiet cove except for the tubas on repeat, much has changed in my town and state and country, surely in the world. At first, reactions to the coronavirus appeared excessive. My daughter's workplace of three thousand employees was the first to shut down in Seattle. Really? There was no mentoring at the middle school that Wednesday back from Chacala. My hiker friends were fearful of carpooling to a trailhead. For a day or two, it seemed silly.

Then, it didn't seem silly at all, and the virus caught my attention, all of it. I listened to White House Coronavirus Task Force reports, wherein the president took over the microphone and said, "We have it totally under control" and looked forward to packed churches at Easter, "a beautiful time." The resurrected Jesus would have said, "Hold everything." Dr. Anthony Fauci, the esteemed epidemiologist, said, "Not so fast."

For the first five months of the pandemic, I acclaimed my good fortune—a house, a garden, a pension. I walked every morning and evening, ate out of the garden, and lost six pounds, which caused me to worry I might have cancer. I listened to a public radio interview with Julie Andrews on the drive home from my first trip to a grocery store and cried at her wisdom and generosity. Then I worried that I infected myself with COVID when I wiped away a tear.

In the sixth month, my daughter and family drove from Washington, D.C. to Oregon without using a single public restroom across the continent. They stopped along the way to see prairie dogs and bison in Teddy Roosevelt National Park and Old Faithful in Yellowstone.

The D.C. family moved into my house to take advantage of my help with virtual school for the five- and eight-year-old boys. Ani and her husband work from the office, a desk in the bedroom, the dining room table, or the garden house. The shelves I recently emptied of forty or sixty years of living are now filled with one-hundred-piece jigsaw puzzles and dozens of books on the solar system, dragons, and how things are made. My cartoonist neighbor Jan gave the boys a few of her Stone Soup collections, along with several Calvin and Hobbes volumes she cleared off her shelves in retirement purge.

The little boys read cartoons every morning at breakfast, and the paperback collections are thick with oatmeal and worn to a pulp.

Sometimes I spin circles in my kitchen, not knowing if I should direct the third grader to the Zoom screen or to count by fours, or if I should clear a flat surface and wash handprints off a window. I start a load of laundry.

I'm good at recess. "Put out the cones," I holler to the boys, who run a pair of orange cones up the street to slow the UPS driver when he careens down into our cul-de-sac to deliver a toothbrush or toner cartridge. Kainoa and I have a record of forty-two catches of the Nerf football, and Kaleo and I are good at tossing a crocheted Frisbee that really flies and doesn't sting the fingers. We bike, cruising to the end of the block and back, more fun than I imagined, for I typically bike to a destination. Sometimes we wind through an obstacle course, zipping on colored chalk pathways between a five-gallon jug of laundry detergent and large planter buckets.

My son-in-law does all the grocery shopping and all the cooking of vegetarian fare with flair. Everything is delicious with cumin and olive oil, buttermilk and butter. Ani pushes a stick vacuum with a headlight (who knew?) every evening to make a clean sweep 'til morning.

I'm happy for the company, noisy as it is. This pair of boys is loud. I made cloth masks and appliqued them with "shhh" for when the noise makes my teeth rattle. When my brother's and my behavior taxed my mother's sensibilities, she asked, "Do you want me to knock your heads together?" or "Do you want me to paste you into the woodwork?" We didn't, really.

When I have had it with the little boys scrapping over Legos or bullying over something, I threaten to hang them from the rafters by the ankles, and when I'm not poised to hoist them in such a way, I adore them. One child has a vocabulary that impresses the teacher, even on screen, and eyes that twinkle as he cocks his head to tell a story or listen to one. The other has a big heart and is best friends with my dog and visits the neighbor dogs. These children make me laugh, and what they take out of me, they add back in good humor. I'm still lucky—a house, a garden, a pension, and a resident family.

While here for the duration, the little boys now under my roof see Pop Pop often. They like his hot tub, his dogs, his penchant for French fries, and him. Ani has time to visit with her devoted father, rather than be annoyed at his repeat phone calls when she doesn't have time to answer.

I won't say "unprecedented times," but the pandemic affords benefits and requires sacrifices I haven't known before.

I miss my Seattle family, the girls who still long for Granny Camp. I miss traveling. I planned a return to Brooke's house in Chacala next winter, for morning walks on the beach and fish tacos, but the pandemic took a bite out of the plan. I miss going to church. Our services are okay on Zoom, but it's too easy to take time out to make coffee or take a shower. The choir collage sends shivers up my spine, but I want to sing, "God's eye is on the sparrow, and I know God's watching me," shoulder-to-shoulder with my ninety-five-year-old friends Jeanne and Jane. I miss the fine people at the YMCA, and I miss a draft beer and good popcorn at the indie theater.

Mine are sacrifices of privilege.

Last fall, I exercised new muscles.

Near the river's edge below his house, Ed built a pizza oven, surrounded in smooth river rock and covered in a roof of timbers. My culinary-and-most-other-ways artist son-in-law baked pizza in the new outdoor oven that's as beautiful as it is serviceable.

Bree came from Seattle with Azra and Kiele on a COVID-tested visit, and along with Ani's family and Ed and wife and dogs, I ate hand-tossed, wood-fired pizza by the river and had birthday cake on the deck. No longer dissolving in tears over what was, I enjoyed the day and looked at *hiraeth, a deep longing for something*, at a distance. I haven't forgotten Joan Didion's sense of the beautiful ordinary in marriage, but I don't long for it.

When Thanksgiving arrived, I was ready to leave the greasy handprints on my windows at home and set a dinner table somewhere else. That place was Pop Pop's house. I knew

I would be offered a slice of turkey, which I was hungry for, and extra to take home. The little boys were a little worried that a big old squawky turkey that roams our neighborhood with a partner and ten poults would be captured, plucked, and set on the table, a few feathers remaining on the pimpled flesh. The real roasted turkey, however, was tucked tastefully away on the kitchen counter. Ed's wife was as gracious and generous as ever. It's infectious. Thankful for my bounty, I was grateful for the holiday and her welcome. I remembered the old French proverb: "Gratitude is the memory of the heart."

Ed and his wife survived a ten-day wildfire evacuation only two months before Thanksgiving. Their house was spared the wind-driven inferno that leveled hundreds of dwellings upriver and licked at wildlands frightfully close to home. Once satellite photos revealed all houses on their road were safe, we worried about the blueberries, but even the berries remained untouched by fire, untainted by smoke, and enriched by ash. Next summer, I'll pick sapphire orbs the size of marbles, again.

I can't get over how lucky they were. And I am. I remember words from an "authentic life" enthusiast who might ordinarily make my teeth ache, but the guru is right about finding joy in the story I'm living rather than longing for a place I cannot return to, that place that "hiraeth" describes.

I remember Azra's words when she was a little girl. "So, when Pop Pop found what he was looking for, why didn't he come back?" He did. We all came back in one way or another, one version or another. I won't say, "It's all good," an expression that does make my teeth ache, because it's not all good, but what isn't good is pretty good.

I often tell Azra and her younger sister, along with their little boy cousins, that we are lucky fish. I'll say it over and again in the years to come, because we are. Much comes to us because we're just plain lucky, or we've been afforded privilege for generations.

After Thanksgiving dinner, I packed turkey and sweet potatoes in the same container, and someone in the kitchen who knows my dessert desires cut me two pieces of pumpkin pie. I set the bundle on my lap for the ride home. The November night passed by my rain-streaked window. The moon, on its way to a Beaver Moon in a few days, moved in and out of towering Douglas fir silhouettes darker than the night.

It was all good, it really was.